THE BRE-X FRAUD

THE BRE-X FRAUD

Douglas Goold and Andrew Willis

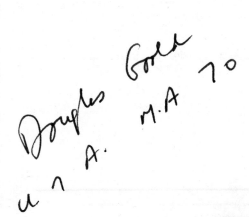

M&S

Canadian Cataloguing in Publication Data

Goold, Douglas, 1946 –
 The Bre-X fraud

ISBN 0-7710-3334-6

1. Bre-X (Firm).   2. Gold mines and mining – Indonesia.   3. Fraud.
I. Willis, Andrew, 1962 –   . II. Title.

HD9536.I544B77   1997   338.2'741'09598   C97-931851-3

Set in Minion by M & S, Toronto
Printed and Bound in the United States of America on acid-free paper

The publishers acknowledge the support of the Canada Council for the Arts and the Ontario Arts Council for their publishing program.

McClelland & Stewart Inc.
The Canadian Publishers
481 University Avenue
Toronto, Ontario
M5G 2E9

CONTENTS

CHAPTER ONE

The Mysterious Death of Michael de Guzman

"He was in good spirits and anticipating getting back to the Busang site." – Bre-X chief David Walsh on de Guzman

On Tuesday, March 18, 1997, Michael de Guzman bought a new suit of clothes. Life seemed to be treating him fairly well. Each of his four wives still knew nothing about the others, and, as one of the geologists behind the world's biggest gold find, his professional reputation was at its peak. Certainly friends sensed that there were health concerns, most of them familiar to hard-living, overweight, forty-one-year-old men who spent time in malarial jungles. And earlier in the day, he had mentioned some assay or mineral testing problems in a phone call to his employee, Rudy Vega. But that evening he sat with Vega in a late-night session in a tiny karaoke bar in Balikpapan, a booming seaside oil town in the part of Indonesia known as Kalimantan, and worked on some local Bintang beer, talking of this and that. Then he took the stage and belted out three songs, including Frank Sinatra's "My Way."

Within twelve hours he was dead.

Within another twelve hours his death was headline news.

De Guzman had become famous all over the world as the man who helped to discover the fabled Busang gold deposit. Just the previous week, the mining community had hailed his presentation at the annual convention of the Prospectors and Developers Association of Canada at the Royal York, the blue-blooded hotel in Toronto where Queen Elizabeth's official Toronto dinner would be held in June. In March de Guzman boasted to his audience that the Busang deposit could contain as much as 200 million ounces of gold. That much gold would be worth about $70 billion (U.S.) and would make the find the largest in history. The audience of professionals buzzed with excited approval. The high point of the conference was the anointment at a black-tie dinner of de Guzman's co-discoverer, the Dutch-born Canadian John Felderhof, as prospector of the year.

That celebratory mood, however, was shattered in the course of the convention by an angry call to de Guzman at the Royal York from David Potter, the chief geologist for Freeport-McMoRan Copper & Gold Inc., the New Orleans-based company that had won the long ownership fight for Busang. Potter's message: Freeport's drilling, part of its due diligence process, had turned up insignificant amounts of gold. Where the hell were all the millions of ounces? Potter's instructions to de Guzman: return to Busang immediately to explain how Freeport could have come up empty on the multi-billion-dollar site.

Early the morning after their midnight session in the karaoke bar, Vega and de Guzman, dressed in an orange Bali shirt, caught an Indonesia Air Transport Alouette III helicopter. Their first hop took them to Samarinda, a timber and mining centre up the coast with a curious combination of mosques, brothels, and an outlet for Kentucky Fried Chicken. The pilot, Edi Tursono, a lieutenant in the Indonesian air force, which had long enjoyed an unsavoury reputation for "losing" unwelcome passengers in mid-flight, was a newcomer to the route and to Bre-X. The helicopter touched down at

Samarinda for ten minutes and Vega got off, unaware of any hint that this would be the last time he would see his boss alive. If de Guzman knew this was to be his last flight, he didn't show it. He left the helicopter briefly, but made no attempt to contact his fourth wife, Lilas, who lived close to the airport.

When de Guzman got back in the helicopter, according to the others in the plane, he took a back seat, an odd choice since the view of the lush terrain is far better from the front. This time the destination was Busang. Seventeen minutes from take-off, while cruising at 150 kilometres an hour 240 metres above the dense green jungle, the pilot and flight mechanic said they felt a whoosh of air coming from the rear left side of the aircraft. When they turned to look, de Guzman was gone – along with his headset, which had been ripped out of its socket. It took four days to recover his body, which had decayed in the 37-degree heat and been partly eaten by wild pigs so that it was barely recognizable.

"It came as a great surprise," a sombre David Walsh, founder and chief executive of Bre-X, told listeners of CBC's "As It Happens" the following night in a call from Atlanta, Georgia. "We were just with Mike de Guzman last week at the Toronto Prospectors and Developers annual convention, where he was in good spirits and anticipating getting back to the Busang site." Echoing the view of the local police, Walsh said the geologist had committed suicide, because after fourteen bouts of malaria he was in constant pain and had just been told he had a terminal case of hepatitis B. "It would have been a very painful, lingering end to his young life," he added wistfully.

De Guzman's death was one of the many startling revelations in the Bre-X saga, and like most of them it left many questions unanswered. Why was a military man at the controls of the helicopter on a routine private flight? Why would a man about to commit suicide buy new clothes? Was de Guzman behind the fraud of the century, and did he anticipate the revelation a few days after his death that there was no gold worth mining at Busang? If he was the culprit, who else was involved, and who knew about it? Could David Walsh and John Felderhof not have known about the dark deeds that had taken place?

The Bre-X story is one of the most compelling tales in Canada's history. It has all the elements: a tiny exploration mining company based in the basement of a former bankrupt that soon came to have a stock market value of more than $6 billion; a stock that turned some people into millionaires and others into paupers; a corrupt government on the other side of the globe, complete with the avaricious, quarrelling "First Siblings" of its wily, long-time president, Suharto; a bare-knuckles, behind-the-scenes fight for Busang by the world's biggest gold-mining companies, who were as shocked as everyone else when they discovered that the gold for which they moiled was fool's gold; and lobbying by former prime minister Brian Mulroney and former U.S. president George Bush on behalf of Peter Munk's Barrick Gold Corp., which was on its way to becoming the world's biggest gold-mining company until fate and President Suharto intervened. After months of struggle, Barrick and the other Canadian contenders, such as Placer Dome Inc. of Vancouver, walked away with precisely nothing. Little did they realize that their apparent defeat was actually a narrow escape from colossal embarrassment and potential disaster.

Instead of being one of the great rags-to-riches finds of the century, Busang is one of its greatest frauds. Yet for almost three years it went undetected by scores of geologists, by the dozens of mining companies operating in Indonesia, by the experts on Bay Street and Wall Street, by the supposedly prudent securities regulators of the Toronto Stock Exchange. All this, despite dozens of red flags raised by the behaviour of Bre-X. How could this happen? Who was to blame, and who was going to pay the price? At the end of the day, the only certainty was that the Bre-X débâcle was poised to create a new set of millionaires – the lawyers, whose battles are destined to stretch well into the next millennium.

The history of Bre-X minerals is the history of hype and promotion, as the company and stock analysts at brokerage firms, in a one-two punch, vied for superlatives about the deposit. The saga is one of short-sightedness and of strong emotions: jealousy, arrogance, anger, and, above all, greed. If love is blind, greed makes blindness infectious. In this case, greed blinded the eyes of everyone from investors to stock analysts. Clearly, when there is a lot of money to be made, few people want to look too closely at just how it is being made. For example, a 1994 report on the $350 million (U.S.) in phantom profits claimed by trader Joseph Jett at investment dealer Kidder Peabody in New York concluded that "employees throughout the firm appear to have deferred to the success of the fixed income division and been unwilling to ask hard questions about Jett, the division's rising star." Then there is Barings PLC, the London-based merchant bank, created in 1762, that survived Napoleon and Hitler but not the criminal activities of Nick Leeson, its then twenty-eight-year-old super-trader in Singapore. Despite warning bells that rang long and loud, Leeson's laughably simple fraud, which included cutting the signatures off documents and pasting them on others, went undetected for years. No one questioned how the trader's huge declared profits could go hand in hand with low risk for so long. Leeson's own answer was that Barings executives "wanted to believe in … the profits that were being reported, and therefore they weren't willing to question."

This book recounts a story in which few people had an interest – or thought they had an interest – in questioning a gold deposit that was a proverbial gold mine for so many. That is one of the reasons why the Bre-X story stands as a fable for our times.

CHAPTER TWO

Banquets for Bankrupts

"When David Walsh decided he wanted to go back to Indonesia, he looked for John Felderhof, who was the only guy he knew there. Why go back? I asked Felderhof that once. He said David had a dream one day and decided to go to Indonesia." – Peter Howe, mining consultant, ACA Howe International Ltd.

"John Felderhof has big arms. You're stretching; you're showing the upside potential of the project, so your arms get bigger and bigger when you describe the project." – Australian geologist Gavin Thomas

A Barbecue in Sydney

The menu was typical of an Australian barbecue, with everyone cooking their own steaks on the grill in Peter Howe's back yard and drinking plenty of beer. But the guest list that day in 1983 had an international flavour. Howe, a Canadian geologist who ran the Sydney office of ACA Howe International Ltd., the mining consulting firm his father had built, had invited a few co-workers to the deck of his harbourside home for dinner. Among those dropping by was a chain-smoking geologist named John Felderhof, who had helped discover an important copper mine in Papua New Guinea sixteen years earlier and hadn't stopped boasting about it since. Felderhof, who grew up in Nova Scotia, worked for Howe. Much of his time was spent in Indonesia roaring around dirt logging roads on a motorcycle and trying to locate gold properties by asking the local villagers where they'd successfully panned for grains of gold.

Howe had invited another Canadian geologist to dinner, a visitor to Sydney named Mike Duggan. He knew Howe from years past, when both worked on gold claims in Timmins, Ontario. Now, Duggan's game was oil and gas, and he brought a colleague to the party, a chubby stock promoter named David Walsh. At the time, Walsh didn't have much to promote. After twenty-three years taking care of other people's money, Walsh had quit his job as a stock trader in Calgary and was suing his former employer, investment dealer Midland Doherty Ltd., for $110,000 in unpaid wages. Walsh was striking out on his own, touring Australia with Duggan looking for promising little oil companies that he could raise money for on the Canadian stock market.

As the sun set and the beer flowed, Indonesia was the main topic of conversation. Howe had been born in Jakarta, though his father's mining interests took the family back to Canada when he was still a boy. He did not return until the 1970s, after the rise of General Suharto paved the way for a pro-business, pro-West regime. After Peter Howe talked about Indonesia's sleazy politics, Felderhof launched into his stories of the country's undiscovered mineral wealth, spinning out a theory of rich gold and copper deposits hidden in the ruins of long-collapsed volcanoes. By the time the evening wound down, Felderhof's tales had hooked Walsh.

With time on his hands and the prospect of money to come from his lawsuit, Walsh decided to visit Indonesia with Felderhof to see this promised land for himself. The pair flew to Jakarta a few days after

Howe's party and spent two weeks touring several islands, with Walsh listening to Felderhof's spiel on geology, a lecture delivered with uncommon self-confidence and a great many Bintang beers. Then they parted, two men with big dreams, both convinced they were on the verge of great things, but both destined to spend the better part of the next decade going nowhere.

Walsh jetted back to Calgary to nurse along a few oil and gas properties he owned in Louisiana; the next year, he turned his attention to diamond plays. Felderhof stayed in Indonesia, where he played a key role in the coming boom – and bust – of the land's junior gold-mining sector. It would be a decade before they met again, this time over dinner in Jakarta.

The Guy on the Barstool at the Three Greenhorns

A few blocks from the sterile office towers of downtown Calgary is a strip of steak houses and taverns on Fourth Avenue S.W. that fill up in the early afternoon with a hard-drinking crowd. Draft beer arrives in dozens of small glasses crammed on huge platters; tastes run to double rye and water if someone else is buying. The guys that gather in these bars spend their working hours pushing stock plays on the Alberta Stock Exchange, home to companies with unproven, sometimes dubious assets – oil fields in distant lands, gold claims that are still moose pasture. The regulars' talk is about companies that promise to be the next big thing, but often fail to deliver. Over a T-bone steak and a few beers – often, more than a few beers – the stock promoters swap gossip, brag, commiserate, and dream about getting rich. Most of the patrons will always be waiting for the big deal to come their way. Many have checkered pasts – run-ins with securities regulators, involvement with companies that went bust, lawsuits from disgruntled former investors and partners. In the 1980s, the Three Greenhorns bar on the corner of Fourth Avenue and Fourth Street was a favourite watering hole for the promoters, and David Walsh was a familiar face.

Even early in the morning, Walsh tends to look like he's just had a few. When he wears a tie, it's always askew. The top button of his dress shirt never seems to stay done up. There's usually a Dunhill cigarette in his hand; his smoking is accompanied by a persistent hacking cough. In another age, Walsh would have been described as cutting a commanding figure. These days, when business executives tend to run lean and mean, Walsh is simply fat. A reminder of every beer he's ever quaffed hangs over his belt, and although he's over six feet tall, lack of exercise means he slouches. His puffy face is often flushed red, the result of high blood pressure. But Walsh is quick to smile and even quicker to launch into a story. If Norm from the television show "Cheers" ever ran a junior mining company, he'd be David Walsh.

"What's he like? Well, he's very persistent," says Barry Tannock, a former Bre-X vice-president who was with the company through its lean years, when the corporate headquarters was the basement rec room of the Walsh family's modest bungalow in Calgary. "He wants very much to succeed. He has a fire in his belly to make it."

Walsh came from a family that succeeded in the financial markets. His grandfather was a successful stockbroker and his father, Vaughan, followed in his footsteps in Montreal. David was born in 1946, when Montreal was still the financial centre of Canada and dominated by an English-speaking business élite. He grew up comfortably in the city's Westmount neighbourhood, then an affluent anglophone enclave of stone houses and shaded streets in the heart of the city.

School never held much attraction for David Walsh. An indifferent student at best, the future multimillionaire quit high school in Montreal at the end of Grade 10. In June 1963, at the age of seventeen, he joined a small trust company in Montreal called Eastern Trust Co., a company that frequently dealt with his father. Walsh worked on the trust's investment desk, buying and selling stocks and bonds on behalf of wealthy individuals and pension funds that kept their money with the company. It was a fun place to be; the market was booming and everyone was making money. Lack of formal education was no real impediment to advancement; many senior financial executives in the 1960s and 1970s had similar backgrounds. Walsh enjoyed what he did and the camaraderie of the desk. At night, he took accounting and finance courses. In 1969, he was named head of the four-person investment department. He was just twenty-three years old, and that same year, he fell in love with a secretary named Jeannette at Eastern Trust (which was taken over by Canada Permanent Trust Co., and is now known as Canada Trust Co.). A year later, they married. Their first son, Brett, was born a year later. A second son, Sean, came along two years after his brother.

Scandal struck the Montreal branch of Canada Permanent in 1976. A Montreal stockbroker at Yorkton Securities, a small investment dealer, had been stealing from his clients. He pilfered securities entrusted to Yorkton and sold them through his own personal accounts, one of which was with Canada Permanent and supervised by Walsh. In March 1976, a few clients complained that securities were missing from their portfolios, and Yorkton conducted an internal audit. The firm could not find about $600,000 worth of stocks and bonds. The broker was caught, convicted of fraud, and sentenced to two years in jail.

No one ever accused Walsh of having any knowledge of wrongdoing in this case. His sin was one of omission. As an executive at Canada Permanent, he had a responsibility to monitor the broker's trading and ensure that sales of securities were authorized by senior Yorkton executives. Trading without authorization should have been a red flag warning that something was amiss. Regulations are in place in the investment industry to ensure that a broker's superiors authorize trades to deter theft and other violations of securities law, such as insider trading. Walsh didn't detect a problem, and he didn't raise a warning flag.

The former Yorkton broker recently said, with regret, that his crimes were a factor in Walsh's departure from Canada Permanent in April 1976. Walsh denies this, saying he left because he wanted to build his own trust company. Nevertheless, he departed under a cloud, after displaying naïveté and negligence in his responsibilities.

After quitting Canada Permanent, Walsh spent three fruitless months attempting to start a new financial services company. In August, he gave up and joined a medium-sized investment dealer, Midland Doherty Ltd. He worked on the institutional equity trading desk in Montreal, buying and selling stocks on behalf of large investors such as life insurers, pension funds, and mutual funds. Success in this world depends in part on the ability to build relationships with fund managers, to buy a few rounds of drinks after work, to come up with hockey tickets for a big game, to schmooze. Walsh enjoyed working in this tight-knit world. The affable stock jockey won a fair amount of business, earning more than $100,000 annually in commissions in the late 1970s and early 1980s.

In 1982, Midland Doherty executives asked Walsh to move to Calgary and set up an institutional stock trading desk. In the lawsuit he later filed, Walsh claimed he packed up Jeannette and his sons and left his home town for the west because the brokerage firm guaranteed him a minimum salary of $50,000 while the business got started. The early 1980s were a terrible time for the oil patch. There was a recession, exploration money was scarce, and whole floors of Calgary office towers sat empty. Home owners faced mortgages worth more than the value of their properties and simply walked away from their problems, dropping off their keys at the bank. Against this dreary background, Walsh had little success. The new equity trading operation fared poorly, and Walsh claimed Midland Doherty cut his pay by more than half, to $2,000 a month. Walsh quit early in 1983, then turned around and sued the company for $110,000, alleging constructive dismissal. The lawsuit was eventually settled out of court, and the terms have never been revealed.

Walsh was out on his own in Calgary with a family to support, and the only game he knew was the stock market. It was time to start working towards a big score. In 1984, he listed a company on the

Vancouver Stock Exchange called Bresea Resources Ltd., the name coming from the names of his sons, Brett and Sean. Walsh talked up the company with friends in financial circles and managed to raise what he needed by selling shares. Part of the money was used to buy oil and gas claims in Louisiana, but the oil industry continued to suffer, and nothing came of the holdings.

In 1985, the focus at Bresea turned from oil to gold. Walsh and Barry Tannock set up a new company called Ayrex Resources Ltd. and picked up claims in the Casa Beradi region of northwestern Quebec; Bresea was a partner in the Quebec claims. Walsh and Tannock worked closely for years, often in unorthodox circumstances. Tannock vividly recalls one memorable night out boosting stock to a group of brokers at Hy's steak-house in Calgary. In the course of the working evening, Walsh got into an altercation with a waitress that resulted in the Calgary police being summoned and Bresea's chairman being led out of the restaurant in handcuffs and tossed in the back of a squad car. Tannock made a frantic late-night call to Bresea's lawyer, who bailed the chastened executive out of jail. In Tannock's laconic words, "The only upshot of this was we were no longer able to spread the good word at Hy's."

Not surprisingly, their working alliance ended with lawsuits after Tannock claimed Walsh reneged on a promised bonus of more than $50,000. Ayrex unearthed nothing of value in Quebec, and money started to run out, so Walsh attempted something of a homecoming. In November 1987, he listed Bresea on the Montreal Stock Exchange, hoping to win new backers for the tiny company, but investors were in no mood to be charmed. One month earlier, the stock market had crashed, and no one was interested in Walsh's collection of claims.

"Yes, We Are Still in Business"

Early in 1988, Walsh incorporated Bre-X Minerals Ltd., listing it on the Alberta Stock Exchange at 30 cents a share. He appointed himself chairman, chief executive officer, and president. Jeanette was the corporate secretary and Tannock was vice-president, investor relations, a job that meant working the phones to find investors for Bre-X as it tried to raise funds. The name this time came from son Brett alone, with the "X" for exploration. Walsh and his wife owned shares in Bre-X directly and through Bresea, which served as a holding company. At Bre-X, the initial search was for diamonds. The company chased the spectacular success of Diamet Minerals Ltd. by purchasing forty-one claims in the Northwest Territories. Investors steered clear, and as a result, Bre-X just bumped along. Shares traded at an average price of twenty-seven cents until 1993 but, at one point, fell as low as two cents. In an otherwise forgettable 1991 annual report, Walsh started his letter to shareholders with the line: "Yes, we are still in business."

During this period, the Walsh household was kept afloat by the $20,000 a year Jeanette brought in as a secretary and whatever money Walsh could make flipping stocks. He was no long-term investor, keeping fourteen accounts at different investment firms. He traded continually and liked to buy stocks in newly formed public companies, then quickly sell into the market. Often, the trading came from tips picked up at the Three Greenhorns.

The pace of stock trading created new problems for Walsh. In 1987, his broker at Pemberton Securities Ltd., now part of RBC Dominion Securities Ltd., mistakenly credited Walsh's account with $40,775 worth of shares that he had already sold. Rather than reveal the error, Walsh again sold the stock, then had Pemberton send the money directly to him. The error was caught by the brokerage firm and Walsh was asked to return the money. He refused to do so, and Pemberton sued. In February 1991, an Alberta court ordered Walsh to pay back the investment dealer. During an interview with *Canadian Business* magazine, Walsh offered a weak justification: "You have to have your priorities, which basically wasn't worrying about bank statements when you are putting out fires running a junior resource company."

By June 1992, the Walsh family's financial situation was grim. Stock trading had proved profitable in the late 1980s, but the market died in the early 1990s. Walsh was making just $1,000 a month. The family survived by drawing on lines of credit, pushing credit cards to their limit, and using cash advances from one card to make the minimum payment on another. They had fifteen different cards from eight banks and trust companies in four different cities, along with plastic from Woolworth's and Canadian Tire. In all, the Walshes owed $59,500 on their credit cards. Then there was National Bank; it had extended $15,000 on a line of credit. Royal Bank had also advanced a loan. Together, the family's debt came to more than $200,000, and Walsh and his wife were forced to declare personal bankruptcy. But creditors got very little; Pemberton received just $1,520 on its claim of close to $50,000.

Walsh walked away from bankruptcy with very little to show for forty-seven years on the planet. In 1993, he and Jeannette still had title to their mortgaged bungalow, along with $1,400 worth of furniture, a 1979 Buick Regal, and a lot of stock in Bre-X and Bresea, which was worth just a few cents a share. Desperate to raise money, he sold some of the Bre-X shares held by Bresea and pulled together $10,000. Walsh decided to spend the money on a return trip to Jakarta, where he went looking for the cocky Dutch geologist he'd last seen a decade ago. "When David Walsh decided to go back to Indonesia, he looked for John Felderhof, who was the only guy he knew there," said Peter Howe, the mining geologist. "Why go back? I asked John Felderhof that question once. He said David had a dream one day and decided to go to Indonesia."

Years later, many would come away from their first meeting with Walsh shaking their head over the thought that this overweight and badly groomed fellow with a terrible financial background could be the brains behind a mining company valued at $6 billion. Walsh had little to offer in a second meeting to dispel this view. His office was always chaotic, six inches deep in letters, geological files, and financial records he would root through when trying to make a point.

The ashtray was always overflowing. In business meetings and interviews, he tended to mouth catch phrases, and he could be arrogant. In 1994, he was pushing Bre-X and visited high-profile San Francisco-based fund manager Paul Stephens. The veteran investor told *Fortune* magazine, "Walsh showed up in our office. He had this massive potbelly and brought this woman with him whose business card said she was secretary of the company. Our checks on him were just awful. He had a history of filing for bankruptcy. And then, when you meet him in person, he was a slob. Bottom line: All you had to do was meet him and you wouldn't have bought the stock."

A *Calgary Herald* reporter once confronted the Bre-X CEO with the widely held sentiment that he was in over his head. "I don't believe I'm in over my head," Walsh replied. "I have two philosophies in life, OPM and OPB – Other People's Money and Other People's Brains. There's an awful lot of talent out there that can be drawn on, an awful lot of brain power. I think the first good management decision I made was getting John Felderhof and his team."

John Felderhof, The River Walker

Friends from early in his career like to tell a story about John Felderhof exploring the deep jungle of Papua New Guinea. Hiking through waist-deep, leech-infested swamp and hills that a government report described as "undoubtedly the end of the world," Felderhof lost his boots. Undeterred, he kept on exploring in bare feet.

Felderhof relishes the tough-guy image of this story. He'll even tell the tale himself over a few beers, along with other assorted memories of a geologist who travelled three continents during thirty years of exploration work. The stories recount fourteen bouts with malaria, weeks spent in jungle villages carrying provisions and rock samples on his back, eating whatever the locals were cooking up, then pushing off the next day to hack through more jungle and wade through swamp. Felderhof tells his stories well, through frequent drags on his ever-present Marlboro cigarette. He enjoys playing the tough tropical rogue. When he's talking, his thick eyebrows dance around, his gaze is intense, and his craggy face and hawk nose are lined from years in the sun and the pain of tropical diseases. "Felderhof was known as a river walker," said Stephens, the fund manager, "someone who would go off for three to six months in the jungle." The river walker is a tough, stubborn, proud man who pioneered a new theory of geology in an unforgiving part of the world. His stories centre on a man who tasted one great success early in his career, co-discovering the rich Ok Tedi copper mine in New Guinea, and then spent the next twenty years trying to regain that glory.

For all his love of geology, Felderhof came relatively late to the field. One of twelve children – nine boys and three girls – he was born in 1940 in Rotterdam, Holland, where his father was a doctor. In 1954, the family moved to New Glasgow, Nova Scotia, where Felderhof's father had a job waiting for him at the town's new hospital. "It was eight or nine years after the war," recalled William Felderhof, youngest member of the clan and a geologist like his elder brother. "Europeans were fed up with all the hardships they'd put up with during the war years. It was a time to move along, move to a place that was a little safer."

Felderhof finished high school in New Glasgow, a decent student and an outdoors man and athlete of some repute. "When he was in high school, he was captain of the rugby team," said Will Felderhof. "I think out here they didn't have football because they couldn't afford the gear." After graduating, Felderhof headed for Dalhousie University, where he enrolled in sciences and considered being a doctor like his father. But he switched majors and graduated in 1962 with an undergraduate degree in geology. Why geology? "One of his early jobs when he went to Dalhousie was in one of the gold mines in Nova Scotia," explained his brother. "Maybe that triggered it. Maybe that was one of the things that really got him interested."

Felderhof's first job after graduation was with Iron Ore Co. in Schefferville, Quebec, a company that would later boast Brian

Mulroney as its president, long before the lawyer became prime minister of Canada and then a director of Barrick Gold. Felderhof spent two years in Schefferville as an open pit engineer, then joined Britain's Rio Tinto Zinc Corp. and headed off to Zambia as a geologist in an underground mine. He spent three years in the African nation and met a South African woman named Denise who became his wife.

In 1967, Felderhof took a job with Kennecott Copper Corp., a U.S. company that was just starting to explore Papua New Guinea. His team based its prospecting on what were then radical geological theories, though they have since been proven valid. The idea – at the time, a largely untested theory – was that rich mineral deposits could be found where the earth's plates collided. Papua New Guinea marked such a collision point.

In July 1967, Felderhof and colleague Doug Fishburn were prospecting along the Ok Tedi River. They sent one native member of the crew out from the base camp to clear a spot for a helicopter to land. The native, named Mangu, came back the next day shouting he'd found *"planti ain i stap"* or "plenty of metal." Felderhof and Fishburn went to the landing pad and found traces of a copper vein that ran for hundreds of feet. They told Kennecott to drill on the site. Within months, a huge copper and gold deposit was mapped out that made both men celebrities among exploration geologists.

What became the Ok Tedi mine made Felderhof famous, though not rich. He didn't own a stake in the discovery, which was eventually developed by Australian mining conglomerate Broken Hill Pty Ltd. No other project he worked on in the next two decades came close to matching this find. In fact, life from this point was a series of disappointments, until the Busang discovery.

In 1974, Felderhof met Peter Howe in Sydney and took a job as a consulting engineer at Howe's father's firm, ACA Howe International. The job filled two needs. Felderhof wanted a change, and his wife, Denise, wanted to go back to South Africa with their two young children. Howe and Felderhof struck a deal to open an office in Johannesburg.

Surprisingly, there was little activity among small mining companies in South Africa. But in the early 1980s, there was lots of action in Indonesia. Howe brought Felderhof back from Africa and had him assemble a team that would explore several of the nation's islands. One of Felderhof's first hires was a bright young Filipino geologist named Michael de Guzman.

In the early 1980s, Felderhof's marriage fell apart. Those who know him say an obsession with work had a great deal to do with the divorce. "John's spent just a little too much time in the forest – he's a little wild," said Rob Van Doorn, gold analyst for investment dealer Loewen Ondaatje McCutcheon Ltd. in Toronto and, like Felderhof, a native of Holland. "He's typical of an exploration geologist, in that he can get totally carried away by what he sees in a few stupid rocks." Barry Tannock got to know Felderhof while working at Bre-X and said, "John's not the kind of guy you picture being married. He's a bit of a rogue, a man's man."

In 1984, Felderhof had remarried, to a woman from Perth named Ingrid, also originally from the Netherlands. She was a stewardess when they met, attractive and poised, with a strong independent streak. The marriage gave Felderhof stability and a daughter named Karen Marie. A strong-willed woman, Ingrid had thrown herself into politics in the 1980s, helping to found the Australian Conservative Party. The movement pushed a back-to-basics approach; in education, it called for moral standards based on the Ten Commandments and singing the national anthem each morning at school, along with military-style boot camps for young offenders. Perhaps anticipating her husband's future success, Ingrid Felderhof also advocated the abolition of capital gains tax. The party never elected a candidate.

Felderhof rode the boom and bust of Indonesian junior gold plays through the 1980s. He took Walsh on a tour when Australian stock market interest in these companies was near its peak. At one point, Felderhof held options worth nearly $19 million (U.S.) in a Perth-based junior mining company named Jason Mining NL, named for Jason, the character of Greek legend who pursued the mythical Golden Fleece. However, Jason's properties didn't pan out and the stock market crashed in 1987, before Felderhof could cash in his options. A number of other Indonesian projects that he was involved in as a geologist or company director also went up in flames. Felderhof was left penniless and out of work.

Felderhof's reputation for exaggeration and binge drinking made finding work tough. He drifted from Australia to Canada and back to Indonesia in search of a job. "At that stage it was a pretty tough time for him," said Colin Hebbard, an old friend of Felderhof's in Perth, Australia. "He sort of spent some time in Indonesia and I think that's where he went through the tough period in his life. He was looked after by various people in Indonesia. His friends sort of took him under their wing over the difficult period." At one point, Felderhof farmed macadamia nuts in Australia. He would later joke that he was so broke late in 1992 that he had to steal a Christmas tree. Felderhof and a friend considered returning to Indonesia not as geologists, but as owners of a combination resort and shrimp farm.

By the early 1990s, the market for junior mining companies was beginning to improve, and Felderhof was back in Indonesia as a mining consultant, evaluating gold and copper claims. He often found himself writing glowing reports on properties that other mining companies never got around to developing. Felderhof longed to prove himself again, to tell a bigger and better story. One of the geologists he met in New Guinea was Gavin Thomas, a native of Sydney, Australia. The two crossed paths frequently over the next three decades and became friends. In an interview with *The Wall Street Journal*, Thomas described Felderhof as "gregarious, flamboyant and excitable."

"John Felderhof has big arms," Thomas said. Like a fisherman, Felderhof's boasts would grow as the night went on. "You're stretching; you're showing the upside potential of the project, so your arms get bigger and bigger when you describe the project." In 1993, while working as a Jakarta-based mining consultant, Felderhof got a chance to get back into the game.

Dinner at the Sari Hotel

The Sari Hotel is one of the most expensive spots in Jakarta. The huge, noisy city of almost 9 million is full of both great luxury and bitter poverty, often in startling proximity. The 400-room Sari, complete with sixty-three penthouses, is a large, cool, reassuring building, set close to the city centre. Affiliated with the Pan Pacific Hotel chain, the twenty-year-old institution is popular with visiting Westerners, who can sample its coffee shop, its delicatessen, or its Mediterranean Bar and Grill, and is definitely ensconced at the luxury end of the local scale. It was therefore an unlikely spot for a down-on-his-luck financier from Calgary to meet with a crew of washed-up geologists. But after ten days of searching the city, David Walsh had finally found his only contact in the country, John Felderhof, and set up a dinner meeting at the hotel. He may have been down to his last few dollars but he still wanted to make a favourable impression. "David flew out to Indonesia and the whole gang was assembled to meet him," recalled Peter Howe. "They figured this Canadian mining promoter had lots of money. Little did they know."

The meal was a resounding success. Walsh got a chance to meet one of Felderhof's best friends, Michael de Guzman, a geologist who shared the faith that gold deposits were hidden in extinct volcanoes. "I told John I had a gut feeling copper and gold was bottoming out," Walsh later told the *Far Eastern Economic Review*. "John agreed with me. Mining companies were pulling out of Indonesia, but we decided to take a contrary view and John said he was aware of several properties."

By the end of the meal, Walsh was committed to raising money to buy properties. Everyone was going to share in the adventure by getting the chance to buy stock in Bre-X at rock-bottom prices.

Felderhof was on his way to secure the rights to three claims, including one he and de Guzman had checked out on the island of Kalimantan seven years earlier. Other companies had worked that property over, even drilled holes and found promising traces of gold, but no one had the cash needed to fully explore the claim. The property on Kalimantan was a 15,000-hectare patch of logged-over rain forest surrounding a creek, an area that lay seven hours by speedboat from the nearest city. The creek was called Busang.

CHAPTER THREE

A Creek Called Busang

"We almost closed the property. In December, 1993, John said, 'Close the property,' and then we made the hit."
– Michael de Guzman, Bre-X exploration manager

"We've got a monster by the tail." – John Felderhof, Bre-X chief geologist

Monkey Pasture

In northern climates, remote gold properties are jokingly referred to as "moose pasture" by geologists. That would make Busang a monkey pasture. In its wilderness days, the rain-forest-covered broken hills were home to orangutans and bulbous-nosed proboscis monkeys. Logging after the Second World War drove away the monkeys, but second-growth forest is now mature in the region, and almost impenetrable, with lush undergrowth and a canopy of leaves that stretches like an unbroken green sea when viewed from the air. Long-extinct volcanoes have been weathered down by centuries of rain, and the

Busang creek flows from these tree-covered hills. Natives have panned traces of gold from the creek for generations. The Bre-X geologists would come to focus their attentions on a rock formation set in a series of hills roughly seven kilometres long and a kilometre across, ridges that look like dolphins cresting the surface of a forest-green sea.

John Felderhof spent a lifetime developing a theory that would produce the golden hills on Kalimantan, a formation 30 million years in the making. According to the gospel preached by Felderhof (and backed by disciple Michael de Guzman), gold sprang from the volcanoes of the Rim of Fire, the 50,000-kilometre circle around the Pacific Ocean that marks the meeting of the great plates that form the Earth's crust. Under Indonesia's 13,000 islands, the Indo-Australian and Pacific tectonic plates collide. The massive forces at play are still shaping the planet; over eons, the Earth's outer layer has been weakened by shifts in these vast continents of rock, lifting mountains and producing volcanoes and earthquakes.

The simple geological explanation for the Busang deposit is known as technomagmatism; it's a theory Felderhof or de Guzman loved to spin over a cold Bintang. The way they explained it, the process started with a thick layer of sedimentary rock covering a volcano. During the late stages of active periods in a volcano's life, its heat turned this relatively soft layer of sedimentary material into a tougher layer of silica, which sealed the volcano. Hot gases or liquids from the still active volcano built up, however, under the silica cap. Eventually the pressure burst through, and hot magma or lava exploded through the fracture, causing an eruption. The magma was already rich in minerals that make up the Earth's core – lead, zinc, copper, and gold – and it leached additional minerals from the surrounding sedimentary rock. The mineral wealth from the centre of the Earth ended up deposited in surface volcanic rock surrounded by fractures in the sedimentary rock cap, hidden by a layer of soil and jungle. This process was repeated over the centuries: the heat of the volcano built a seal, pressure grew, and it erupted. When the volcano finally fell silent, its presence was recorded in a smattering of rock and minerals pulled from the Earth's core.

The plug of rock that makes up Busang measures five kilometres by twelve kilometres – a volcanic footprint on the face of the Earth. For Felderhof, finding this footprint was his life's ambition.

Several years later, the mining and financial communities would pick up the habit of faithfully regurgitating these theories in their studies on Bre-X. Then outsiders would run a short explanation in accessible English to let the public in on the good news. Analyst Bruno Kaiser, then at CIBC Wood Gundy, cranked out a report to clients in July 1996 that was typical of the genre. "Busang is appropriately classified as a carbonate-polymetallic pyrite dominated epithermal deposit genetically associated with a high level emplacement of dome complex within a maar diatreme," he explained helpfully in the course of a ten-page report on the company. The description was cribbed from a presentation de Guzman had given to a Toronto audience a few months earlier. For those readers who didn't hold graduate degrees in geology, Kaiser drew a map of a deposit that showed a pocket of volcanic rock surrounded by worthless sedimentary stone. The analysts explained how tough it was to find such riches and how smart prospectors had to be to find it. After reading these reports, outsiders came away with the impression that individuals far more knowledgeable than they had diligently worked over Bre-X's calculations and found that they passed muster.

Gold on Kalimantan was no big surprise to the mining community. Indonesian schoolchildren learn that gold was first mined on the island by the Chinese in the fourth century – the name Kalimantan means "rivers of gold" in the local dialect. The deposit's existence, de Guzman explained in poorly delivered lectures to audiences of geologists, bankers or university students after he discovered Busang, was first suspected by Dutch missionaries who saw locals pan gold in Kalimantan's highland rivers. These God-fearing souls occasionally worked the rivers shoulder to shoulder with the indigenous Dayak people as the region was settled after the Second World War.

Bre-X's presentations, used to sell the property to investors and the world at large when Busang was being explored, built an image of a region awash in unclaimed wealth, a land where simple rice farmers used to fill their pans with river gold. The mother lode awaited someone diligent and persistent enough to uncover its secrets.

In beer halls, university classrooms, and investment bank board-rooms, Felderhof and de Guzman preached often and at length on their theory and their property at Busang. Felderhof in particular possessed a faith in the volcanic origins of Indonesia's gold that bordered on fanaticism. An unyielding man, he had the unshakable belief common to his Dutch Calvinist ancestors. He enjoyed credibility with financiers because of his apparent knowledge, cockily displayed, and because of his past success at Ok Tedi in Papua New Guinea.

To be worth mining, a deposit in a relatively remote spot like Borneo would have to contain at least a million ounces of gold. Mount Muro, a mine about 300 kilometres southwest of Busang that Felderhof once worked on, holds an estimated 1.8 million ounces. The Kelian mine just 200 kilometres away boasts reserves of 5 million ounces. The world's largest gold deposit is on the neighbouring island of Irian Jaya, the 53.4-million-ounce Grasberg mine owned by Freeport McMoRan Copper & Gold Inc. of New Orleans. Of course, the other key factor in determining if a gold deposit can be mined is the cost of production. Indonesia's mines are open pits, which are far cheaper to exploit than the deep underground shafts of mines found in much of Canada and South Africa. Bre-X's geologists painted a picture of Busang that was ideally suited to a low-cost open-pit mine, from which gold could be extracted for less than $90 (U.S.) an ounce, at a time when it traded for about $350 an ounce.

The Allure Of Gold

Gold has a special charm for investors. It has an ancient, storied history, which pre-dates paper money by several millennia. Indeed, much of history revolves around the quest for gold and its display. The innermost of Pharaoh Tutankhamen's three coffins was made of solid gold, weighing 240 pounds. In 550 B.C., King Croesus of Lydia in Asia Minor established the first currency of pure gold and gave the language a simile, "rich as Croesus," which lives on 2,500 years later. Judas betrayed Jesus for thirty pieces of silver, gold's sister metal. In the Middle Ages, European merchants transacted business in Troyes, France, using a specific weight of gold, the troy ounce. During the early Renaissance, Florence issued its renowned gold florins, while Venice countered with its gold ducats. Britain's currency was originally based on silver, with 240 silver coins making up a pound sterling. Timbuktu, a major African commercial and smelting centre in the fourteenth century, was the "city of gold." Spain opened up the New World as a result of its successful search for gold and silver, which it found in Peru and Mexico.

Beginning with Britain in 1821, many countries have operated under a gold standard, by which the basic monetary unit is defined in terms of a fixed quantity of gold. President Richard Nixon took the United States off the gold standard in 1971, a decision that ultimately allowed the price to soar above $35 (U.S.) an ounce, the level at which it had been fixed. According to William Greider in *Secrets of the Temple*, a book on the Federal Reserve, this was "the precise date on which America's singular dominance of the world's economy ended." The list of gold's historical antecedents is endless and explains why for centuries gold has had a unique position in the hearts of princes, merchants, capitalists, communists, and ordinary citizens in all the parts of the world.

Gold is unlike any other commodity in another way: virtually every ounce that has been produced since ancient times still exists. Much of it is in the hands of the world's central banks, which the U.S. Federal Reserve holds for them in vaults under the sidewalks of Manhattan. Twice a day for decades, representatives of five major gold dealers have met at N. M. Rothschild & Sons Ltd. in London, where they set, or "fix," the current price, or "spot," by raising and lowering tiny Union Jacks that indicate the price they are willing to support.

South Africa, built on gold and diamonds, remains the world's largest producer of bullion, though its lead is slipping badly as its mines become depleted and its costs escalate, in large part because the end of apartheid has meant higher wages for miners, most of whom are black. A few years ago, the United States replaced Russia in second place; the United States is now followed by Australia, Canada, China, Russia, and Indonesia, even without Busang. Anglo-American Corp. of South Africa, the child of Cecil Rhodes and the Oppenheimers, is overwhelmingly the biggest gold-producing company in the world; Barrick Gold Corp. of Toronto is second; Placer Dome Inc. of Vancouver is sixth; while Freeport McMoRan Copper & Gold Inc. is ninth.

The average world-wide cash cost to produce an ounce of gold in 1996 was $262 (U.S.), though many producers, particularly in the Americas, can get the metal out of the ground for less. For example, Barrick, which bills itself as the lowest-cost major producer, had an average cash cost of $193. The average world-wide total production cost, which includes accounting items such as depreciation, was $317, making many operations marginal as the price of gold slumped.

Most of the demand for gold comes from the jewellery industry, with consumption highest in Asia, particularly in India, where it is firmly rooted in the culture. Across the subcontinent, it is trusted more than paper currency; it can easily be hidden or worn, is portable, and is an important part of dowries. In fact, as much as 200 grams of gold can change hands at each of the 5 million weddings that take place in India every year. "Farmers' profits rarely, if ever, are invested in anything except gold and silver," says Gold Fields Mineral Services Ltd.'s *Gold 1997* report, the Bible on gold markets. "It is for this reason that the monsoon is so important to the subsequent level of demand."

Investors buy gold for many reasons. More than anything else, they favour gold as a medium of exchange that – unlike paper currencies – has always had value. It can be hoarded and hidden, but it cannot be devalued by a government, because its price is ultimately determined by supply and demand in many countries. The price of gold does particularly well in times of inflation. The decline in inflation since the early 1980s largely explains why the price eroded from the 1980 high of $850 (U.S.) an ounce to an average of $388 in 1996, and skidded to its lowest level in years, $325, in July 1997. Nonetheless, there are still legions of fanatical devotees, called gold bugs. They're the incurable optimists of the investment world, eternally convinced – despite years of evidence to the contrary – that the Midas metal is poised to soar. Most of them have a bleak view of the planet's future, and work from the dark conviction that the yellow metal alone provides security in a frighteningly troubled world. As George Bernard Shaw once commented, "If you must choose between placing your trust in government or placing your trust in gold, then gentlemen, I strongly advise you to place your trust in gold."

A Claim No One Wanted

Felderhof had first heard of Busang in the early 1980s, when he and his Australian colleague Mike Bird were exploring the logging roads of Borneo on rented motorcycles. They roared from village to village, asking the locals to point out where they had found gold nuggets in stream beds. Bird, an Australian geologist, spoke the local dialect and was plugged into the Indonesian establishment through his marriage to the daughter of one of the country's high-ranking army officers. "There were no maps," Felderhof told the *Northern Miner* newspaper. "It took years to figure out where the prospective areas of Kalimantan were."

Felderhof and Bird worked with two Australian junior mining companies – Pelsart Resources NL and Jason Mining Ltd. – as they staked claims across Borneo. One of those claims became the Mount Muro mine. Another claim offered to Felderhof by a Kalimantan family, the Syakeranis, and its partner, a small Australian mining company, was a 15,000-hectare site that contained the Busang creek. He decided the patch of rolling hills and rain forest 500 kilometres north of his base camp was too remote and too expensive to explore. Then, following the stock market crash of 1987, Pelsart and Jason collapsed amidst acrimony and scandal. Felderhof held nearly $19 million in stock options in the Australian companies, but never cashed in and emerged from the period bitter and nearly bankrupt. He drifted between countries in an attempt to cobble together a living. But like a moth around a flame, he kept circling back towards Indonesia and the claims that once had made him rich, but had then turned to nothing.

Busang remained in the hands of the middle-class Syakerani family, who lived on Kalimantan. To determine if the property could be turned into a mine, the family enlisted the help of Indonesian geologist Jonathan Nassey; a local businessman and politician with a controversial past named Jusuf Merukh; and an Australian junior mining company, Westralian Resources Projects Ltd.

In December 1986, this foursome pulled together a joint venture, called Westralian Atan Minerals, to explore Busang. The Australians owned 80 per cent of the company, the locals kept 20 per cent. That kind of ownership structure was typical because the Indonesian government required that local interests have at least a 10 per cent interest in any mining development. Twelve months later, a second Australian company called Montague Gold NL took a 50 per cent stake in the Indonesian gold venture. When the two Australian mining companies found enough money to back the drilling of nineteen holes on the property in 1988 and 1989, the exploration program hit traces of gold. But the cash ran out before anyone discovered if there was a worthwhile deposit. Busang remained jungle. It would be more than three years before anyone came visiting again.

In January 1992, Scottish businessman William McLucas bought control of the two Australian companies and went looking for knowledgeable geologists. McLucas hired John Felderhof and Mike de Guzman, which is how the pair first encountered the three-year-old Busang drill results. The property seemed to fit Felderhof and de Guzman's volcano theories. After de Guzman visited Busang early in 1993 and collected rock samples that again showed promising traces of gold, the two geologists wrote an upbeat report for McLucas, stating that Busang might contain 2 million ounces, and pressed for further exploration. But McLucas was strapped for cash and more interested in properties in Alaska, so he put the property up for sale early in 1993. The scene was set for Bre-X's arrival.

By May 1993, three months after the decisive dinner at the Sari Hotel, Walsh and his wife had raised enough money through Bre-X to buy an option on an 80 per cent stake in the Busang claim from McLucas for $80,100. (U.S.)

The three separate claims in the Borneo hills that make up the Busang property form a rough "L" shape. Each claim came to be owned by a different local partner and Bre-X. The mineral rights Bre-X purchased from Westralian Atan Minerals in May were in the bottom portion of the "L," known as the central zone or Busang I. Although this had been the site of drilling during the 1980s, the 15,062-hectare central zone proved to be only an appetizer.

In 1994, Bre-X and the Syakerani family established a partnership that acquired the land adjacent to the central zone, extending their holding on the horizontal part of that "L." The joint-venture company they established was called Askatindo Karya Mineral, and it was 90 per cent owned by the Canadians and 10 per cent by the Indonesians. This claim became the famous southeast zone or Busang II, and it was where the richest concentrations of gold would be found. At 45,221 hectares, the southeast zone was three times the size of the central zone and was the scene of almost all of Bre-X's eventual exploration.

In November 1995, Bre-X took another bite of Busang, buying a 90 per cent interest in a partnership called PT Amsya Lyna. Again, the Syakerani family was the local partner. This joint venture was labelled the northwest zone or Busang III, and was on the upper vertical segment of the "L." Its 127,448 unexplored hectares of land represented another major increase in Bre-X's holdings. Felderhof and de Guzman identified two rock formations that looked promising in Busang Northwest but never got around to exploring the area, as they were completely occupied with exploration of the southeast zone.

Buying a property was the first part of a two-stage process Bre-X needed to complete to open a mine in Indonesia. The second stage is getting government approval. In Indonesia, that means the president's signature. For such an openly corrupt nation, it is surprising that Indonesia has an internationally respected, standardized method of dealing with mining claims. Companies apply for a Contract of Work, or COW, an agreement between the government and a foreign company that spells out the terms for tax payments, royalty payments, employment quotas, and environmental safeguards. While approval of a contract is normally routine, it is ultimately a political act, as it requires the attention of the president himself. But with a contract in hand, a foreign company like Bre-X can usually operate without worrying about changes in its terms for thirty years or more.

Check and Checkmate

Busang's central zone covered a patch of virtually untracked wilderness the size of a small city. Late in 1993, Bre-X began drilling holes in this massive claim, working on the central zone where Felderhof and de Guzman's early work had shown the potential for a million ounces of gold.

The first two holes near the yellow rock came up empty. "We almost closed the property," de Guzman later told a *Fortune* magazine reporter. "In December 1993, John said, 'Close the property' and then we made the hit."

The hit was a hole 120 metres deep that showed gold concentrations of up to 6.58 grams of gold per tonne. As a general rule, anything over two grams is considered excellent. The central zone was shaping up as a decent candidate for a small open-pit mine. These early promising results were used by Walsh to raise money for Bre-X in Canada, funds that would be used to pay for drilling operations.

Felderhof and de Guzman later bragged that they had found gold where so many others had failed. Geologists from a dozen companies had walked around Busang over ten years and Montague had sunk nineteen holes, finding only traces of gold. "They were all in the wrong places," Felderhof said with a dismissive laugh to one reporter. Rivals didn't dig deep enough. They used the wrong drilling technology. Or they just didn't focus on the job at hand. "Geology wasn't on their minds," Felderhof said. "They were too busy spending all their time in town chasing girls and naming creeks after them." There was some truth in his statement. When Bre-X took over, there were creeks named Karen, Jenny, Martha, and Ann flowing through Busang. De Guzman consulted with local tribes and reinstated the traditional names.

Originally, Felderhof and Walsh assumed they were working on a deposit similar to Mount Muro, the small mine 300 kilometres away. Walsh told investors he expected to prove that 2 or 3 million ounces of gold lay under Busang's hills. The pair believed the deposit would move Bre-X's 30-cent share price up to $4 or $5 before a major mining company took over the deposit, a prospect they comfortably embraced. Felderhof and Walsh wanted a quick score, then it would be on to the next exploration project; in fact, Felderhof already had started preliminary drilling programs on two other Indonesian properties. Clearly, neither Bre-X executive ever dreamed of running a senior mining company. That all changed when the potential of the southeast zone became clear.

Early in 1994, de Guzman, under instructions from Felderhof, began exploring the limits of Busang's potentially gold-bearing rock in the southeast zone. The way he later told the story, de Guzman and an assistant hiked into the jungle, 32 kilometres from the nearest village, Long Tesak, and built a rough hut with a thatched roof that would be their home for a week at a time. Dinner each day consisted of noodles; so did lunch. On one excursion, at the end of an exhausting five-kilometre traverse of a broken, low-lying ridge of volcanic rock, a bit of yellow rock on a river bank caught de Guzman's eye. "Check it out," he wrote on a plastic strip that he attached to the rock, leaving the stone for an assistant. When the assistant, a fellow Filipino named Cesar Puspos, picked up the tag, he scribbled, "Checkmate."

In May 1994, Bre-X drilled its first hole in the southeast zone. In June, the company reported results. They were promising, with gold grades of up to 4.5 grams per tonne. However, the bulk of Bre-X's drilling was still being done in the central zone. It took until January 1995 before a rig could be freed up for work on the new project. A second rig was moved into the southeast zone in February and a third in April.

The drill rigs came from a reputable Indonesian company called PT Drillinti Tiko. They were top-of-the line machines. In everything they did at Busang, the Bre-X geologists used the best possible equipment, which sent a message that they were in for the long haul. Rigs were about ten metres in height when operating, each with a crew of four. Hitched behind pick-up trucks, the contraptions were hauled down paths carved in the rain forest by Bre-X's bulldozers. Every fifty metres, the drills would stop and sink a hole, usually boring on a slight angle to create a better picture of the rock. When drilling was in full swing, the crews worked long days at the isolated camp: six weeks on, two weeks off. They sank lengths of hollow pipe tipped with a diamond-studded cutting bit 500 metres down into the bedrock. The rock cores that were pulled from the centre of the pipe were the thickness of a fire hose. After the core came out of the ground, it was broken with a sledge-hammer into baseball-bat lengths. Then it was washed, packed into wooden crates, and carried by truck back to the base camp. From here, it would be partly crushed and prepared for the trip to the assay labs. Felderhof and de Guzman became more excited about their deposit as the drilling showed gold existing right at the bottom of their samples. Analysts following the company would say the deposit was "open at depth," which meant that the gold extended deeper than drilling could reveal.

When a hole was drilled and the rock core pulled, the rig would move another fifty metres down the hacked-out path between the trees and bore another hole. Over the next two years, more than 400 such holes were drilled and promising samples sent to the labs to be assayed. Rich core samples were known as "bonanza intersections." The southeast zone, Felderhof bragged, featured an incredible number of bonanza intersections. The first results from assays on rock samples out of the zone, done in April 1995, showed 3.03 grams of gold in every tonne of rock. By July, the company had pumped out assays on three more core samples; the grades were fabulous, ranging up to 6.38 grams per tonne. While evidence of what lay under the ground was only beginning to emerge, Felderhof offered an estimate that 8 million ounces of gold would be proved within four months. Suddenly, Busang was shaping up to be a big-league mine.

Riches in the Ground

The discovery seemed the stuff of fairy-tales. A down-on-his-luck geologist spots a promising rock in a river bank, gets his intrepid assistant to crack off a chunk, and finds gold. In fact, such stories are at the heart of great mining discoveries, from the nuggets in Sutter's Creek that started the California gold rush to "Siwash George" Cormack in Rabbit Creek in the Yukon, all the way to South Africa's Witwatersrand. Single-minded prospectors tend to find the big prizes. Often, they are working for companies with dodgy backgrounds. But once the geology is proven, respectable players in the mining industry sweep in and take over.

Two mining success stories in as many years at Vancouver-based companies had made millions for investors and made Bre-X's tale more credible, since early investors in both companies became incredibly wealthy. One was Diamond Fields Resources and its stunning Labrador nickel find. As its name implies, Diamond Fields was originally conceived as a diamond exploration company by controversial stock promoter Robert Friedland. Two geologists working for Diamond Fields spotted a rusty streak in the rocks while flying over central Labrador in a helicopter. To their eyes the colour signalled nickel, and closer inspection revealed rock formations that had never been identified, despite the earlier mapping of the region by government geologists. Drilling unveiled the largest nickel and zinc find in decades. In its early days, Diamond Fields stock went for pennies. Just three years later, in August 1996, a spirited take-over battle saw Diamond Fields acquired for $4.3 billion by Inco Ltd., the world's largest nickel miner.

The same magic played out for investors in Arequipa Resources Ltd., which struck gold high in Peru's Andes mountains. A tiny family-run junior mining company, Arequipa's stock went from $1 to $34 in nine months. Ultimately, Barrick Gold grabbed the company with a $1-billion hostile take-over. Barrick based its bid on results from core samples that pointed to the potential for a 10-million-ounce gold deposit.

Strange theories, strange lands, fast-talking stock promoters, minimal drilling results – it didn't seem to make any difference. There were riches in the ground that turned into huge wins for daring investors.

CHAPTER FOUR

The Selling of Bre-X

"The stock was a bit of a punt." – Garrett Herman, chief executive officer, Loewen Ondaatje McCutcheon Ltd., on Bre-X Minerals Ltd.

"National brokerage houses do not finance junior mining companies without doing a lot of due diligence." – Stephen McAnulty, vice-president, Bre-X Minerals Ltd.

"I know for a fact the gold is there. I've seen it." – Egizio Bianchini, gold analyst, Nesbitt Burns Inc.

"Let Me Tell You About David Walsh"

The selling of Bre-X Minerals Ltd. began on a rainy spring afternoon amid the walnut panelling and tasteful oil landscapes of the Yorkville offices of investment dealer Loewen Ondaatje McCutcheon Ltd. It was April 1994, and in Indonesia, Bre-X's crews were running drill rigs and swatting away mosquitoes in the jungles of the central zone. In Toronto, Paul Kavanagh, the recently retired head of exploration at American Barrick Resources Corp. and a respected player in the mining industry, had been talking up the junior mining company whenever he ran into Robert Van Doorn, Loewen's gold analyst. The two saw each other often; their offices were side by side in the trendy Toronto neighbourhood just north of Bloor Street.

Kavanagh had visited Busang twice while trying to win Barrick a stake in the claim, which Bre-X had just begun to explore. Although talks had fallen apart five months earlier over the issue of who would control the property, creating bad blood between the two companies' executives, Kavanagh's interest was still strong. So strong, in fact, that he had joined the Bre-X board of directors in late March. In his first few weeks with the company, Kavanagh helped raise money by introducing Bre-X management in Toronto financial circles, and Van Doorn had agreed to meet with David Walsh and John Felderhof. The location of their property – in Indonesia – meshed nicely with the brokerage firm's aim of financing Canadian companies in Asian markets. In fact, the firm's millionaire founder Christopher Ondaatje was in the process of starting several companies in his native Sri Lanka. The meeting was a big step for Bre-X; until this point, the company had raised money by selling a few thousand shares at a time on the Alberta Stock Exchange, appealing mainly to Walsh's cronies.

"I sat down with Walsh and Felderhof and went over the drill results from Busang that the Australian companies compiled, plus a few of their own results," Van Doorn recalled. "Then I listened to Felderhof explain his theory on how it was different and what the deposit really looked like. It all made sense."

Van Doorn made a few phone calls and put together a second meeting to give gold analysts and investment bankers from other firms a chance to hear Walsh and Felderhof. He remembered that second gathering with a smile. "Walsh made the presentation, and by the end of the meeting, people were just drifting out of the room," Van Doorn said. "It was a bit embarrassing. He wasn't very impressive."

With outside interest in Busang tepid at best, like a good investment dealer Van Doorn shouldered the burden of raising money himself. The former mining engineer made calls to Australia to check up on Felderhof and received endorsements of the geologist's technical skills and track record. Van Doorn, Dutch-born like Felderhof, was impressed with the geological picture emerging from Busang's central zone – no drill results from the supposedly rich southeast zone had been released. He went to his boss, Loewen chief executive officer Garrett Herman, and suggested the firm consider going solo and raising a few million dollars for Bre-X.

Herman is a stockily built, incredibly intense, major player in Toronto financial circles. At one time, his dispassionate and cutting ways on a stock trading desk won him the nickname "Robobroker." He had drifted in and out of the unsuccessful meeting with Walsh and Felderhof, so he knew the Bre-X story. "We had results from previous owners, nothing impressive, but not bad, and we knew the region was elephant country," Herman remembered, repeating the geologist's pet phrase for large deposits.

Herman decided the deal was a good fit with Loewen's strategy, so with help from Walsh and one or two investment bankers and stock salespeople, the brokerage firm sold 300,000 units in Bre-X at $1.50 each. Each unit consisted of one share and half a warrant; a whole warrant allowed the holder to buy an additional Bre-X share at $1.75 at any time over the next two years. Arranging the details of the financing took a series of meetings over several weeks, but once the paperwork was done, Loewen's staff sold the Bre-X shares in the space of a day. Walsh made a few calls and placed an additional 300,000 units at the same price; much of the stock went to Bresea, his holding company. At the time, the stock was trading at $1.85, so the price was attractive. On May 2, 1994, Bre-X collected a cheque for just over $4 million from Loewen – $4.5 million from the financing, less a 10 per cent fee. Herman is nothing if not direct in his assessment of the deal: "The stock was a bit of a punt."

Financings such as this are commonplace among small mining companies. Deep-pocketed investors such as mutual funds and insurance companies buy blocks of shares and warrants in chunks of $150,000 and up. The relatively high threshold allows a company like Bre-X to raise money without filing paperwork with a regulator such as the Alberta Securities Commission. Buyers are assumed to be sophisticated and able to make their own analysis of the company – or capable of withstanding the loss of their entire investment.

Normally, after a financing is closed there's a celebratory dinner, with plenty of booze and an extravagant menu. If there was a celebration to mark the Loewen financing, none of the brokerage firm's executives made it. "Taking them out for a night of boozing just isn't our style," said Herman. "Maybe if we had gotten them drunk, we would have kept them as a client."

Loewen's role as the chief money-raiser for Bre-X lasted through one more deal, a $7.5-million stock sale done in May 1995. "Let me tell you about David Walsh," said Herman, recalling a memory that clearly was not pleasant. "These deals worked in spite of him."

As Herman recalls, Loewen had enlisted the aid of rival brokerage firm Nesbitt Burns Inc., a leader in mining financing, and arranged to sell 2 million Bre-X shares at $3.75 each. The deal was all but wrapped up when Walsh began to fiddle. "He wanted to be the mastermind, the guy who was running the show," Herman said.

The Bre-X chief executive wanted two more investment banks, ScotiaMcLeod Inc. and McLean McCarthy Ltd., the Canadian arm of Germany's Deutsche Bank, included among the sellers, despite the fact that neither institution knew Bre-X. Walsh's goal was more exposure for his obscure little company, but he was also trying to show just who was boss. The Bre-X CEO also wanted the new stock and the commissions generated by selling it split equally among the four dealers; normally, the brokerage firm that leads the deal does most of the work, sells the bulk of the shares, and collects a larger slice of the fee. Messing with commission fees is bound to upset the investment bankers. The situation got worse when ScotiaMcLeod and McLean McCarthy made little progress selling their part of the deal, which was hardly surprising, as neither company knew anything about the stock. Executives at Loewen and Nesbitt spent three frustrating days waiting to close the deal, then took back all the Bre-X shares and sold the paper themselves. The other two dealers got 25 per cent of the $750,000 fee and did almost no work. Herman was livid. He said, "After that, we never really dealt with Walsh again."

Followers on the Fringes

The world had first heard about Bre-X's investment in Busang on May 6, 1993, a few weeks after the dinner at Jakarta's Sari Hotel. The stock was trading at 51 cents a share when Walsh announced Bre-X had bought the rights to the Kalimantan property for an initial payment of $80,100 (U.S.). It's doubtful anyone outside Walsh's buddies at the Three Greenhorns took much notice. The vast majority of these penny stocks – so called because they trade for less than $5 and a rise or fall in their price is measured in cents, not in nickels, the fractions of dollars seen in senior stocks – never amounted to anything and were left to speculators.

Bre-X's head of investor relations, Stephen McAnulty, made much of the company's first news on Busang three years later, when he launched a Bre-X Web site on the Internet. "Today, such a news release would attract immediate attention, but in early 1993, Indonesia was an unknown entity," he editorialized. "Bre-X will keep shareholders informed of future developments in a timely manner." Like most of the company's claims, this promise was not kept.

Bre-X's early followers dwelt on the fringes of the investment community. They were analysts and newsletter editors known only to those investors who played the penny stocks, taking a chance on the junior mining companies with promise, but no proven reserves. This tightly knit group had seen many scams, many failures, and the occasional huge win. Walsh and Felderhof were charter members of this club, and there was nothing unusual about the two men step-ping up for another spin on the junior mining roulette wheel.

The first analyst to really follow Bre-X was Dorothy Atkinson, who watched the gold stocks for Pacific International Securities in Vancouver, a small investment dealer that catered to mining com-panies. She advised her clients to buy Bre-X in late June 1994, when the stock was trading at $2.40. "I was new to the investment indus-try, although I'd been a geologist for twenty years," recalled Atkinson, who had supervised diamond mining claims for the federal govern-ment in the Northwest Territories and consulted on potential gold projects for Vancouver companies such as Royal Oak Mines. "I went looking for an area with lots of potential but little analyst coverage. In Indonesia, you had Grasberg [a huge gold mine] and Newmont [a major U.S. mining company] doing well, but no one looking at juniors."

In her search for start-up companies, of which she found very few, she stumbled across the Bre-X team. She liked what she saw in Felderhof and his research; over the next few months, she had dinner with the geologist twice and talked frequently to Bre-X executives on the phone. "At the time, they were trying to prove a 1-million-ounces resource. They had a geological anomaly with high potential. It seemed logical." Three years after writing her first recommendation, Atkinson was able to use her stock-picking acumen to win a job at Whelan Beliveau Associates, a larger, more prominent shop in Vancouver that catered to institutional investors.

Investor newsletters, which are often closely tied to the junior mining companies they write about, also began to follow Bre-X. These early reports had a strongly promotional air, and it was clear that the writers were taking everything Walsh and his colleagues said at face value. Such enthusiasm was customary in newsletters, but Canada's largest brokerage firms were supposed to be more dis-criminating; this, however, was not the case with their approach to Bre-X. A sky's-the-limit tone would come to flavour many reports on the company, right through to the stock's spectacular crash.

Walsh designated Felderhof the company's exploration manager in September 1994. Mike de Guzman moved into the slot of Busang's exploration manager. With the two geologists working the jungle sites and Walsh and McAnulty manning the printing presses and working the phones with potential investors back in Calgary, Bre-X became a machine that cranked out news. The news story they told soon featured a larger project than previously imagined. Busang had started out as a poor candidate for a small open-pit mine – 1 million ounces just wasn't enough gold. But that April 1994 estimate of Busang's riches was based on results from twenty-four drill holes, many of which were drilled by the previous owners, whom Felderhof portrayed as incompetent.

By January 1995, forty-four holes had been sunk under de Guzman's supervision in both the central zone and the new, previously unexplored southeast zone. Bre-X began to tell the world what the drills were turning up. In press releases and in conversations with players in the tightly knit mining community in the spring of 1995, Bre-X estimated it was working on a reserve of 2.5 million ounces. But as more of the southeast zone was revealed, Felderhof boldly projected reserves of 5 million ounces by year-end. In a late-night call from Indonesia to Walsh at the chief executive's Calgary home, Felderhof uttered a phrase that was to become famous: "We've got a monster by the tail."

Suddenly, the deposit was 5.3 kilometres long by 900 metres across. According to Felderhof, in addition to the pit mine, it might be necessary to go underground to get all the gold.

With the benefit of hindsight, it's clear how Bre-X maintained its credibility. While excited by the wealth being hinted at, the company took pains to suggest that mature hands were on the wheel. Bre-X, for example, insisted on using the best mining equipment. When announcing results from one hole, the company qualified the report by saying they planned to go down 300 metres, but "aborted due to a sheared core barrel." Felderhof promised the broken drill would be fixed and its assay would be published with the next batch of results.

The Indonesian crew always took pains to show the world they were running a tight ship.

Oh, What a Tangled Web ...

Stephen McAnulty was the man to help Bre-X hit the right buttons with analysts and investors. Like his boss David Walsh, McAnulty was no stranger to the Street. He had spent twenty-seven years in finance and mining, including a stint at Pemberton Securities Inc., a large investment dealer based in western Canada that was acquired in 1988 by RBC Dominion Securities Ltd. There he was a vice-president – admittedly a common title within the firm – and his job in Vancouver was to buy and sell treasury bills for the firm's individual investors. By all accounts, McAnulty was good at his work, but the stress proved too much to handle, and he left the investment business, moved to Calgary, and joined Bre-X in 1994.

In joining the junior mining company, McAnulty had turned his back on the $150,000-plus pay package enjoyed by successful brokers at RBC Dominion. In his first year at the junior mining company, he worked in the basement of the Walshes' home, a sharp contrast to RBC Dominion's grand Vancouver office on Burrard Street. What no ordinary broker could dream of, though, was the fortune to be made from Bre-X stock options.

Long a favourite way to reward executives for boosting their company's stock price, options give their holders an opportunity to buy shares at a set price. Often, that level is well below the stock's price on the market. Seldom has the market seen an option deal as sweet as Bre-X's. Buying shares through the option plan and selling them in the open market made McAnulty and his wife Nancy $22.2 million in 1996. Giving up downtown Vancouver, with its views of the harbour, Stanley Park, and the north shore mountains, came to seem less of a sacrifice.

McAnulty had a broker's typically upbeat view of the world. He developed the Bre-X web site, as he said, to "boost public awareness" of the stock. "These days, even very junior companies have some kind of presence on the 'Net, even if they don't have Web sites as such," McAnulty explained. "We want to reach the same audience – people who are on-line now or who will be in the future. It's a whole new market segment for us." He presented the site as a "partnership" between Bre-X and software giant Microsoft.

When Bre-X began to ascend into the stock market stratosphere, McAnulty was the voice that spread the word on the Internet. His imaginative approach to Indonesian cartography on the 'Net included using images of large bars of gold to represent producing mines. Pictures of smaller gold nuggets represented recent gold discoveries. To an Internet surfer, the jungles of Borneo seemed studded with a broad belt of gold bars. Over time, Busang became the biggest, richest bar.

Bre-X published charts contrasting Busang's reserves, which had never yielded an ounce of gold, with reserves at the twelve producing gold mines in Indonesia. Like a sprinter charging through a crowd, Busang roared past its rivals. McAnulty used his charts to show how estimates of Busang's reserve base grew from 2.75 million ounces in October 1995 to 25 million ounces in April 1996, then on to 47 million ounces in July, which left it trailing only the huge Grasberg mine as the region's largest deposit. Over time, Bre-X attracted a huge and rabid following of Internet users, many of whom based their decision to buy the stock on what they found on McAnulty's Web site.

Like most junior mining company executives, Walsh and McAnulty made sure a steady supply of upbeat news flowed out of the basement office. Walsh's scrape with bankruptcy had taught him to raise money when it was available, not when it was needed. As a junior gold company, Bre-X was years away from owning a mine that produced revenue, and the war chest would require frequent cash infusions in order to meet this goal. As a result, Bre-X's early releases tended to put the best possible spin on every drill hole the company sank in the central zone. The reports were bait, meant to reel in investors. Just before Christmas 1993, Bre-X's lure was taken by an unexpected fish: American Barrick Resources – renamed Barrick Gold Corp. in 1994 – known as the biggest shark in gold mining seas because of its love of acquisitions.

Bre-X had sent out a news release in December 1993 detailing the rich gold concentrations found in three drilling samples; a fourth hole was started, but petered out after just 22 metres when a drill rig broke. Felderhof helpfully noted that prior to the accident, even that hole showed excellent grades of gold. Suddenly, a 5-million ounce deposit in this one spot was beginning to seem possible – and the vast majority of Busang remained unexplored.

Paul Kavanagh, Barrick's head of exploration, was among those who read about the drilling results. He called Walsh and arranged for a tour of Busang. After his first visit, Kavanagh liked what he had seen so much that he visited again. But he was retiring from Barrick, so he ended up handing over the file. Two Barrick executives, Alan Hill and Alex Davidson, Kavanagh's replacement, picked up the negotiations. As usual, Walsh needed money and he offered Barrick 14 per cent of Bre-X for $500,000. Barrick's philosophy, however, was to control any property with which it was involved, effectively ruling out Walsh's proposal. Weeks of negotiations could not break the impasse and Walsh called them off in January 1994. Later he would tell *Canadian Business* magazine, "Just because you're small doesn't mean you're stupid."

Although no deal was struck, these early negotiations with Barrick did yield two dividends. The attentions of a major producer legitimized Bre-X's claims, while the Calgary junior's promise attracted Kavanagh to the Bre-X board of directors. Adding the respected outside executive to the board was a huge event in Bre-X's short history. Here was a proven mining executive and independent director from the big time joining a tiny junior mining company. In a press release issued on March 24, 1994, Bre-X noted that the recently retired senior vice-president of Barrick and former president of Newmont Mining of Canada had done postgraduate work at

Princeton – a considerable improvement on Walsh's academic back-ground. Rumours started to circulate; the gossip was that Kavanagh had seen incredible grades of gold in samples from Busang and that he had quit Barrick in exasperation over Barrick chairman and guiding light Peter Munk's failure to snap up this gem. Suddenly, Bre-X was making a name for itself. With its new-found credibility, the junior mining company was able to raise money through Loewen Ondaatje McCutcheon.

In Indonesia, the focus of exploration had shifted to the emerging southeast zone. In January 1995, a second drill rig appeared at Busang's southeast zone, paid for by the money from Loewen Ondaatje McCutcheon. A third would arrive in April. The push was on to make good on Felderhof's boast of 5 million ounces in reserves by the end of the year, but the drilling was eating up cash. The company had already spent more than $3 million in the field, and Walsh needed more money. He raised the cash in May 1995 through the company's second financing for $7.5 million with the syndicate made up (somewhat unevenly) of Loewen, Nesbitt Burns, ScotiaMcLeod, and McLean McCarthy. Felderhof now had the money he needed to drill hundreds of holes. On the Web site, the always optimistic McAnulty wrote, "National brokerage houses like the ones above do not finance junior mining companies without doing a lot of due diligence. This stamp of approval is a signal of what Bre-X has been saying all along, the company has a lot of merit to it."

The exultant boast would come back to haunt both McAnulty and the investment dealers. In fact, no due diligence or independent testing had been done. None. Bre-X supplied all the geological data that sold the stock. At the time of the financing, no one from outside the company had drilled holes at Busang, and few outsiders had made the ten-hour journey up the muddy Mahakam River and over the rough thirty-kilometre logging road to visit Busang. Those who did arrive were carefully shepherded around the site, were shown what was appropriate, and were told many good things.

The new year brought a new wrinkle to the information Bre-X was sending to the public. Until January 1995, claims about the size of the Busang find came from the mouths of two executives: Felderhof and Walsh, with amplification from McAnulty. There were no independent, outside voices backing up the Bre-X story. To add authority, Walsh announced in January that "an independent mining engineer familiar with Southeast Asia geology is preparing a resource calculation." He promised the consultant's report would be delivered within six weeks.

The independent calculation came from Roger Pooley, a well-regarded independent geologist. His degree from the Royal School of Mines in England gave his work on Bre-X lustre, as did his thirty-five years of experience. In late February, he put his name on a report that stated that reserves were at least 1 million ounces of gold. Just how much more was part of the guessing game. However, according to Felderhof, incomplete drilling results that Pooley hadn't considered were expected to add another million ounces to reserves. Pooley based his calculations on rock samples and maps supplied to him by de Guzman and Felderhof. Like the many other consultants who would come to work on Bre-X's rocks, the experienced geologist followed industry practice and, trustingly, did not extract his own core samples.

A pattern was developing that would propel Bre-X's stock price upward in months to come. The company would fire out a press release announcing independently audited results that showed decent gold reserves. Then Felderhof would chime in with a line or two about the further potential of the site. Analysts in turn would translate Felderhof's projections into even larger gold reserves, pumping up the stock price. As the number of followers grew, so did the momentum behind Felderhof's claims.

Many of Bre-X's fans remained outside the mainstream of the mining industry. A British newsletter writer, Jim Taylor of *Gold and Gold Stocks*, labelled Busang "a major world class open pit gold mine" with strong managers who "expressed confidence that an open pitable resource of between 3 million and 6 million ounces will be delin-eated." He recommended the stock as it traded around $1.80 in early March 1995.

In Indonesia, John Felderhof was banging the drum again, talking up the size of the reserves. In early May 1995 he said, typically, "With results from the phase III drilling program being better than anticipated, an updated reserve calculation scheduled for release by June 20 should be better than initially anticipated." Felderhof boldly stated that Busang's reserves would total 6 to 8 million ounces within a few weeks. When proven reserves came in at just 2.3 million ounces on June 20, stock market players didn't seem to care. They believed in the 8-million-ounce figure.

Analysts who got on the Bre-X bandwagon early had reason to crow. In Vancouver, Whelan Beliveau's Atkinson began a report by saying, "It is with pleasure we update Bre-X," then went on to explain that $100 invested in Bre-X at the time of her first recom-mendation was now worth $415. The stock was at $12 and Atkinson called for it to go to $20 within the next six to twelve months. She based the projection on an 8-million-ounce gold deposit. Like the rest of the Street, Atkinson had bought into the story outlined by Felderhof's big arms.

Bre-X Goes Mainstream

The *Northern Miner* newspaper wrote its first major article on Bre-X as the stock hit $14. This was a ground-breaking event, because the *Northern Miner* is the geologist's bible of what's going on in Canadian mining circles. A dry, fact-filled article in late July 1995 explained that the company had proven reserves of 2.4 million ounces. The newspaper went on to report that reserves could be 8 million ounces within four months and noted that the gold was near the surface, which meant an open-pit mine was practical. In dull, respon-sible prose, the *Northern Miner* portrayed Bre-X as a respectable, promising company.

The mainstream media also began to buy in. The first substantial article on Bre-X came out in July as the stock rose above $14. The home-town *Calgary Herald* ran a story on July 19, 1995, headlined "Bre-X shares soar on news about gold find." In the article, Stephen McAnulty happily predicted, "We think it's going to be the largest pure gold find in Indonesia by the time we finish off."

McAnulty never missed a chance to beat the drum. Most companies publish restrained annual reports, erring on the side of boredom when describing the past year. Bre-X ladled out the hype. The 1995 annual report quoted Indonesian director general of mines Kuntoro Mangkusubroto as saying, "Bre-X has found a 40-million-ounce gold deposit at the Busang," despite the fact that even Felderhof was only claiming 30 million ounces at the time. The report went on to quote Alberta Stock Exchange executive vice-president Gerry Romanzin as stating, "It's our most significant trading of all time." That year, Bre-X ranked first on the ASE in its price gain, up $50.12, and in trading value, statistics that were written up in the company's statements in bold typeface.

The boyish enthusiasm of Walsh and McAnulty back in Calgary showed up in the way Bre-X approached drilling. Rather than explore Busang with a series of carefully plotted, closely spaced holes, the company occasionally took a flyer and moved a rig out several kilometres. The process is known as step-out drilling, an aggressive practice aimed at dramatically increasing the size of a deposit. In late July, Bre-X sank two holes 1.25 kilometres away from the heart of the southeast zone. Both holes hit strong concentrations of gold: Busang was again larger than expected. Steve McAnulty celebrated the results on the Internet by writing: "This is an enormous step-out, opening up the possibility for doubling the reserves on the Busang property."

The company also announced that "visual analysis" of four new holes in the southeast zone suggested "considerably more mineralization than originally anticipated." In other words, Bre-X geologists were dramatically inflating the size of their find because the rock looked like it could contain gold, rather than waiting for lab tests to prove their claim. Like most gold deposits in the world, the gold grains at Busang would not be visible to the naked eye.

The step-out drilling program was seen as dramatically increasing the potential size of the ore body that lay under the jungle in Indonesia. In his initial report on the company – a buy recommendation, naturally – respected ScotiaMcLeod analyst Ted Reeve wrote, "Bre-X has discovered another large gold zone. These results vindicate the company's comments on building a resource of six to eight million ounces by next year." Toronto's mining fraternity was now accepting eyeball estimates from the Bre-X geologists. The Busang boom had begun in earnest.

Professional geologists also were becoming giddy about Bre-X. In a widely read and respected newsletter called the *Global Gold Stock Report*, editor Michael Schaefer raised the possibility of a 10-million-ounce deposit and targeted a $40 price tag for the $13 stock. "The Busang discovery is a once in a lifetime situation," Schaefer wrote enthusiastically. "Deposits of this caliber and potential do not happen very often. We are by no means close to determining the ultimate size and economic value of this gold deposit."

On September 5, 1995, from his Toronto office at First Canadian Place at King and Bay Streets, Nesbitt Burns analyst Egizio Bianchini started to cover the tiny Calgary company. Buy it, said his first report. When the endorsement came from the analyst regarded as the top gold stock picker in Canada, people bought. Quick to smile, well-spoken, and a consummate story-teller, Bianchini also has that wonderful characteristic of making those he talks to feel special – a genuine warmth combined with an excellent memory for names and the ability to recall exactly what you told him the last time you talked. With a geology degree and years of industry experience under his belt, Bianchini was every inch the experienced, credible analyst. He had picked winners, and just as importantly, he had witnessed some of the gold sector's notorious scams, including the Vancouver-based New Cinch crash, which had seen salted core samples used to fleece investors for millions of dollars. Investors assumed Bianchini brought all his geological training and investment acumen to bear when he wrote, "After reviewing all the drill data and all available cross sections of Busang, we have developed the view that the project is likely to develop into a world-class gold mining operation." He added that Busang was covered by a large Contract of Work permit, then went on to explain the Contract system was an accepted, respected part of Indonesian mining culture. The notion that Bre-X's control of the deposit was secure was implicit in his reports, and in those of most other analysts. In fact, problems with Indonesian partners in Busang and the greed of the government were combining to make Bre-X's hold shaky.

Bianchini was quick to note that Bre-X shares were speculative – all his reports stressed this fact – but he also gave credit to Felderhof and his colleagues, writing, "Management is very competent technically and has a long track record of exploration and development in the Pacific Rim." Bianchini's first report came out on September 5, 1995, when Bre-X was trading at $14. He predicted the stock would hit $21 within a year. It took just three weeks to reach that mark.

If Felderhof had big arms, Bianchini had a big reach. He worked for what was then the largest brokerage firm in Canada. Every morning at 7:30, a sales force of 1,200 stockbrokers could listen to Bianchini's views, then turn around and pass these recommendations on to thousands of clients. The same instructions – buy this gold stock, sell that one – flew out to mutual fund companies, insurance companies, and pension fund companies. When Bianchini talked, he spoke to more potential Bre-X investors than any other analyst in Canada. And Bianchini did talk.

"You got in a situation where Egizio was running down the street with no clothes screaming about this stock," said Barry Allen, gold analyst at Gordon Capital Corp. "The rest of us felt we had to match him or be left behind."

Before long, reports from Bianchini and his competitors spoke with the authority of those who had been to Busang and typed their reports with mud from the jungles of Kalimantan under their fingernails. Teams of Canadian analysts made the twenty-hour flight to Jakarta, then hopped in a Bre-X helicopter for the flight to Busang base camp. When one early Bre-X enthusiast, Michael Fowler of the Montreal-based brokerage firm Lévesque Beaubien Geoffrion, visited in the spring of 1996, he wrote, "It is certain from visual inspection of outcrops that the mineralization continues. We therefore believe that our estimate of 52.94 million ounces is conservative."

In simple language, Fowler, a crusty ex-patriate Brit, said he walked around and saw lots of new rocks that looked like the old rocks, so chances were there was a lot more gold.

Bianchini was even more explicit. In an interview with *Globe and Mail* mining reporter Allan Robinson, he said, "I know for a fact the gold is there. I've seen it."

There were ten major gold company analysts watching Bre-X stock in October 1995, when the price blew through $30 on October 20, a level that meant investors valued the company at more than $700 million. Normally, analysts move up their target price for a $30 stock by a few dollars at a time. Not with Bre-X. Targets rose in leaps and bounds. By October 23, 1995, Bre-X was changing hands at $43 and Lévesque's Fowler, still enthralled by his "visual inspection," set out a one-year target of $62, which would rank Bre-X as one of the five largest gold companies in Canada. In Indonesia, the geologists stayed true to form. Rather than verifying the existing deposit, Felderhof and de Guzman continued to do step-out drilling. Three new holes were drilled that extended the size of the deposit to a strip 2.75 kilometres long. All three found gold. The stock soared on the news.

Like players in a poker game, brokerage firm analysts continued to raise one another's bets on how much gold was at Busang and what price the stock would reach. Traders at rival firms swapped stories about the estimates and share price targets, and many invested their own money in Bre-X. Even the rumour that a major analyst planned to raise his estimate in the next few days was enough to get traders buzzing and raise the price of Bre-X.

In late October, Lévesque's Fowler had set a share price target of $63. Three weeks later, on November 20, with Bre-X already up to $51.25 from $43 he told listeners on a morning conference call from his office in the Aetna building at Toronto's King and York Streets that he was taking the target higher. The next morning, Fowler's $62 bet was topped by a Bianchini estimate of $70 and 30 million ounces of gold. Three days later, on November 23, from the Toronto boutique Eagle & Partners in Scotia Plaza, John Hainey stepped up with a $75 estimate. On December 4, Yorkton Securities weighed in from London, England, with a $100 estimate.

This was all highly congenial to Bre-X's McAnulty, who kept busy by electronically posting upbeat forecasts within hours of their publication. The computer bulletin board never featured those who took a dim view of Bre-X's potential. Gold analyst John Ing at Maison Placements, for example, told investors to steer clear because of problems he detected in Bre-X's ownership of the site; he was not allowed to visit Busang. Jonathan Cunningham, head of research at Nesbitt Burns, complained Bianchini's reports were edited before being posted on the Internet – McAnulty had chopped out any negative comments. At first, Cunningham was not aware of this editing. When he realized Nesbitt Burns's material was being used without permission, the firm's lawyers faxed a warning letter to the Bre-X head office, and McAnulty stopped using the Nesbitt Burns research in his reports posted on Bre-X's Web site. By that point, though, thousands of Internet users had already seen Bianchini's endorsements.

Brokerage houses such as Nesbitt Burns rarely showed restraint when it came to Bre-X, and the enthusiasm began to spread to the entire junior mining sector. At a June 1996 presentation to hundreds of clients in Toronto's Sheraton Hotel Centre, Nesbitt Burns's mining team set out its favourites. Bianchini said, "I still think Bre-X is a buy here, though the easy money has been made, and all we have left now is a double. I remember when doubles used to be great," referring to a stock that doubles in price. His colleague Julian Baldry set out loftier expectations for the sector. He called mining stocks "a once-in-a-life-time investment opportunity."

"It starts with a premise as follows," Baldry told a packed ballroom. "Are Diamond Fields – which went from pennies to $160 presplit – and Bre-X isolated events, or are they the vanguard of a wave of similar opportunities that are going to be presented to us? We believe that they represent a vanguard of what is to come.

"Ladies and gentlemen, welcome to the made-in-Canada mining boom," Baldry told a rapt audience. "I hope you enjoy it."

The game of upping the ante on Bre-X's target price continued into the New Year. ScotiaMcLeod's Ted Reeve bumped his $62.20 target up to $88 on January 5, 1996. Ten days later, Felderhof fanned the flames by stating that 30 million ounces was "readily obtainable." The next day, Nesbitt Burns's Bianchini stated the stock was worth $110 – just seven days after that, from his office tower one block west, Fowler moved the standard up to $128 a share.

At this point, take-over speculation began to bubble around Bre-X, adding to the stock market frenzy. In January, newsletter writer Michael Schaefer fired off a report that was typical of the time. "Bre-X doesn't have the technical expertise to build a mining operation of this scope, but I doubt it would be difficult to entice the best talent in the world from any of the major mining companies," he wrote. "Any offer from a major that would even be considered by Bre-X management will have to be at least twice the current share price if not more. I doubt if we will have to wait much longer before such offers are made." Schaefer would soon be proven right.

On February 24, 1996, Walsh confirmed what everyone knew, that Bre-X was open to the idea of being bought out at Busang, either in a joint venture on the property or an investment in Bre-X. "We've never intended to sell out," Walsh said. "We will negotiate with a mining company that's experienced in mine development and operation. We intend to retain 75 per cent, minimum, of the property." The spectre of a battle for a stake in Busang between senior mining companies added to the already rich premium investors gave to Bre-X.

At the same time, the analysts just couldn't leave their targets alone. Fowler upped his estimate to 40 million ounces and targeted $160 on February 20. The next day, Bianchini said $180 was achievable within the next twelve months and set an eighteen-month target of $220. Six days later, Fowler also went to a $210 target. The stakes were raised to the roof when in Vancouver Dorothy Atkinson put her name to a report that said Busang contained 70 million ounces of gold and Bre-X was worth $270 a share. Ultimately, Bre-X stock would justify the analysts' targets, but it would not remain at these stellar levels for long.

"30 Million Ounces, Plus, Plus, Plus"

With Bre-X enjoying the unqualified support of mainstream analysts and the adulation of its shareholders, Walsh decided it was time to fill the vault. In a private placement done on March 1, 1996, Bre-X sold 250,000 shares for $120 each, with Nesbitt Burns leading the deal. The company banked $30 million for additional drilling in Busang.

The hype around Bre-X now became deafening. At The Madison, a popular pub for the University of Toronto crowd, a group of geology students said Paul Kavanagh had boasted that Busang contained 100 million ounces of gold. The comment surfaced in newspapers within days. Kavanagh denied making the claim, but the number added to the excitement around Bre-X's future.

There was no denying what was said at a packed Bre-X annual meeting on March 14, 1996, in Toronto's venerable Royal York Hotel. During an affair defined by rambling speeches and poorly illustrated presentations, Felderhof was asked about the size of the deposit. While he admitted he'd "stuck his foot in it several times," Felderhof said, "I think it's 30 million ounces, plus, plus, plus." No one attempted to slow Felderhof down. When asked after the meeting to define some of those pluses by commenting on rumours of a 100-million-ounce property, de Guzman said, "At the back of my mind, the deposit has that tendency." The pair's optimistic projections reflected the fact that their crews had sunk their drills into only 25 per cent of the property.

For his part, Walsh said he was "conservative and comfortable" with the 30-million-ounce claim, and again raised the possibility of a take-over, telling his fellow shareholders that he intended to spend the second half of the year negotiating a deal with a senior mining company that would bring Busang into production.

At the same time Bre-X shareholders were meeting, the company was making the transition from the Alberta Stock Exchange to the big leagues of the Toronto Stock Exchange. It was a significant event. The TSE gave Bre-X respectability – investors assumed that only legitimate businesses gained entry to the country's oldest and largest market. And because the TSE listing meant Bre-X shares traded in Ontario, the company was now filing reports to the Ontario Securities Commission, the nation's largest securities regulator. "I think people are going to take comfort in the fact it's Toronto-listed," said David Thomas, a gold analyst with Goepel Shields & Partners. In an interview conducted just before Bre-X made the move, he said, "There are certain regulatory requirements that have to be met before it's Toronto-listed so in a way there's been added due diligence on this company."

Bre-X began trading on the TSE April 23, 1996, at $187.50 a share – by the end of that first session, the price was $192.50. On May 10, 1996, Bre-X shareholders gathered again in Calgary to approve a ten-for-one split in Bre-X shares. The move was meant to make the stock more affordable for small, individual investors. Shareholders also voted in favour of a shareholder rights' plan, better known as a poison pill, designed to ward off unwanted suitors.

Bre-X peaked at $28.65 in late May, or $286.50 on a pre-split basis, giving the company a market capitalization of $6.2 billion, the highest value it would ever hit. The stock made its American debut on the NASDAQ stock market on August 19, 1996, a move that meant it fell under the jurisdiction of another regulator, the U.S.

Securities and Exchange Commission, or SEC. The stock arrived on the Montreal Exchange, Walsh's old stomping grounds, on September 3, 1996.

Meanwhile, the analysts continued to fly into Busang and gaze approvingly at the new holes being drilled. On June 17, Bianchini came back from the site and promptly tossed out an estimate that it held 62 million ounces of gold. He projected a $32 stock price, $6 above its level at the time.

Once again, Bre-X announced its claims were backed by independent geological consultants. Roger Pooley, a solo operator, had given way to one of the largest and most respected mining engineering companies in Canada, Montreal-based Kilborn SNC-Lavalin Inc. In late July 1996, not only did the company back a reserve estimate of 47 million ounces – with gold at $350 (U.S.) an ounce, the deposit was worth $16.5 billion – but the consultant began a discussion on the feasibility of mining the site. Maps were drawn to show where to dig a pit and locate a mill that could crush the rock. Busang seemed on the verge of becoming a real mine. Gold bars were expected to be coming out of the site by the year 2001.

In August 1996, however, with its market capitalization over $6 billion, Bre-X suddenly stopped being a story about a gold mine and became a tale of political intrigue and corporate scheming.

CHAPTER FIVE

The Bombshell

"So why does the [Indonesian] government have to give Bre-X a $5-billion gift, for the little money it put up? Bre-X has to give up a good chunk of it." – The story's original "Deep Throat," August 1996

"It's possible that the Alberta Stock Exchange should build a statue to David Walsh and put it in front of its front door." – Paul Kavanagh, Bre-X director, February 1996

The Phone Call

It was just after three o'clock on a slow, muggy Friday afternoon in late August 1996. In the vast and largely deserted *Globe and Mail* newsroom in Toronto Douglas Goold's phone rang, and the newspaper's financial markets columnist picked it up, to hear a conspiratorial voice. "Bre-X now has a market capitalization of more than $5 billion and is up for the renewal of its exploration permit," the caller whispered. "The company already knows it hasn't got the permit, because it has been cancelled by the corrupt Indonesian government."

The caller then offered the phone number of one of the most promi-nent members of Canada's business community, who had agreed to provide details first thing Monday morning.

This was devastating news. Cinderella, it seemed, was not going to the ball after all. And the fairy-tale of Bre-X was not going to have a happy ending. Could this be possible? If so, it defied the traditional plot line. From the start, the Bre-X story had been the perfect fairy-tale. Although the tiny Calgary exploration company had no revenues or profits, it had become one of the most successful stock market plays in Canadian history. Shares had skyrocketed to $240 (on a pre-split basis) by that summer from pennies in 1994, creating overnight millionaires out of ordinary investors and gold rush fever reminis-cent of the Klondike of the 1890s. Thanks to the investment research of a single loans officer at the local credit union, one in every fifty residents in St. Paul, Alberta, a remote town of 5,000 people, owned shares in Bre-X. Many of them became millionaires, but some fam-ilies were feuding because some family members had been let in on the hot tip and others had not.

Although no one in Indonesia, Canada, or elsewhere doubted that the gold was in the ground, Bre-X still had to navigate the treach-erous shoals of the Indonesian bureaucracy. On July 25, the company's SIPP – the Indonesian acronym for an exploration permit – was set to expire, and would have to be renewed. But the big prize, which had so far proved elusive, was the final signing of Contracts of Works for the critical southeast zone and the undrilled northwest zone. Signing would give the company clear title to the properties.

The Monday morning phone call to the well-placed source shattered Cinderella's glass slipper. "Here is my understanding," the source began almost inaudibly. "Bre-X is real, as far as the gold reserves and quantity is concerned. But what isn't real is what it will cost the company to get its interest retained. Walsh was told by the government that he has to give up a very significant interest in order to get the work permit. And the work permit is not something symbolic; it gives you the right to the property. Without the work permit, you own nothing. . . . They are putting pressure on the company now, and one of the pressures is that they did not renew their exploration permit for the southeastern zone, the prolific zone where all the gold is.

"You have to understand how the government is looking at it. Here is a bunch of guys who put up very little money and their company has a market capitalization of $5 billion. Walsh is a drunk, and when the government told them [Bre-X executives] about the cancellation [of the SIPPS], they got drunk and were pretty nasty. So why does the government have to give Bre-X a $5-billion gift, for the little money it put up? Bre-X has to give up a good chunk of it. That means major partnerships or joint ventures, or the government telling them who should be their partner, and the terms.

"But the government can't do this outright," the informant continued. "And it can't do it in a very brutal form, because it doesn't want to alienate foreign investors. But my feeling is the company is not coming out [with the news]. There were nine analysts in Busang last week and they all wrote reports. They all basically say what a great ore body it is – and it is. But it does not explain what it takes to convert that into ownership.

"This is the most corrupt entity in the world. . . . But when you are talking at this scale, then Suharto wants to be involved."

These were stunning revelations. What the source said about Bre-X and its problems turned out to be uncannily accurate, apart from the view – which was then shared by everyone – that the gold was real. If anyone at this stage had taken a step back from the story, he or she would have realized that it indeed was too good to be true. Now, it appeared, the Indonesian government was playing hardball with Bre-X. Never before had it cancelled a company's work permit, as Kuntoro Mangkusubroto, Indonesia's director general for mines, later confirmed in an interview in his office in Jakarta. The message was that Bre-X would not be allowed to keep its current interest but would have to "share" its $5-billion "gift" with the government and unnamed partners.

Bre-X, of course, had long said that it would do what junior exploration companies normally do when they hit pay dirt: Find a senior partner to finance, develop, and build a mine, and then move on to the next promising piece of land or jungle. In May, the company had announced it would sell a 25 per cent stake in the property, with the bidding starting at a cool $2 billion. But if the source was correct, Bre-X would not be the one calling the shots in any negotiations.

Bre-X had not made any of its problems public, leaving both its shareholders and stock analysts in the dark. A typical report dated July 15, which a Toronto-based brokerage firm circulated internally, said that conventional wisdom would lead investors to sell their shares in Bre-X, since its Busang project was beginning the feasibility phase, when mining stocks normally falter. "However, a visit to the property is necessary to grasp the magnitude of what is going on and to justify throwing out the rule book," its author enthusiastically concluded.

It was difficult for Goold and his *Globe* colleagues to know how to proceed with the tantalizing revelations the source had provided. Phoning the company without any hard evidence would give Bre-X the chance to deny anything was amiss, or to downplay the cancellation of the permit. It would also be difficult to get information out of an authoritarian government on the other side of the planet. Interviews with mining executives in Toronto and late-night phone calls over the next few weeks to government and investment sources in Jakarta yielded some information, but no confirmation of the leak.

In early September, the company snubbed Toronto's Bay Street by choosing two New York banks, J. P. Morgan & Co. Inc. and Republic National Bank, as its financial and strategic advisers. J. P. Morgan was already well-acquainted with the company. David Neuhaus, one of the analysts on the recent tour of the Busang site, had gushed in July that "150-million ounces is a conservative guess as to what Bre-X will ultimately come up with." That much gold would be worth $52.5 billion (U.S.), greater than the combined reserves of the four largest gold producers in North America. But soon there were hints that Bre-X was not completely in control of its fate. At the end of September, the company announced for the first time that it was considering a full range of options, including a joint venture with a partner, an acquisition, a full merger, or the sale of a majority stake in the deposit. "There are many ways to carve this up," said Walsh. "We are not tied to the 25 per cent option. We want to be flexible and show investors we are covering the entire spectrum of options." A Bre-X official said the decision had nothing to do with delays in signing Contracts of Work.

The Letter

On October 1, the *Globe* contacted the Indonesian government's representatives in Canada to check on the status of Bre-X. The initial official explanation for the delay in the Contracts wasn't any help. Jean Anes, the vice-consul for investments in Toronto, said the loss of the First Lady – President Suharto's wife of forty-nine years and closest adviser, who was commonly called Ibu Tien, had died in April at the age of seventy-two – "certainly will delay letters which our president has to sign." However, he added reassuringly, "I am sure the government has decided to continue its commitment and will do nothing to jeopardize international investors."

But just when the trail had been getting cold, a second key source had faxed critical documents, in Indonesian and English, to *The Globe and Mail*'s veteran mining reporter, Allan Robinson. The document that turned an intriguing lead into hard evidence, and framed the story for months to come, was only three brief paragraphs long. It was a letter dated August 15 "for the attention of" the director of PT Askatindo Karya Mineral, Bre-X's local partner in the southeast zone. The bland, bureaucratic text that appeared above the signature and seal of Kuntoro Mangkusubroto, the dapper, Stanford-educated director general for mines, disguised the letter's formidable punch. This is what the letter said.

"1. Due to a pending administrative problem with your partner (Bre-X), we with regret would like to inform you that we have to cancel your SIPP [preliminary approval letter for exploration].

"2. Your deposit of $100,000 (U.S.) will be returned to your account and also your fee of $1,135.59.

"3. With issuance of this letter we declared that our letter number 1911/2012/DJP/96 [extending the exploration approval] dated July 25, 1996 has never been issued."

What was effectively a death sentence ended, rather ludicrously, "Thank you for your co-operation."

A second letter, addressed to the minister of mines and energy, Idus Bagus Sudjana, a sixty-year-old former three-star general and one of the few Balinese members of the cabinet, revealed the existence of a high-level government committee "formed in connection with the problems surrounding Bre-X." What all this boiled down to was that the government was applying pressure to Bre-X, as the original source had predicted.

After an initial telephone conversation with vice-consul Anes, the *Globe* faxed a series of questions to him, enclosing copies of the documents to prove that the paper had access to secret information. "We plan to publish a story on this subject within the next day or so," the fax warned, in order to force a quick response. Surprisingly, two days later Anes faxed full, written answers from the mines ministry in Jakarta, basically confirming what the paper had learned.

The government said it cancelled the exploration permit because of a complaint against Bre-X by PT Kreung Gasui, one of its two Indonesian partners in the central zone. Both partner companies were controlled by Jusuf Merukh, the Indonesian businessman and former politician one Indonesian source referred to as "a wily old fox." Furthermore, Bre-X "had broken the Indonesian rules," Anes explained, by failing to get the government's permission before acquiring Busang's central zone from its previous offshore owner in 1993.

Not mentioned in the fax was the fact that Bre-X had broken the rules by aggressively drilling on its properties before it had full title. The Calgary company had also upset Indonesian mining officials by relentlessly promoting its drill results in Canada before the ministry in Jakarta even knew about them.

"The government does not have any special preference concerning the share ownership in the Contract of Work of Bre-X," the fax continued. "The government only is concerned about the development of the project soon. To get the president to sign a final contract of work, Bre-X has to give or submit genuine information concerning these problems, supported by authentic documents to prove that Bre-X didn't violate the convention, which may cause losses to the Indonesian partner, PT Kreung Gasui, as well as to the interests of the government of Indonesia."

"I feel sorry for Bre-X shareholders," the affable Jean Anes offered as he dispatched the documents at 3:33 on the afternoon of October 3. As indeed he should have. The story that appeared the next day across the top of the front page of the Report on Business revealed for the first time the formidable road-blocks that Bre-X faced. The story contained a chipper comment from Walsh that "positive discussions" with the Indonesian government were continuing.

The news led to a four-hour halt in trading of Bre-X shares on the Toronto Stock Exchange. At 11:39 that morning, Bre-X issued a press release in response to the story, which it complained contained "incomplete" information. What was notable was that it did not say the story was inaccurate. The company rejected its Indonesian partner's complaint and argued that it hadn't needed the permission of the Indonesian government when it acquired the central zone from the previous owner. "Bre-X believes it will shortly resolve all outstanding issues relating to the Busang project and remains confident that the Indonesian government will proceed with the issues of COWs," said Walsh.

When the stock reopened, a million shares changed hands in the first five frantic minutes of trading, as spooked investors erased

$510 million from the value of the company. By the end of the day, they had traded a whopping 5.8 million shares. Though more money would be lost over the following weeks, the company's legions of true believers remained just that – true believers.

The news was no big deal, analysts argued. And lawsuits were to be expected, given the size of the find. After all, that is what had happened with Diamond Fields Resources Inc. of Vancouver, the company run by free-wheeling entrepreneur Robert Friedland that had discovered the largest nickel deposit in history at Voisey's Bay in Labrador. Bre-X's many supporters loved to compare their story to that of Diamond Fields, whose stock had skyrocketed on the basis of the massive find, once investors had overcome their scepticism about its size. Friedland himself realized that the success of Diamond Fields helped to make the Bre-X story believable. As he explained in a March 1997 interview in his spacious office overlooking the skyline in Singapore, "Once having willingly suspended disbelief, it became a lot easier for people to believe that lightning could strike twice." What Diamond Fields faced were "just nuisance suits in the end, and people paid them just to make them go away," said Wayne Deans, a money manager with Deans Knight Capital Management Ltd. of Vancouver. Bre-X was now in a similar position, he suggested.

Jusuf Merukh, Bre-X's disaffected Indonesian partner, later alleged in a $2-billion (U.S.) suit filed in an Alberta court that he had been defrauded by Bre-X. He claimed that the company had used confidential information it gained from their partnership in the central zone to discover and lay claim to the much richer, contiguous southeast zone. Merukh claimed 30 per cent of the southeast zone, the richest part of Busang. The only good news for Bre-X in this welter of claims was that Merukh was heartily loathed by Suharto's family, the mines department, and many of the mining entrepreneurs with whom he had done business.

Throughout 1996, the mining community and analysts had been reassuring about Bre-X at every point in the saga. Few came close, however, to the gloss the company put on its own discoveries.

"It's possible that the Alberta Stock Exchange should build a statue to David Walsh and put it in front of its front door," director Paul Kavanagh said in February. More disarming was the sensible-shoes advice to investors from David Walsh in an interview with the *Calgary Herald* that same month: "You've got to do your due diligence checking. You've got to look for a company with management, a technical team, money in the bank and a decent property."

Walsh was, of course, right. The problem was, Bre-X was not one of those companies.

CHAPTER SIX

The Land of the Shadow Puppets

"It's Indonesia. It's the puppet thing. You see the characters move, but you don't really knows who controls them." – Steve Bugg, exploration manager, Barrick Gold Corp., Jakarta

"I look on it [corruption] as an inverted taxation system. It's pretty systematic." – Tim Scott, commercial manager, Barrick Gold Corp., Jakarta

"There is a much more personal side to business in Indonesia which really says: Is that person or institution somebody that we can count on?" – Harvey Goldstein, chairman, Harvest International Inc., Jakarta

A Nation in Waiting

Jakarta is a sprawling city where visitors encounter ugly, Stalinist public monuments; worshippers on prayer rugs that jut into the street; the unspeakably luxurious Shangri-La Hotel, with its shapely pool and view of the large, white-domed mosque at the end of the

75

property; and the all-too-predictable corrugated tin shacks with chickens running freely in dirt yards just down the street. Indonesia's capital is a city of open sewers, closed sewers, sewers perpetually under repair and streets packed with vendors who materialize out of the ether at the same time every evening, selling fruit, pop, and cigarettes and preparing noodles and satay on the spot. The bustling, chaotic Javanese city includes kids who march by your car at intersections selling everything that can be sold, including popcorn, bright blue globes of the world, decals of Disney characters, flowers, watermelons, scissors, furry toy animals, cell phones, and sculptures of fish. "There's an entrepreneurial instinct here," says Chris Green, as he drives to the Dusit Hotel, where he is the manager. "If you don't have something to sell, you don't eat. But there's no abject poverty, as there is in Bangladesh."

Like many third-world capitals, Jakarta is a dirty, polluted, fascinating city, where taxi drivers, none of whom has a map, are content to sit indefinitely in gridlocked traffic. "I had three car accidents in my first three months here," groaned one Canadian investment officer. "I just argued them out in the police station." The city has no discernible centre, and life is lived in the streets. With almost 9 million inhabitants, and counting, labour is plentiful – and so is poverty, pain, prosperity, and prostitution. "You like younger, mister?" offers a spurned prostitute in front of the Grand Hyatt Hotel.

Even literate westerners know little about Indonesia. As often happens with distant, unknown lands, their brief moment in the sun when they come to the western world's attention is an unhappy one. Apart from the Bre-X story, Indonesia's most memorable appearance in the world's press in recent months has centred on the contributions Indonesian financier James Riady, whose family founded the powerful Lippo Group, has made to the Democratic Party and the influence he might have wielded as a result on his old friend, President Bill Clinton.

To most westerners, Indonesia lacks familiar historical signposts or a clear identity, beyond the idyllic island of Bali and the theatre of shadow puppets. Yet this nation of more than 200 million souls is the fourth most populous on Earth, and is the largest Muslim country. Though its Muslims are far from united, they account for more than 90 per cent of the population. This vast citizenry on more than 5,000 inhabited islands, of which Java is the most crowded, is spread over three time zones along 15,120 kilometres, the world's longest archipelago.

Indonesia is unknown in part because President Suharto, its ruler since 1966, has kept a low international profile. He became only the second president in the country's history after he staged a coup – in which hundreds of thousands were killed – against its first ruler, Sukarno. His excuse was that a communist take-over was imminent, though the existence of a plot has never been proved. Before Sukarno achieved independence for Indonesia in 1945, the country suffered under the unenlightened colonial rule of the Dutch, which helps to explain its latent anti-western sentiment. Sukarno has a living legacy in the form of his daughter Megawati Sukarnoputri, the popular Indonesian Democratic Party opposition leader whom the government successfully removed from her position in time for the May 1997 parliamentary elections. It is that trump card of control, and a willingness to employ any means to ensure it, that has kept the same regime in power for so many decades.

All roads in Indonesia lead to the wily, authoritarian Suharto, who has been in power for longer than any other international leader except Fidel Castro. "Don't turn your head too obviously," Barrick Gold Corp.'s commercial manager, Tim Scott, warned a passenger as they drove by the president's house in a prosperous, leafy section of the capital. "There are soldiers between the houses and there is often an armoured personnel carrier blocking each end of the street." Suharto, so familiar in his brimless hat, has brought political stability and considerable economic progress to his people. Growth after accounting for inflation has been an impressive 6 to 7 per cent a year for the past several decades. Per capita gross domestic product is around $1,400, marginally less than that of the

Philippines, but less than half that of Mexico. Indonesia could become an economic powerhouse sometime next century, thanks to its abundant, cheap labour force and wide array of natural resources, which include oil, timber, spices, and many minerals.

But prosperity has come at a price, and that price is obvious to those familiar with the censorship, the excesses of the army, and the repression in East Timor, the former Portuguese colony that Indonesia invaded in 1975. And it would be hard to imagine a more glaring gap between the Mercedes class, with its blatant display of wealth, and the bulk of the people. The authoritarian, paternalistic political system, which was cobbled together to deal with the crises of the 1960s, is increasingly out of date. Thanks to Suharto, political progress hasn't matched economic advancement, a disequilibrium that the élites realize will have to be addressed soon.

Indonesia is "a nation in waiting," the title of a book by Adam Schwarz, the best work in English on the country (visitors to Jakarta are told, helpfully, that although the book is banned in Indonesia, it is in plentiful supply in the airport in Singapore). Indonesians are waiting for the Suharto era to end, and to discover what will succeed it. It is assumed he will go either by death or by choice; no one expects him to be overthrown. One key is to see whom Suharto will choose as his next vice-president, since the appointee could be his successor. Potential choices range from the current vice-president, Try Sutrisno, to the president's eldest daughter, forty-nine-year-old Siti Hariyanti Rukmana. Tutut, as she is called, has a senior position in the ruling Golkar party and would ensure continuity for those with a vested interest in the status quo. In the May 1997 parliamentary elections, which were as always tightly scripted by the government, Golkar registered its sixth consecutive win, amid accusations of election fraud. It received 74.27 per cent of the vote, well ahead of the 70.02 per cent (that exact number!) the party's wonderfully named "Department of Winning the Election" predicted. Now all eyes are focused on whether the president, who is seventy-six in 1997, will run for a seventh and presumably final five-year term in 1998. Suharto is in reasonable health and determined to appear fit, recently posing in a leather jacket and cap astride the Harley-Davidson motorcycle with an attached sidecar that he rides around the presidential grounds.

Anything could happen after Suharto is gone, from an ethnic conflict similar to Yugoslavia's once Tito was gone, to a military dictatorship – as it is, the military is guaranteed 75 of the parliament's 500 seats. Certainly there has been a noticeable rise in ethnic unrest in the last few years. Indonesia experienced the worst riots in thirty years last July, triggered by political, economic, and social discontent, and in particular by the government's ouster of Megawati. The government has a clear idea of how to deal with dissidents, who are often accused of being communists. "Opening fire is simply shock therapy," Field Marshal Tjokong Tarigan of the armed forces faction opined a few months before the election, in a discussion over the forces' shoot-rioters-on-sight order. While some observers anticipate a relatively smooth transition to a combined civilian-military government, as opposed to rule by the military alone or by a Muslim faction, no one denies that Indonesia is approaching a critical period of formidable risks. As economist Hartojo Wignjowijoto sees it, the Indonesian government is a "one-man show," and when Suharto goes, the "filing system in his head" will go with him.

Business Culture in Indonesia

In this elusive land of shadow puppets, nothing is quite what it seems. It's easy for westerners to mistake the meaning or miss the nuance of what is said or done. Yes can mean no. Politeness can mask hostility. Devout Muslims turn out to be not so devout after all. The person ostensibly in charge may not be the one in charge at all. "It's Indonesia," said Barrick's exploration manager Steve Bugg during a wide-ranging conversation in the Texas BBQ Restaurant in Jakarta. "You see the characters move, but you don't really know who controls them." Indonesian values are very different from those of North America and Western Europe. Saving face and avoiding embarrassment are critical. As in the rest of Asia, relationships and trust count for more than money and have to be built up and nurtured – on the spot, not from afar – in offices, in homes, and on the golf course over many years. Business is conducted much differently than it is in the West. For outsiders to succeed takes a lot of patience and understanding, qualities that would be found wanting in some of the Canadian players in the Bre-X drama. "Team Canada" visits by a fly-in, shake-hands, fly-out cheerleading prime minister, with a planeload of businesspeople in his wake, do very little to bridge the chasm.

Not that corporate Canada is unfamiliar with Indonesia. Business ties have burgeoned, particularly in the past few years, with the result that there are more than 100 Canadian companies operating in the country. Most of them are in the oil and gas and mining exploration sectors. Participants include TransCanada Pipelines, Nova Corp., SNC-Lavalin Group Inc., Manulife, and Bata Shoes Canada Ltd. In February 1997, for example, Gulf Canada Resources Ltd. and Talisman Energy Inc. signed a $450-million (U.S.) financing deal for a natural gas project in Sumatra. Three months later, the Bank of Nova Scotia bought a small, profitable Indonesia bank. Scotiabank had left the country ten years earlier, in part because of its corruption.

The culture of Java, a small island with 115 million inhabitants with Jakarta at its heart, dominates Indonesia. The Javanese like developing relationships and trust over many years; they do not like to be rushed; they do not like decision-makers from afar determining their fate; they base their decisions on much more than money; and they favour progress through consensus, not through conflict. A low-key approach can succeed where an aggressive one fails, as Barrick Gold would discover.

No one knows this better than Harvey Goldstein, chairman of consulting firm Harvest International Inc. and a consultant in Jakarta for twenty-seven years. Goldstein coaches multinationals such as Shell, Procter & Gamble, and Esso on the nuances of Indonesia's business culture. How else would they know, for example, that putting your hands on your hips is as rude to Indonesians as putting your feet up on the table is to westerners?

"The threshold of being insulting or offensive is much lower to a Javanese person than it would be to a western person. And the signals are much less perceptible to a western person," says the portly, animated Goldstein. "During negotiations, the westerner can become oblivious to the transgressions, and if they think it's only money and quality and time and delivery that are important, they're wrong. It has something to do with attitudes and trust.

"President Suharto is the ultimate of Javanese gentlemen, because you go in and speak to him and you'll never know when you pass the point of no return, unless you can read him very carefully. And that's an art.

"There is a much more personal side to business in Indonesia which really says: Is that person or institution somebody that we can count on? Is he a person who is loyal and friendly to us, and is he a person or institution that we can trust?

"And if all those things are so, we can look at the financial side of the picture, or the quality side of the picture. But if that person or institution has had a disloyal or an offensive relationship, even though he comes with the best mousetrap at the best price in the best time delivery, he will fail."

These attitudes are deeply embedded in Javanese culture and are not about to be changed by western companies who are used to getting their way, and getting it quickly. Goldstein explains that "when companies say, 'They can't do that to us,' I say, 'Look, you have to understand this is their country and their game, and they've been colonized for so many hundred years. And they've fought their revolution, and they died for their freedom and they are going to do it this way. Now do you want to play it? Maybe it's not in your rule book.'"

Thirty-year-old Ranjeet Sundher, president of Indogold Exploration Services, who was awaiting final approval in the summer of 1997 for fifty-six "seventh generation" Contracts of Work for his clients, has similar advice. "Respect the culture, learn from the way they do business, and be down here," the Vancouver native said in his office in Jakarta. Sundher, who says he feels like a pioneer, has not lost his boundless enthusiasm for the "fantastic, very helpful" mines ministry, "which wants us to be successful."

"The Contract of Work is a very simple contract which they stick to if you stick to." It's important to keep in close touch with the government, he said, adding that he has at times made trips almost daily to the mines ministry to apply for exploration permits or to stake claims on the ministry's sophisticated, computerized map, a far cry from the traditional wooden stake approach.

PT Inco, whose majority owner is nickel giant Inco Ltd. of Toronto, is the second oldest and second largest foreign-owned mining company in Indonesia, after New Orleans-based Freeport-McMoRan Copper & Gold Inc. PT Inco has maintained a discreet, successful presence in Indonesia for more than a quarter of a century. And it makes money, earning $61 million (U.S.) in 1996. In January 1996, after two and a half years of negotiations, Inco signed a coveted new Contract of Work, extending its agreement with the government to the year 2025. The company first agreed to spend $580 million (U.S.) to expand its facilities. PT Inco's respected Indonesian-born chief executive, Rumengan Musu, laughed when asked how the company avoided the environmental and human rights problems of Freeport. He recounted how he had stayed for three weeks with the village chief of Soroako on the island of Sulawesi, when Inco was first exploring the region in the 1960s. The bonds he and his colleagues established there continue to this day. Although the chief died in 1972, he says, "I continued with his family – his daughter and his son – like they were my own family. And every time I visit Soroako, I always pop in. We automatically became a leader in the community, and we maintained a relationship with the people. We have to understand their culture and respect all the people, especially the elder people in the village." Over the years, Inco has contributed to health, education, and cultural activities in the areas in which it operates, while staying clear of religion and politics. More than 99 per cent of its work force is Indonesian. Inco's Toronto-based president Scott Hand expresses it this way: "I've been told by Indonesians and I've learned from it: 'Scott, you've got to become more Javanese.'"

There are two other aspects of business in Indonesia that played a role in the Bre-X story: ethnicity and corruption. There are 50 million ethnic Chinese in southeast Asia, and everywhere they play a leading role in business. Their economic power is widely resented, most visibly in Malaysia, where rioting in 1969 led to laws restricting their activities and affirmative action programs for the Muslim majority. The tension is less visible in Indonesia, but it is there. The ethnic Chinese, many of whom are Christian, make up only 3.5 per cent of the population, but control more than 70 per cent of the wealth. That imbalance is greater than in any other country in southeast Asia. Muslims resent this domination, which in the last several years has touched off bouts of civil strife.

Suharto hasn't helped matters with the support he has given to some of the most powerful Chinese businesspeople, for reasons that are not entirely clear. One view is that by giving the Chinese concessions, he has achieved a measure of control over them and prevented them from gaining political power. In *A Nation in Waiting*, Adam Schwarz calls the ethnic Chinese "the race that counts."

Muktar Widjaj is the youthful-looking managing director of the Sinar Mas Group, whose Chinese family controls dozens of companies in Asia and Europe in businesses ranging from cooking oil to paper and is the second largest business group in Indonesia. Over a buffet breakfast at the Dusit Hotel, he says he is very positive about the business environment in Indonesia. Growth has been swift, taxes are reasonable, there are no foreign exchange controls, and the government has done a good job of controlling monetary policy and inflation. But, he adds, you have to "adjust to the society" and have a sense of social responsibility. "I was born here. We go to Singapore, Hong Kong – we go everywhere – but I prefer Indonesia."

Mohammad "Bob" Hasan, a twice-a-week golfing buddy of the president's and the powerbroker in the Bre-X saga, is one of these

Chinese businesspeople. Born The Kian Seng, he became associated with Suharto in the 1950s and later converted to Islam and changed his name. The *Far Eastern Economic Review* has dubbed him Suharto's "First Friend." He is frequently referred to as the timber baron, because he controls 2 million hectares of forest lands, most of them in Kalimantan. More than anyone else, he called the shots for the export of Indonesia's hardwood plywood, an industry worth $4 billion (U.S.) and the country's second largest export after oil. Hasan established this control by dominating the Indonesian Wood Panel Association and other trade groups. According to Adam Schwarz, "Hasan wields considerably more influence over the forestry sector than the ministry of forestry." Although he was a member of the World Business Council for Sustainable Development, environmentalists – and the World Bank – have criticized him for the aggressive logging of tropical rain forests. "I'm the greenest guy of all," he retorts. The sixty-six-year-old timber baron also had major interests in banking, insurance, autos, airlines, and construction, giving him an estimated fortune of £700 million, or about $1.6 billion, according to Geoff Hiscock's *Asia's Wealth Club*, a book published in the middle of 1997 that profiles Asia's top 100 billionaires. Hasan is an avid sports activist and a member of many sports organizations, including the International Olympic Committee. While he is feared by competitors, he has adopted an easy-going persona and claims to be as interested in sports as he is in business. Asked about his powerful relationship with Suharto, he replied with a laugh, "What do you mean powerful? My friends say my main business is sports."

"Have you ever been asked for a kickback?"

The final Indonesian ingredient in the Bre-X mix is corruption. In mining circles in Indonesia, it is widely believed but unproven that unauthorized payments were made to officials in an attempt to win their support. While the United States has a Foreign Corrupt

Practices Act, outlawing the practice for U.S. companies operating abroad, Canada does not. The suspicions of bribery are hardly surprising, given the stakes that were thought to be involved and the fact that most international surveys finger Indonesia, despite its bedrock of Muslim faith, as one of the most corrupt countries in the world. That, of course, doesn't prevent seasoned travellers from pleading, "But you haven't been to Pakistan – or Venezuela – or Nigeria." Mines minister Sudjana was called before parliament in December 1996 to answer charges that he diverted $21.4 million (U.S.) from a state-owned coal company into his personal bank account. The general's explanation: he needed to supervise the money personally to prevent it from being wasted.

"Have you ever been asked for a kickback?" *The Globe and Mail* bluntly asked Alex Van Hoeken, the amiable senior vice-president of Vancouver-based Golden Panther Resources Ltd., a junior mining exploration company, in his Jakarta office. "Big ones or small ones?" the towering twenty-eight-year-old native of The Hague in the Netherlands responded. "Put it this way," he continued. "In certain situations, we have been given a fee for what it would cost us to do something. This costs so much: you don't question the fee. Now, I think there's a big difference here between little kickbacks and big kickbacks. The guy in the bottom level of the ministry makes 200,000 rupiah [$150] a month. How's he going to live? Guys like that, it's normal. Guys make suggestions: hey, if you want to speed things up, you put something in a little envelope. Now, here's the difference between big companies and small companies. Big companies have a lot of political power and people, and they can use a lot of avenues. Small companies have to go with the flow.

"Those big companies who have policies [of avoiding corrupt practices] are the companies with the staying power. Small companies don't have that luxury.

"Everybody facilitates things on a smaller level. You give the guy 20,000 rupiah or whatever to process the visas. On the bigger things, I haven't actually been asked for a big payment yet." Van Hoeken remained hopeful, adding that if you develop the right relationships, you don't have to make payoffs.

"The corruption question inevitably comes up," says the affable, well-connected Tim Scott, commercial manager of Barrick's Jakarta office of twenty, nodding to an employee headed to the office's prayer room. "I find if you generally stick to the rules, you don't have to [make payments]. If you're asking officials to bend the rules, it's a different matter. I think if the game is being played on the top of the table, that is open for everyone to see, you don't have any problems.

"I look on corruption as an inverted taxation system," says Scott. "It's pretty systematic." The native of Perth, Australia, who favours loafers with no socks, recalled how some twenty years ago he was asked to pay $500 (U.S.) to clear his car through customs, an amount he considered outrageous. So he found a young man who was able to tell him exactly what each official expected to be paid. One got 5,000 [$3.75] rupiahs, while the next demanded 7,000 [$5.25].

"I didn't have any 1,000 rupiah notes, so I gave him a note for 10,000 [$7.50], and he gave me three single 1,000 rupiah notes back in change," explained Scott. "In my thinking of corruption, if you bribe somebody with $20 and all you have got in your pocket is $100, you are lucky to get your $80 change back. You know, the recipient thinks you are so far in, plus the deal is already immoral, why not take all your change of $80? But no, this whole thing was all organized: a proper schedule of rates. What they didn't have was a sign up on the desk which said: My signature costs 7,000 rupiah."

A Canadian mining executive in Jakarta was describing the problems of conducting business in Jakarta to *Globe* reporter John Stackhouse when a secretary interrupted to announce the arrival of an immigration official. "I don't believe it," said the executive, shaking his head. "We gave these people $1,000 (U.S.) last week," but "it's never enough." The official could, if he was bloody-minded enough, order the executive to leave Indonesia within forty-eight hours. "It takes a lot to stay in this country, a lot of graft and a lot of hardship," groaned the executive.

Corruption is endemic in Asia. But it's not viewed there with the same sense of disgust as it is in the West. The most common explanation for low-level corruption is the dismal pay of most officials. Others say it is the way in which a poor country, with a startling gap between rich and poor, attempts to bring about a more justifiable distribution of income. At higher levels, corruption is variously ascribed to greed, a sense of entitlement, or part of the cronyism that has long dominated the country's politics. It remains unchecked, in part at least, because of the lack of a free press and a slow, ineffective legal system. Virtually everyone in Indonesia who has views on the subject notes that at a time when even the Lincoln Bedroom in the White House is available in return for political contributions, the West is in no position to point fingers.

Asked how executives at Canadian companies should handle requests for payments, Kuntoro, then the director general of mines, made no attempt to deny the problem. "I can't say anything," he replied. "They should ask their colleagues." Ironically, until Bre-X, the mines ministry had one of the cleanest reputations in the government.

"The First Siblings"

Nowhere is corruption more visible, more egregious, or on a grander scale than with "the first siblings," the ironic name given to Suharto's six children. Critics have called Indonesia "the land of the rising sons and daughters." Several other relatives, including a cousin and a half-brother, also receive huge benefits from the president. The late First Lady was derisively referred to as "Madame Tien Per Cent," a reference to allegations that she demanded a 10 per cent kickback on public projects. The family looks good only by comparison to the Philippines' "kleptocratic" Marcos family.

It may be that Suharto just lacks critical distance from his own family, whose greed and squabbles have frequently caused him huge embarrassment. Or he may simply believe that they all deserve to share the spoils of office. The most memorable expression of the view that politics is for the benefit of the participants came from billion-aire and former mayor of Mexico City, the charming Carlos Hank Gonzalez, when he said that "a politician who is poor is a poor politi-cian." After so many years in power, Suharto seems less interested in governing than in ensuring a prosperous future for his children.

Geoff Hiscock's *Asia's Wealth Club* puts the Suharto family in ninth spot among Asia's billionaires, with assets of £3.9 billion, or $6.4-billion (U.S.). The siblings have been granted huge conces-sions in the automobile, petrochemical, telecommunications, broad-casting, toll road, and other sectors. According to *Business Week*, the children's interests are worth at least $4 billion (U.S.). Leading *Business Week*'s list is Suharto's forty-three-year-old son Bambang Trihatmodjo, with estimated assets of $2.2 billion, and partnerships with multinationals Hughes, Deutsche Telekom, Siemens, Hyatt, and Hyundai. Three other offspring are worth half a billion or so each. They are eldest daughter Tutut, forty-five-year-old son Sigit Harjojudanto, and the brash, aggressive thirty-four-year-old son, Hutomo Mandala Putra, who is called Tommy.

Although Indonesia is an authoritarian state, there is a degree of open expression, and criticism of "the Royal Family" is not uncom-mon. As Indonesia moves increasingly to a market economy, even the normally conservative business community finds it hard to accept concessions freely given to the children, since they disrupt the normal competitive environment, raise prices, and anger foreign investors. For example, many Indonesians and virtually all foreigners were out-raged when Suharto granted Tommy the exclusive rights to produce a national car, the Timor, with joint-venture partner Kia Motors Corp. of South Korea (brother Bambang, who also has auto inter-ests, stopped speaking with Tommy as a result of the award). The partners were given the right to import parts without paying duties and to sell cars without paying luxury taxes, which would allow them to produce cars that are 30 to 50 per cent cheaper than their rivals. This has led to rare unanimity among Japanese, European, and North

American auto manufacturers, with the Japanese pressing for a ruling on this blatant nepotism by the World Trade Organization. Ford says they are putting their investment in Indonesia on hold "until this situation is cleared up."

A Strategic Alliance

Canadians had their chance to see the First Family in action the morning of Monday, October 28, 1996. Trading in Bre-X was halted so the company could announce that it had formed a "strategic alliance" with PT Panutan Duta, a private Indonesian company "controlled by Mr. Sigit Harjojudanto." Noticeably lacking from the press release was mention of the fact that Sigit was Suharto's eldest son. It is thought that the omnipresent Bob Hasan introduced Sigit to Bre-X. The problem was that though Sigit had substantial business interests (in, for example, the Bank of Central Asia, Indonesia's largest private bank), he was less influential or credible than several of his brothers and sisters. According to several accounts, a few years ago Suharto had to have money flown in to bail out Sigit, who had lost at least $25 million (U.S.) gambling in Las Vegas. Even his not easily embarrassed family were embarrassed. According to a mining executive who does business with one of Suharto's children, the incident was shocking in a Muslim society and caused Tutut to complain to her father that Sigit was making the family look like a bunch of tinpot dictators. "It was more scandalous than Fergie's toe-sucking," the executive quipped.

Panutan was to act as a consultant "to assist in administrative, technical and other support matters within the Republic of Indonesia, including the identification of issues concerning the acquisition, exploration, development and production from mineral resource properties and other interests." Although the job description was bland, the financial terms were not. The arrangement was to run for up to forty months at $1 million (U.S.) a month, plus a 10 per cent interest in two zones of the deposit, including the one that counted. Sigit would own 40 per cent of a newly formed support services company, which would provide utilities, petroleum, and limestone to any projects in Indonesia. The agreement was conditional upon the issuance to Bre-X of Contracts of Work for its properties.

The deal was a ham-fisted, transparent, and astonishingly expensive attempt by Bre-X to gain political support for the go-ahead on Busang. What other company would offer to give away 10 per cent of its assets, through an agreement that could cost more than half a billion dollars, in return for help in solving an ownership dispute? Although this was Indonesia, and many foreign companies found that it took big payments to get things done, this had the look of desperation about it, suggesting there was more going on than met the eye. While professors of business ethics were given a rare chance to moralize in the press, Bre-X investors – however much they pretended to be appalled by how business was conducted in the archipelago – were delighted. When trading resumed at 11:08 the morning of the October 28 announcement, Bre-X shares soared $3.45 to $24.25, a gain of almost 17 per cent, with 7 million shares changing hands.

Few observers had any doubt as to what the deal meant: that with Sigit's high-powered help, Bre-X would quickly resolve its fight with its minority partners and get the go-ahead from the government. "If you have any trouble understanding what it all means, I assume you also believe in the tooth fairy," commented Doug Leishman of Yorkton Securities. "Welcome to Indonesia." Even the Indonesian government had trouble keeping a straight face. Asked if it was easier for a foreign company to get a Contract if it had a Suharto sibling working on its behalf, Chaidir Siregar, head of the economics section at the Indonesian Embassy in Ottawa, replied, "It might be, yes. I think it's not only in Indonesia, it's all over the world. If you are very close to power, it's easier for you. This is – what do you call it? – the nature of business."

The nature of business for Bre-X was its agreement with Sigit. It was a response to an arrangement made in the summer – the details of which were never publicized – between Barrick Gold, which had long been interested in Bre-X, and a construction company controlled by Suharto's powerful daughter Tutut. Obviously, the construction company would play a major role if Barrick decided to build a mine in Indonesia. And it was Barrick, under the determined leadership of its founder and chairman Peter Munk, that was on the point of concluding a deal of its own that would transform the Bre-X story.

CHAPTER SEVEN

The November Coup

"I don't think I'm ambitious, but my family does, so maybe I am." – Peter Munk, chairman of Barrick Gold Corp., October 1996

"Something has been going on that is not kosher in the West." – John Willson, chief executive officer, Placer Dome Inc., December 1996

Barrick Behind the Scenes

In the fall of 1996 it became clear that Suharto's son Sigit was failing miserably in his mission to help Bre-X resolve its ownership problem, despite the enormous financial incentives he had been offered to do so. Bre-X was getting the worst of both worlds; its Indonesian partners continued to claim 30 per cent of the mother lode, yet the company still had not been granted its Contracts of Work, which would give it clear title to Busang. Worse, there were now two Suharto siblings backing rival players in the unseemly battle for control of the property; in Sigit, Bre-X had chosen by far the weaker.

For months, Barrick had been stealthily wooing key Indonesian decision-makers, starting with the memorable Tutut, Suharto's daughter. With her support Barrick had won over the minister of mines, Sudjana, his son, the son of another minister, and Sudjana's powerful adviser, Adnan Ganto. Ganto, an interesting figure, had close ties to the military and had been instrumental in the purchase of Skyhawk fighter jets from Britain. An article entitled "Adnan's Shadow Behind Sudjana" in the Indonesian weekly magazine *Forum* observed that because Ganto was not appointed under the usual presidential decree, "it is not surprising that there is suspicion that it is the advisor who is the real authority at the department of mines and energy." Ganto was to remain a shadowy background figure. And a hard-hitting article in *Gatra* (owned by the billionaire businessman Bob Hasan, whose fingerprints seemed to be everywhere) claimed that Sudjana had undermined his officials. It also recounted the "mystery" of the missing millions that ended up in the minister's account in the coal-mining scandal. From the top down, the mines department was in turmoil.

Barrick sold itself to these powerbrokers as the only company with the political clout to break the ownership log-jam, and with the financial resources and experience to build a world-class mine. It flew mining officials and members of the Indonesian media on a well-catered trip to Nevada so they could see for themselves the fine things the company had achieved. Barrick's efforts were helped by Bre-X's missteps, which had raised the hackles of the government and had led to the cancellation of the company's exploration permit in the first place.

The optics were not in Bre-X's favour.

On the one side, you had the rough-hewn Felderhof with his smoker's cough and the flabby unimpressive Walsh, fresh from bankruptcy, a man who had moved his office out of his Calgary basement only in March. On the other side, you had the elegant, jet-setting Peter Munk, who in a little more than a decade had transformed Barrick into a world-class money-spinner with a market value that has topped $14 billion. And while Walsh was used to drinking beer and exchanging stories at the Three Greenhorns in Calgary, Munk traded ideas with the world's élite at Davos, Switzerland. Barrick had an international advisory board that included the powerful former U.S. Senator Howard Baker; Karl Otto Pöhl, at one time the chairman of Germany's central bank; Paul Desmarais, chairman of Power Corp.; and former U.S. president George Bush. The advisory group was chaired by the former Canadian prime minister Brian Mulroney, who was responsible for selecting other members. The fifty-eight-year-old Mulroney had been named a director of the company in November 1993 and was also a director of Munk's holding company Horsham Corp., (which in 1996 was transformed into TrizecHahn Corp). Clearly, Barrick had major-league connections. And Indonesia is a country where connections count for a great deal.

Did Barrick's powerful supporters pressure Kuntoro, the director general of mines, into revoking Bre-X's exploration permit, as the weekly *Forum* alleged, so that Barrick could come in and pick up the pieces? In an interview in his spacious office, decorated with Van Gogh prints, Kuntoro was asked to respond to these allegations. He replied, "Maybe they are right. But from my point of view, I am just following procedures. I will never proceed if there is a dispute between partners. They have to settle it first."

Certainly during the fall Barrick was making stupendous progress at the expense of Bre-X. In mid-October 1996, in his role as minister, where he was widely regarded as incompetent, Sudjana stripped Kuntoro of his control over the Contract of Work process. (As one observer noted in a typical comment about Sudjana: "No one knew why he was picked, except that he was a loyal soldier." One mining executive said that when several people complained at a private meeting with the minister about a lack of maps, Sudjana responded, "What would you need maps for?") In mid-November, the minister told ashen-faced Bre-X executives in a confidential meeting in his office that their new partner was Barrick.

Mulroney and Bush were part of Barrick's blitzkrieg. According to *Canadian Business* magazine, at a private dinner in the minister's honour in June at the Indonesian consulate on Jarvis Street in Toronto, Alan Hill, Barrick's executive vice-president for development, had handed Sudjana a letter signed by Mulroney. The letter described Barrick's interest in Busang. In September, George Bush wrote directly to Suharto, praising Barrick and suggesting that the company should be given an opportunity to develop the Busang site.

No one should have been shocked by these revelations, though they were. In mid-November, Bre-X faxed to analysts a story written by John McBeth, the Jakarta bureau chief for the *Far Eastern Economic Review*. The article was the first to claim that Barrick "has tried to push Bre-X into a less-than-favourable deal with phone calls to top-level Indonesians" from Bush and Mulroney. The article was greeted with derision. "That's absolute rubbish," commented one analyst. "It's so outlandish." But opinion had changed by the following month, when the *Financial Post* ran an editorial page cartoon showing George Bush saying "Read my lips" to a beleaguered Bre-X shareholder who responded, "I was afraid he'd say that!"

"Mr. Mulroney's Presence"

Peter Munk pays his directors very well and expects a lot in return, including help in fighting political battles. That's legitimate. He wants to be able to phone them in the middle of the night and use their political knowledge and connections to get things done. The rewards are spectacular. In 1993, four directors and five officers of Barrick exercised options worth $31.4 million.

As a corporate lawyer by training and a schmoozer by inclination, Mulroney had much to offer as a director. His work for Barrick was useful to the company and to himself, since it allowed him to get involved in business and politics outside Canada; at home his reputation was still controversial. Barrick has used Mulroney to help with a number of deals, including setting up an arrangement with his old friend Paul Desmarais of Power Corp. to develop gold deposits in China. In 1994, Barrick paid the former prime minister $141,000 for advisory services and expenses. At Barrick's 1995 annual meeting, Munk told shareholders that "Mr. Mulroney's presence has been larger and more meaningful than we anticipated." After the meeting, pressed for details, Mulroney said, "I couldn't quantify it, but I spend a fair amount of time in Latin America and China and Africa working with senior management and governments around the world."

In late 1993, Mulroney was granted options to buy 250,000 shares of Horsham at $18 each and 250,000 shares of Barrick at $34.87 each. While the options were worth $1.5 million at the time, Mulroney had to wait at least a year before exercising them. William Riedl, president of Fairvest Securities Corp. of Toronto, a firm that provides advice on shareholder rights, commented: "It blows you away. Those are big numbers. Are Mr. Mulroney's contacts worth that much?" Barrick granted the former prime minister another 250,000 options in September 1994, with an exercise price of $33.87. Yet according to the 1997 proxy circular, Mulroney had purchased only 700 Barrick shares for himself, which would have cost something over $20,000.

Mulroney, of course, does not devote full-time attention to Barrick. He is also an independent director of Archer-Daniels-Midland Co., the agricultural products giant located in Decatur, Illinois, which is dominated by the family of Dwayne Andreas. A survey of institutional investors published in *Business Week* voted the company's board the worst in the United States. In October 1996, Mulroney helped to broker with Washington the settlement of a price-fixing scandal involving the company. Archer-Daniels agreed to plead guilty to two charges and pay a $100-million (U.S.) fine, the largest such fine in U.S. history.

Munk was candid about what he expected from his directors in an editorial meeting at *The Globe and Mail* in October 1996, at which he was asked point-blank why he rewarded directors with millions of dollars in stock options.

"What you said is true, I reward them with millions of dollars," he replied, rapping the boardroom table for emphasis. But "I don't pay them millions of dollars. I use stock options. The stocks go up and they become worth millions of dollars because, let's say, gold doubles. What I am trying to do is to tie them intellectually and emotionally and to the maximum extent I can to my cause. I don't want them to sit there [slams fist down] like a bunch of bureaucrats, just nodding and passing resolutions. I want people to care [slams fist]. I want people at the board table that I can call in the middle of the night and say, hey, Brian Mulroney, I've got U.S. Interior Secretary Bruce Babbitt who is threatening to increase mining royalties in Nevada, and we have to do something about it."

"You want to tie them [directors] to you so that they have identical, deep-seated interests in what you're trying to do. One way of doing that is by making them buy shares. Well, sometimes, Mr. Mulroney has got no money. Mickey Cohen [a director] has no money. So I gave them options. . . ."

And if someone makes a lot of money through options? "Bully for him. It could have happened that the shares went nowhere. . . . Brian Mulroney's stock options for a year-and-a-half were under water. And I used to go to bed thinking: how can I make money for him?"

Peter Munk: The Man with the Midas Touch?

Peter Munk is a capitalist's capitalist. His speech is sprinkled with references to free enterprise and the solemn duty of maximizing the return to his shareholders. He is the first to point the finger at himself when he believes he has fallen short. At the 1996 Horsham annual meeting, Munk told shareholders, "We have failed in the most fundamental responsibility that a public company has toward its shareholders and that's the delivery of value to you. . . . It's not acceptable, we shall not live with it, and we shall do something about it." Munk did just that within months, transforming the cumbersome, ill-defined Horsham into the tightly focused TrizecHahn.

The fiercely competitive, fiercely demanding, sixty-nine-year-old Munk grew up in a wealthy Jewish family in Budapest that was forced to flee Nazi-occupied Hungary in 1944. Like many immigrants, he was forever grateful for what Canada offered him. It is fair to say, however, that his rise to the top of the Canadian business élite was anything but smooth. Munk's earlier years were filled with an odd array of big hits and big misses, which made the business community and the media view him with some scepticism.

Armed with an electrical engineering degree from the University of Toronto, Munk began his career with a disaster. In the late 1950s, he founded Clairtone Sound Corp., which made elegant, advanced hi-fi systems, and, later, colour televisions. The company rose and then fell, the victim of mismanagement and Japanese competition. Its collapse in 1967 left the government of Nova Scotia, which had helped to finance a plant in the province, with a $20-million bill – a special embarrassment for Munk, the devotee of pure free enterprise. Munk settled a lawsuit out of court that alleged he had sold his own shares in Clairtone before he informed other investors of the company's problems.

The Clairtone failure haunted the notoriously thin-skinned Munk for years. Reporters were warned about bringing the subject up in interviews. Even his fellow Hungarian and friend, the late Andy Sarlos, wrote in his 1993 autobiography, *Fireworks: The Investment of a Lifetime*, that "Clairtone made Peter famous, then infamous."

Other unusual ventures followed. Munk successfully ran and then sold a chain of hotels in the South Pacific. In one of the most bizarre episodes in Canadian corporate history, Munk allied himself with Adnan Khashoggi, the Saudi Arabian arms dealer, the controversial figure who was involved in the Iran contra affair and at one time was thought to be one of the richest men in the world. They planned to build a resort and golf course at the foot of the Pyramids. Not surprisingly, the thought of Titleist golf balls zinging past one of the seven wonders of the world provoked howls of protest, and the idea was dropped.

In the early 1960s, Munk bought a company called Barrick Petroleum and renamed it American Barrick Resources Corp. (the name was changed again to Barrick Gold Corp. in 1994). Munk knew nothing about gold, but believed that with all the problems in South Africa, the world's largest gold-producing country, a large, stable North American–based producer could do very well. He was right. Barrick hit the mother lode in 1986 with the purchase of the Goldstrike property in Nevada for $81 million (U.S.). Its 30 million ounces in reserves, the largest in the United States, was to make it one of the most valuable mining properties in the world.

Barrick embarked on an aggressive campaign of acquisitions. In 1994, the company paid $1.2 billion for Lac Minerals Ltd., after fighting a bitter take-over battle with Peggy Witte's Royal Oak Mines Ltd. In fact, Munk's companies may have set a Canadian record that year by spending $3.35 billion on take-overs in the space of two months. Munk shocked everyone in August 1996 by paying $1.1 billion for upstart Arequipa Resources Ltd. on the strength of a few drill core samples in Peru.

Barrick duly emerged as a global mining powerhouse, as Munk correctly called it, and as a company with the third highest stock market value in Canada, after BCE Inc. and Seagram Co. Ltd. Certainly Munk's obsession with the share price paid off for shareholders, who saw it rise to as much as $43 from a bit over a dollar in 1985. Although he was certainly lucky with Goldstrike, he proved he could be successful in a completely unrelated field. In 1996, he created TrizecHahn out of the debris of Trizec Corp. and quickly developed it into one of the largest and most aggressive real estate companies in North America. So far he has avoided the excesses of debt and ego that brought down Robert Campeau and the Reichmann brothers, despite their lifetimes of experience in real estate.

Even with his failures long behind him, Peter Munk has never been far from controversy. After the 1996 annual meeting of Horsham, which has operations in Chile, Munk saw fit to offer words of praise for former Chilean dictator General Augusto Pinochet, whose human rights record was well known as terrible. "That man, albeit you may not approve of the methodology, had the courage to single-handedly change the whole direction of a whole continent. That man created a model that today, several years later, has generated more profit per capita in a forgotten Latin American country than in any other comparable period, in any other comparable country, with the exception of the last four years in North America." While Munk refused to comment on human rights, he allowed that the ends justified the means.

"I think it does because it brought wealth to an enormous number of people, I mean in my terms. If you ask somebody who is in jail, he'll say no. But that's the wonderful thing about our world; we can have the freedom to disagree." And disagree is exactly what readers of his comments did, as the avalanche of critical letters showed. In response, in a letter to the editor of *The Globe and Mail*, Munk seemed to apologize without quite apologizing at all. His remarks, he told readers, "were not placed in a proper context and may have been misunderstood, and as such, appeared insensitive. This was not my intent and I regret if they were so interpreted." What one cannot quarrel with, however, is his forthright conclusion. "What I did not convey was my abhorrence of any abuse of human rights that occurred during his [Pinochet's] regime. My mother was at Auschwitz. I personally escaped from Nazi terror in 1944. I want to assure you that democracy is not something that I take for granted. I cherish it."

Peter Munk told journalists at the *Globe* in October 1996 that "I don't think I'm ambitious, but my family does, so maybe I am." His family is clearly right, but it's an ambition that has been remarkably focused and disciplined. "I have a vision of what to do with Barrick," he continued. "First, I wanted to be number one in North America, and we got there. Then I wanted to become global, and we're getting there." But does becoming global mean moving heaven and earth to become number one in the world, by, for example, winning control of Busang?

The answer, surprisingly, is no, despite the widespread assumption that Munk is obsessed with turning Barrick into the number one producer in the world. Certainly Busang, if it did have 47 million ounces of gold – let alone the far higher estimates that were to come – would be essential to any attempt to vault past South Africa's Anglo-American Corp. into the top spot. Barrick had 51 million ounces of reserves in 1996 and eleven producing mines in Canada, the United States, and Chile. It appeared that adding a single mine at Busang would double the company's reserves and eventually its production.

However, Barrick's point of pride was not just quantity, but quality. It endlessly repeated that it was the world's most profitable gold mining company and had the lowest cost of the major producers. As the 1996 annual report boasts, "No other gold company makes more money for its shareholders than Barrick does." The company was also quick to point out how conservatively financed it was, with the result that it was the only gold company in the world with an "A" credit rating.

Randall Oliphant, Barrick's executive vice-president and chief financial officer, nicely summed up the company's creed at the 1997 annual meeting at Toronto's Royal York Hotel. The gathering attracted a standing-room-only crowd of 500, beneath a huge sign entitled "Reserves increase 40 per cent," and huge model core samples. "We are only interested in acquiring assets that will be under our control and that will add quality, low-cost ounces to our production," said Oliphant. "Barrick's strategy for growth is not simply to get bigger – not at all. Our strategy is to provide better returns to our shareholders." This insistence on control – so critical to Munk in his personal and corporate relationships – was to be an important theme in the Bre-X story.

But Barrick's on-going task of getting bigger and better was becoming much tougher. The only way to keep spoiled shareholders happy and the stock price up was by making more acquisitions. With 3.1 million ounces of production a year, sixteen times that of a decade earlier, acquisitions had to get bigger and bigger to have any effect on the bottom line. And to find new deposits, companies like Barrick had to go farther and farther afield, to parts of the world that were largely unexplored. They had to travel to countries like Indonesia, where the geology was promising and the mining laws attractive. Significantly, even before the battle for Busang, Indonesia had become Barrick's top choice in Asia. The company had an Indonesian office and field staff of sixty, and Barrick held more exploration properties in the country than any of its competitors. Many of these properties, some of which were owned by Yamana Resources Inc., which Barrick financed, were on Kalimantan near Busang.

At the end of the day, it was inevitable that a company like Barrick, quite apart from its particular corporate culture, would be interested in Busang. No major international mining company with the resources to acquire an interest in the deposit could afford not to consider what was thought to be one of the biggest and lowest-cost mines in history. When Barrick had tried to march in and strike a deal for Bre-X in late 1993 and early 1994, it had been rebuffed by Walsh, who found Munk's company too demanding and too arrogant. "Bre-X has declined Barrick's offer and no further discussions are contemplated," Walsh had said in a terse press release in February 1994. The failure of the talks had left a sour taste in Walsh's mouth.

The same went for Peter Munk in spades. The pale, intense Munk, often photographed striding to meetings in his trademark fedora, was a relentless stalker. He had pursued Lac Minerals for six years before he succeeded in taking it over. He had tried and failed to acquire Bre-X in 1993; he was determined not to fail again. Munk "is easily one of the most persistent people I have ever met," wrote his friend Sarlos. "Once Peter has latched on to something he wants, he will not rest until he gets it." And Peter Munk wanted Busang for Barrick.

Indonesia Holds Bre-X to Ransom

Only a handful of people knew about Barrick's behind-the-scenes manoeuvring. The remainder had their eyes opened on November 26.

In what ranks as one of the most extraordinary press releases ever – more a ransom note than anything else – Bre-X announced that the Indonesian government had "given guidance" to the company to form a joint venture between itself and Barrick on a 25 to 75 per cent basis.

It didn't take much insight to figure out that if the government hadn't dictated the release, it might as well have. Bre-X added wanly that it had asked if a different arrangement would be acceptable, but had not received a reply. The government warned that if a deal was not finalized by December 4, it would "take the necessary steps to prevent a delay in the development of the Busang gold deposit." But that's not all. Barrick would be cut in, and so would the Indonesian government, in a not very subtle way. "The Indonesian government would appreciate it if the parties could consider a 10 per cent participation being given to the Indonesian government." The same day, Barrick confirmed that it had been negotiating with Bre-X.

At first blush, the reaction to the news was all that Barrick could have hoped for. As the press and analysts saw it, Munk had intrigued masterfully behind the scenes and had now emerged triumphant. Bre-X had been squeezed. "Munk had played his imperial hand beautifully," crowed *Maclean's* magazine. Everyone agreed that Barrick would soon have Busang. And Bre-X, it appeared, could be left with nothing if it failed to meet the government's deadline, a possibility that knocked more than 10 per cent off the value of its shares, which closed that day at $20.25.

If Bre-X and its shareholders were upset, so were potential bidders like Placer Dome of Vancouver, which expressed disappointment that Barrick had "the inside track." As John Willson, the scrappy chief executive of Barrick's arch-rival, phrased it, "Something has been going on that is not kosher in the West." It was time to put the cards – or at least some of the cards – on the table. Placer revealed that it had been negotiating with Bre-X since October and had discussed a conditional offer of more than $25 a share, or $5.5 billion for the company and its deposit. Placer also said that Vancouver's Teck Corp.

and Denver-based Newmont Mining Corp., the largest gold producer in the United States, had approached it about forming a consortium to make a bid, but Placer had decided to proceed on its own.

While Placer complained that the usual auction had been pre-empted, it had not lost all hope. It referred in an early December press release to comments in *The Globe and Mail* by Jean Anes, the Indonesian official in Toronto who had played a part in the cancellation of Bre-X's exploration permit in October. Anes had said the government would still consider other offers. Of course, what an official said in Toronto was not necessarily what was going to happen in Jakarta.

With its announcement (albeit through the mouth of Bre-X) of November 26, the Indonesian government had indeed pre-empted a normal auction, whereby bidders are free to bid for a property or company. Under that process, everyone has a fair shot. No one is prohibited from competing and the take-over target is in a position to get the best price for its shareholders. That's exactly what had happened with Diamond Fields Resources, which skilfully engaged Inco Ltd. and Falconbridge Ltd. in an intense bidding war, which Inco won with a $4.3-billion offer. This time an auction was what everyone wanted, except for the Indonesian government and Barrick, which appeared assured of victory without it – and at a lower price than it would have had to pay in a competition.

The government's December 4 deadline came and went. Nothing happened. A dense fog settled over the private negotiations between Bre-X and Barrick, which were based on the 25–75 split decreed by the government. Since no details were forthcoming, it was unclear how the joint venture would be structured, and what Barrick would pay Bre-X for its participation in Busang. And what did a 25–75 division really mean? While the government had ordered a 10 per cent portion for itself, would another 10 per cent go to Bre-X's Indonesian partners?

Most analysts started with the assumption that the government would get its portion, leaving 67.5 per cent of the deposit for Barrick and 22.5 per cent for Bre-X. They valued the deal at anywhere from $15 to $35 a share for Bre-X, a range of values that showed just how unpredictable the outcome was, with the government calling the shots. There was, however, a widespread belief that Barrick would treat Bre-X shareholders fairly, as it said it would.

There were several reasons why Barrick's offer would have to be reasonable. First, the company had to keep the approval of its powerful institutional investors, such as pension funds and insurance companies, many of whom also had substantial positions in Bre-X. Second, there was the risk of lawsuits from unhappy Bre-X shareholders, who could sue in the ever-litigious United States because Barrick was now listed on the New York Stock Exchange. The Loewen Group, the giant funeral concern based in Burnaby, British Columbia, had seen what that could mean. In late 1995, a Mississippi jury made a stunning – and preposterous – $500-million (U.S.) award against the company, in an apparently routine breach-of-contract lawsuit involving assets of only $8.5 million. (Loewen ultimately settled for $85 million.) Lastly, Barrick would have to be fair in order to maintain its reputation in the capital markets, which it would have to tap in the future to raise debt or equity. "The constraint on Barrick is that they have to go back to the capital markets from time to time doing other deals," one analyst commented. "It's a question of sawing off somewhere where it [this deal] smells, but doesn't smell too bad."

Bre-X's 13,000 shareholders should have been aware since October, when the government questioned the company's claim to Busang, how risky their shares were. They had now been doubly warned, since their future was clearly being driven not by the agenda of the company, but by that of the Indonesian government.

Barrick had triumphed – or had it? There was trouble on the horizon from a number of directions. Bre-X's shareholders were unhappy at – again – being kept in the dark by their company, and displeased by the revelation that they were having a partner forced on them. Greg Chorny of Aurora, Ontario, who said he owned about

1 per cent of Bre-X's outstanding shares, urged other shareholders to protest to Barrick and Bre-X. In a form letter faxed to the two companies, Chorny "put both Bre-X and Barrick on notice that any transaction struck between them must fully represent full and fair value to Bre-X shareholders." If not, he said, he and others were prepared to "take appropriate action to ensure the rights of Bre-X shareholders are fully respected." That sounded a lot like the threat of a lawsuit. In fact, Chorny and some other activist shareholders were represented by Tom Ajamie, a smart, cool, youthful lawyer then with the Houston firm Baker & Botts, the second-largest law firm in Texas. Ajamie would eventually spend weeks holed up on the fourth floor of the posh Regent's Hotel in Jakarta, working his sources. Baker & Botts had successfully fought an apparently losing battle on behalf of Pennzoil Co. against Texaco Inc. in the 1980s, winning one of the biggest settlements in U.S. history. The Baker in the name of the firm, which was founded in the nineteenth century, was the family of James Baker, secretary of state under President Reagan. Baker & Botts had also performed magic on behalf of the Loewen Group, which it defended against the unwanted entreaties of its larger arch-enemy, SCI International Ltd.

Barrick's apparent victory was also tarnished by the fact that the deal the government outlined looked about as bad as a deal can look. "We're dealing with a Third World group of – I wouldn't call them government officials, I'd call them quasi-gangsters – that basically didn't want to be involved in this project until it became successful," said Brendan Kyne, the manager of the 20/20 RSP Aggressive Equity Fund in Chicago, which had made a lot of money on Bre-X. "It's a joke. I mean, everything's Etch-a-Sketch, and if the deposit changes, we just shake the thing and then we write new rules."

Finally, Barrick's position was threatened by the fact that the actions of the government of Indonesia triggered protests even from the country's mining community. The Indonesian Mining Association met with Kuntoro in late November, and with Umar Said, secretary general of mines, at the beginning of December. The association argued that Bre-X should be able to proceed "without any unsolicited interference" from the government, and that the ownership question was best decided by "an international tender." According to the IMA's newsletter, Umar Said assured the organization that Busang was "an isolated case . . . a combination of administrative mistakes by the operator, ambition of the government to see its potential gold deposit developed for the benefit of the economy of the country, and the availability of an interested, strong company to take part in the venture," a reference to Barrick. Not mentioned was the fact that there were other interested, strong companies equally available – and eager – to take part.

On December 11, the government supplied more evidence – if any was needed – of how erratic its policy was, and how hostile it was to Bre-X. Emerging from a commission hearing in Jakarta on his performance in office, mines minister Sudjana said the government had cancelled parliamentary approval for Bre-X's Contracts of Work. "We cancel it," he told reporters. "The Bre-X Contract of Work will be processed from the beginning." His underling Umar Said tried to repair the damage the next day, telling Bre-X executives that their Contract applications remained in good standing. Not that he had suddenly gone soft; he went on to warn them that the government was checking to see if Bre-X had made false ownership claims to the New York Stock Exchange. "We have obtained a series of documents through our lawyers that show that Bre-X said it owned Busang II and III," he said, referring to the two zones without Contracts. "Maybe that was meant to push up the price of its shares. We are checking with Bapepam [the markets' supervisory agency] to see if this is criminal."

"A Scarlet Pimpernel Kind of Thing"

If ever there was a time when Bre-X should have been front and centre presenting its case, this was it. But Walsh was missing in action, as he had been to most of the media throughout this crucial period.

He simply refused to talk to outlets that he thought were unsympathetic to his company. A secretary at Bre-X headquarters in Calgary said on December 11, "I don't know where he is, and I don't know if anyone knows. It's a bit of a Scarlet Pimpernel kind of thing, I suppose."

All of this should have been enough to spook shareholders. But it wasn't, even though Bre-X had no clear title to its single significant asset and a shotgun marriage was in the offing. Investors were still willing to pay from $17.75 to $22.20 during December for a share of the company, which meant that the market valued it for as much as $5 billion. Maybe that shouldn't have been a surprise, because some of the biggest mining companies in the world appeared to agree with that lofty valuation.

In fact, the apparent value of the Busang deposit had just gone up again. On December 3, Bre-X announced it had mineral resources of 57 million ounces, up from 47 million only four-and-a-half months earlier. At $350 (U.S.) an ounce, that 10-million ounce addition was worth $3.5 billion.

"The Integrity of the TSE Indices"

Bre-X had been trading on Canada's senior exchange, the Toronto Stock Exchange, since the spring. In a comedy of errors, Bre-X was added to the TSE's 300 composite index in December, following a series of flip-flops by the exchange. After announcing its intention to add the company to the index, the TSE prudently announced on December 12 that "in view of the continuing uncertainty concerning Bre-X Minerals and the need to maintain the integrity of the TSE Indices, the TSE announces that it will not be adding Bre-X to the TSE Indices at this time." But after the receipt of unspecified additional information from the company less than an hour later, the decision was again reversed; Bre-X was in.

The inclusion in the 300 index, like the move to the TSE earlier in 1996, gave Bre-X credibility, even though that wasn't part of the

TSE's intention. Many ordinary retail investors bought shares in Bre-X in the belief that Canada's premier exchange had bestowed its blessing on the company. Sadly, no doubt impressed by the TSE's talk of "integrity," they were unaware of the fact that the criteria for entry are not qualitative but quantitative, based on such things as trading volume and market value. For example, Imperial Oil Ltd., the bluest of the blue chips, had been dropped from an apparently even more exclusive index, the TSE 35 index, solely because its shares did not trade often enough (largely because it was 69 per cent owned by its U.S. parent, Exxon).

Bre-X's inclusion in the 300 index was also important because many big institutional investors and "index" investors automatically buy shares in every company in the index. All this meant a greater demand, and in all likelihood a higher price, for Bre-X shares. There would later be a fierce debate about the appropriateness of adding such a speculative company to such an important and supposedly responsible index, with the Toronto Stock Exchange taking much of the flak. Of course, the exchange is owned by its members, the very investment dealers, such as Nesbitt Burns and First Marathon Securities, that were so bullish on Bre-X stock. "Bre-X met all listing and disclosure requirements," TSE president Rowland Fleming explained later.

Barrick Triumphant

There are two telling and memorable images from this juncture of the Bre-X saga. The first, which was noticed in Jakarta, was the December 9 issue of *Maclean's* magazine. Peter Munk is on the cover, staring intently at the camera, his right foot propped up on three giant gold bricks tied with a red ribbon, as if to suggest a gift. "King of gold," reads the headline. "The daring deal that makes Peter Munk the world's biggest gold miner." Inside, under a column entitled "Peter Munk: a dreamer who became a king," Peter C. Newman tells readers that while the dreamy king is lucky, "he also has a sixth sense about timing, moving in on his corporate prey – Goldstrike, Lac, Bre-X – with the sophistication of a skilled swordsman, knowing precisely when to feign and when to thrust."

The second image is of Barrick's loud and triumphant annual Christmas party at Rodney's Oyster House in downtown Toronto. By a happy coincidence the well-attended celebration was held on December 4, the Indonesian government's deadline for an agreement between Barrick and Bre-X. Smugness was in the air at the lavish food and drink fest, with its free-flowing open bar and mountains of oysters on ice. In conversations around the room it was hard to miss the defiant attitude towards other mining companies and even potential legal difficulties; Barrick would happily remain the successful, envied outsider. As the revellers donned their overcoats and stepped out into the cold and dark of a Toronto winter evening, there was no doubt in anyone's mind: the deal would be done by Christmas.

CHAPTER EIGHT

Indonesia Pushes Barrick Aside

"It's like a fog, I can hear two fog horns out there but I don't know who they are." – Norman Keevil, chairman, Teck Corp., January 1997

"I think Mr. Hasan is in effect conducting a competition between ourselves and Barrick." – John Willson, chief executive, Placer Dome Inc., February 1997

Suharto Steps In

President Suharto was unhappy about Busang. Here was what everyone said was one of the biggest gold mines in history and yet it was causing Indonesia no end of embarrassment. Nothing could be worse than that in a country where saving face counted for everything, as it did throughout much of Asia. Two of the president's own children had joined competing companies in the seemingly endless ownership dispute. And the domestic and, much worse, the international mining community was upset by the way the mines department was handling the issue. Almost none of the deluge of publicity about

Indonesia was favourable: virtually every story drew attention to the corruption of the country and the greed of the First Family. And as the saga dragged on, nationalists began to ask exactly how much Indonesia would get to keep of its own resources, after Barrick, the most profitable gold mining company in the world, and Bre-X, one of the luckiest and least impressive, had taken their cut.

Suharto, of course, could have done anything he wanted to to resolve the Busang tangle; his word was effectively law in Indonesia. But as luck would have it, he wasn't the only powerful figure in the country who was unhappy with the way the problem was being handled. Two businesspeople also felt that way, two men who had far more clout in Indonesia than Peter Munk, let alone David Walsh. The two heavy hitters were granted a meeting with Suharto at his 600-hectare Tapos cattle ranch outside Jakarta at the beginning of December. According to the *Far Eastern Economic Review*, at that decisive meeting they urged the president to allow an open, international auction for the Busang property; that, after all, is what most foreign investors, whose capital was vitally important to the country, wanted. The two men, both of whom were to play a critical role in the resolution of the impasse, were Suharto's buddy, the ubiquitous billionaire Bob Hasan, and the Texan James "Jim Bob" Moffett, chairman of Freeport McMoRan Copper & Gold.

What Hasan didn't reveal at the time – and which was not reported in Canada until mid-January – was that at the beginning of December he had quietly acquired a 50 per cent interest in PT Askatindo Karya Mineral, Bre-X's minority Indonesian partner in the zone where all the gold was thought to be, and an interest in another minority partner, PT Amsya Lyna. In fact, he was named president-commissioner of Askatindo, which put him in charge of the company. Hasan's purchase gave him a direct 5 per cent stake in the Busang deposit, a position that was all the more powerful because as the local partner, Askatindo held what was called a KP, a mining authorization available only to Indonesian companies. Even more astonishing – but not perhaps in a country where the line between the government and big business was a thin and wavering one – the acquisition was actually made by the Nusamba Group. Although run by Hasan, it was 80 per cent owned by three charitable foundations headed by Suharto "in his private capacity"; 10 per cent owned by the president's son Sigit; and 10 per cent by Hasan. Yet again the government, led by the First Family, had cut itself in.

Both Hasan and Suharto were on good terms with tough-talking Jim Bob Moffett. In fact, as if to complete the circle, in January Hasan bought a stake of almost 10 per cent in Freeport's Indonesian subsidiary, PT Freeport Indonesia Co. through Nusamba. Freeport's $3-billion (U.S.) investment in Indonesia makes the company the biggest foreign investor in the country and the largest mining company, well ahead of second-place Inco. The company's Grasberg complex in remote Irian Jaya, where some of the most primitive tribes to be found anywhere live, is the world's largest open-pit gold mine and has 17,000 employees.

Jim Bob Moffett: "You Know He's There"

Moffett is the proverbial larger-than-life Texan who is the "Mo" in McMoRan. The profane, fifty-nine-year-old executive, who is known for his impersonations of Elvis Presley – he is said to have his own custom-leather version of the king's jump suit – is an odd success story in a country whose culture favours those who take a low-key approach. Every year at the end of Ramadan, Moffett flies into Jakarta in his Boeing 757 to dispense gifts and greetings. "He is not the kind of person who comes or goes softly in the night," says Michael Levy, publisher of *Texas Monthly* in Austin, Texas. "You know he's there."

Few corporate leaders head such controversial companies. Environmentalists and social activists have long criticized Freeport. In March 1996, near Grasberg a company employee accidentally ran down a local man named William Kogoya. Mistakenly believing he had been killed, thousands of natives rioted with sticks, spears, knives, and arrows. The army had to call in reinforcements to restore order and the mine was closed for three days. That a minor accident could trigger such a strong response among the local people was testament to the anger that had built up towards the company.

"You and your workers live in luxury on our property," a tribal leader told Moffett. "We, who own the rights to the property, sleep on rubbish. Therefore, from today, we don't give you permission for this company, and close it." A few months earlier, the Overseas Private Investment Corp., an agency of the U.S. government, had cancelled a $100-million (U.S.) risk insurance policy for the company because of its environmental policies. Critics claimed that Freeport was poisoning local waters and causing harm to the local population and the delicate ecosystem, because of the way it disposed of its tailings, the waste left over after ore is processed. Freeport has also faced allegations that its security force of more than 300 works hand in glove with the Indonesian army in improper ways, including a case involving the torture of a native woman in a shipping carton. While Freeport says the government insists that the company provide supplies and transportation to military personnel around its mine site, it denies all of these allegations.

Even Moffett's donations to the University of Texas and to Loyola University in his home town of New Orleans have created huge storms of protest. After Loyola students picketed Moffett's fine Charles Street house chanting, "Jim Bob Moffett kills for profit," he asked for his donation back, but the university refused. Washington-based Ralph Nader's *Multinational Monitor* listed Freeport as one of the ten worst corporations of 1996, alongside Archer-Daniels-Midland (for price fixing), Shell (for its role in Nigeria), and Caterpillar (for its relations with its unions). In recent years, Freeport has aggressively fought its critics, taking out advertisements in *The New York Times*, commissioning independent environmental and social audits, and winning back its risk insurance by agreeing to a $100-million (U.S.) environmental trust fund. The company's 1996 annual report devotes seven pages to reports on the environment, social responsibilities, and health programs.

Despite all these controversies, Freeport is a formidable company. Its board includes Henry Kissinger and Leon Davis, the chief executive of the RTZ-CRA Group, the former Rio Tinto Zinc and the biggest mining company in the world; RTZ owns 12 per cent of Freeport's Indonesian operations. Jim Bob Moffett is the most powerful foreign executive in Indonesia, with close ties to the president, who visited Grasberg in 1995 to show his support. Freeport is helped by the fact that it has operated in Indonesia since 1973, longer than any other mining company, and – in what was to become a mantra – is the country's biggest corporate taxpayer.

The Waiting Game

It's easy to forget that the Bre-X story had appeared to be over on October 28, when Bre-X announced its alliance with Sigit. At the time everyone believed that Suharto's son would ensure that the company got its Contracts, and then Bre-X would sell part or all of its interest in the world's largest gold deposit to the highest bidder for billions of dollars. Walsh and Felderhof would be fêted as heroes, and shareholders would make millions cashing in. That never happened. The story again appeared to be over on November 26, when the government decreed that Bre-X would form a partnership with Barrick. The details would all be worked out by the deadline of December 4. But they weren't. In fact, more deadlines were to come and go.

By mid-December, it was clear that what the government had ordered was not necessarily going to happen, even though minister Sudjana had a new deadline, the end of the year. Not that it was easy at the best of times to understand what the minister had in mind. "I will wait for them," he said, referring to Bre-X and Barrick. "This also is the advice of the president . . . give them a chance until the end of December. I forget the date, but there is a limit."

On December 12, Walsh wrote to Sudjana that "Bre-X Minerals Ltd. is very pleased that President Suharto has apparently personally intervened, according to a Dow Jones newswire article dated

December 11, in the complicated deliberations surrounding the Indonesian government's earlier decision to compel our company to enter a partnership with Barrick Gold Corporation for the development of the Busang gold deposit." It's hardly surprising that negotiations weren't going well when Bre-X believed – correctly – it was "compelled" to take on a partner of the government's choice. Nor was it a good sign that Bre-X had to rely on the media for information. But negotiations with other parties now seemed possible.

Nonetheless, Bre-X and Barrick submitted a joint proposal to the government four days later. Though the document wasn't made public, the two companies proposed a 10 per cent stake for the government, 67.5 per cent for Barrick, and 22.5 per cent for Bre-X. No one knew where that would leave the Calgary company's Indonesian partner, Askatindo. Certainly its fate was of particular interest to shareholders of Minorca Resources Inc. of Montreal; in return for providing for development costs, Minorca had the right to a 70 per cent interest in Askatindo's share, or 7 per cent of the Busang deposit.

The year-end deadline passed with no announcements. And none seemed likely for weeks, as the month-long celebration of Ramadan began on January 10. During the holiday, many in government worked only partial days or were too weak from fasting from dawn till dusk to make major decisions. Busang continued to hold out great promise, and great problems. On January 13, 1997, Bre-X reported that their engineering consultant Kilborn had confirmed their estimate of 57.3 million ounces of gold at Busang, and that one of the drill holes revealed ore containing five grams of gold per tonne, which was 5.5 times richer than the average for the deposit. That obviously made its acquisition all the more attractive. Chad Williams of Research Capital in Montreal issued a brief report the same day, arguing that the results greatly improved the economics of a mine, and suggesting that announcements would continue to "exceed expectations, confirming our view that it may well become one of the largest gold deposits ever discovered." Williams rated the stock a speculative buy, with a one-year target price of $30. Less happily, Indonesian businessperson Jusuf Merukh filed his $2-billion (U.S.) lawsuit in the Court of Queen's Bench in Alberta, alleging that he had been defrauded by Bre-X, and claiming a 30 per cent stake in the apparently gold-laden southeast zone. While Bre-X said the suit was "frivolous" and "completely without merit," it added yet another layer of uncertainty to a very uncertain future.

Placer's $6.2-Billion Merger Offer

In what was to be the decisive move Suharto delegated his old friend Hasan to sort out the Busang imbroglio. With his wife gone, the president needed to be able to turn to someone he could trust – who had solved business problems for him before – to broker a deal, particularly since two of his children were on opposite sides of the dispute. Hasan had played this role before. He had, for example, bought a stake in auto maker Astra International through Nusamba in part to help end the fight between sons Bambang and Tommy over a national car, and indeed went on to become Astra's chairman. In effect, Hasan had become the First Family's good uncle. As for Busang, "Suharto brought Hasan in to settle the nursery dispute," quipped one mining executive in Jakarta. Luckily for Placer, Hasan didn't like Barrick and their heavy-handed ways, and did like Placer and the idea of an auction.

Paul Waldie of *The Globe and Mail* was the only journalist to interview Hasan at this turning point in the story, contacting him on January 16 in a hotel room in Indian Wells, California. Hasan was there as a wealthy, well-connected amateur golfer – the guest of forest product giant Georgia Pacific, one of his partners – to play with Fuzzy Zoeller in the Pro-Am Bob Hope Chrysler Classic in Palm Desert. (Fuzzy, a fine golfer, later drew unwelcome attention to his talents as a comedian with his comments when Tiger Woods won the 1997 Masters championship.) Hasan made it clear that because of his stake in Askatindo, the fate of Busang rested with him, and that he had not yet made a decision. Even though "we are the actual licence holder," Barrick hadn't approached him, he said.

A deal "should be done by people who are really in the business like Bre-X, Placer Dome or any other company who is at home in this field," Hasan said, and "not necessarily Barrick." While Placer Dome was a good company and he had met its chief John Willson before Christmas, Hasan said he had never met Peter Munk.

"I saw a report that Placer Dome and Bre-X are going to talk," he said. "I think that's a good thing. Together they will be stronger. If the shareholders of [the two companies] are confident that they should get together, then I think it will happen." Hasan was casual about his position and his power. "We are just good listeners," he said of his role as powerbroker. "I have many interests," he explained, modestly. "I'm in insurance, I've a few banks, I've quite a lot of interests."

In addition to his broad public hints via *The Globe and Mail*, the timber baron privately encouraged Placer to bid for his new partner Bre-X, and that's precisely what Placer did.

The mining companies that came together in 1987 to form Placer Dome had been part of Canadian mining lore for eighty-six years, unlike Placer's upstart rival Barrick. The successor to the famous Dome Mines Ltd., Campbell Red Lake Mines Ltd., and Placer Development Ltd., Placer Dome produced 1.9 million ounces of gold in 1996 and had 26.5 million ounces of reserves, putting it well behind Barrick on both counts. Placer, however, was the more international of the two companies, with operations throughout the Americas, in Australia, and in Papua New Guinea, which shares the island of New Guinea with Irian Jaya, Indonesia's most easterly province. The Vancouver company needed Busang to avoid falling further behind its major competitor. Many large institutional investors had room in their portfolio for only one major gold-mining company, and if Barrick got Busang, those investors would never choose Placer. Like Munk, fifty-seven-year-old John Willson was a tough, determined executive. As president of Western Canada Steel Ltd., he had closed

British Columbia's only steel mine during a lock-out in 1988, and sought to deny severance to the workers, on the grounds that they had acted unreasonably.

In a "Dear David" letter dated January 13, 1997, Willson made Walsh a clever and intriguing offer, "a tax effective, stock-for-stock merger of equals" worth an estimated $6.2 billion. If consummated, the deal would have been the second biggest in Canadian corporate history, behind Seagram's $7.8-billion take-over of MCA and ahead of Amoco's $5.2-billion buy-out of Dome Petroleum. What was remarkable was that one of the biggest and oldest gold-mining companies in the world, with sales of $1.2 billion and 8,300 employees, was proposing an alliance of equals with an exploration company that had until recently had been run out of a basement office, with a single dubiously held asset, no sales or production, and only 400 or so employees.

Placer's bid had a lot of appeal for Bre-X and for the Indonesian government. The companies would have equal standing, and Walsh would emerge as the new company's biggest shareholder. It would be a merger rather than a take-over, which meant that under accounting rules Placer would not get hit with big charges against its earnings. Indonesian interests would get participation of up to 40 per cent, quadruple what Barrick was offering. Willson said his company would spend $1.7 billion (U.S.) on a mine, more than anyone else had proposed, and that it would be producing gold as early as 1999. Although the bid contained few details, there were more than there were for the weeks-old Barrick proposal, which had never been made public. The ultimate size of the mine would depend on "additional data collection and studies carried out in the first nine months."

Bre-X shareholders were heartened, as were other potential bidders. By throwing down the gauntlet, Placer was pressuring the government to hold an auction. The company's first aim was to force an auction; its second aim was to win that auction. In response, Walsh said Bre-X would consider the offer. Meanwhile, the government announced yet another deadline. Unless Bre-X and Barrick had come to an agreement with their partners by February 15, the week after the High Holiday of Idul Fitrie, which signals the end of Ramadan, the government would either find new investors for Busang or take it over itself. Speaking on behalf of the government, the secretary general of mines, Umar Said, in an interview from his home in Jakarta, declared, "Nobody owns that area. There is no formal Contract of Work given to any party. If there is no deal, then it is the government who decides." What this meant was that Bre-X and Barrick had to come to an agreement with Hasan, who was the eyes and ears of the president. As Willson correctly observed, "I think Mr. Hasan is in effect conducting a competition between ourselves and Barrick." This time, mercifully, the deadline would be met, but not without an ugly war of words first between Barrick and Placer.

The War of Words: "A Very Inappropriate Game"

Certainly the claims each company made about its ability to proceed with Busang were fair enough. In a call to analysts, Munk – in a reference to the Goldstrike property in Nevada – boasted that Barrick has a "unique mine development team – the only team, the only team, gentlemen – that can point to putting on stream a mine operation of the scale of Busang . . . in the last few years with the latest technology, from scratch, on budget, on time, without a single hitch." He continued, "Environmental stewardship is of the highest importance" in a rain forest where "a mistake can turn a small problem into a catastrophe." For its part, Placer noted that it had constructed $3.5 billion (U.S.) in new mines since 1985, and over a four-year period had invested $1.1 billion in its operations in Papua New Guinea, which was similar to Kalimantan.

But according to Placer, Barrick went much further than this.

An anti-Placer fax was spewing out of machines across Jakarta, and John Willson said it had Barrick's fax number on it. A Barrick spokesperson admitted to *Canadian Business* that the number was theirs, but denied that the company had circulated the material. The fax highlighted Placer's environmental problems in the Philippines – which Munk, no doubt, was alluding to when he happened to mention environmental stewardship – where the failure of a drainage tunnel in March 1996 sent millions of tonnes of mining waste into the river at Placer's 40 per cent owned Marcopper Mining Corp. location. The government cancelled Marcopper's mining permit and charged three of the company's senior officials with negligence and violation of the Philippine Mining Act. "I don't call it playing hard ball," commented Willson, "I think it's just a very inappropriate game."

According to *Fortune* magazine, Barrick hired Kroll Associates, the detective agency, to compile dirt on Bre-X. The company also hired Montrealer Luc Lavoie, who had been the highly effective spokesperson for Brian Mulroney in his libel suit against the Canadian government in the Airbus Affair. His role was to co-ordinate its public relations in Jakarta, where he was soon holed up at the Grand Hyatt with the rest of the Barrick team. Lavoie denied any involvement in a dirty tricks campaign.

The points made in the fax against Placer were soon being repeated by the government. "We have reliable information that Placer Dome Inc. has had problems with the governments of the Philippines, Venezuela, Kazakhstan and Canada," Umar Said told a House of Representatives commission at the end of January 1997. What was particularly embarrassing was the fact that the government of the Philippines shut Marcopper's operations down because of the spill. "As a member of the Association of Southeast Asian nations, we should not permit a company rejected by another member to operate in our country," said Umar Said. "Similarly, we can feel how it would be if the Philippines government let Ramos Horta enter its country." Horta was a thorn in the side of the Indonesian government for fighting for the independence of East Timor, particularly after he won the Nobel Prize, so this was a very powerful comparison to choose to make. The Indonesian official also said that, according to estimates made by J. P. Morgan, Barrick was stronger than Placer in cash flow, earnings, and gold reserves. Even Willson admitted that of the two companies, Barrick had the deeper pockets, and that the criticisms of Placer's environmental record in the Philippines were fair comment. However, he complained, "there are some people, including Umar Said, who have been sort of anti-Placer, incredibly anti-Placer, for a long time. I actually have a very good idea where that [attitude] comes from," he said, referring to Barrick.

The Dark Horses

Though investors, analysts, and the media lavished all their attention on the open battle between Barrick and Placer, several other major mining companies expressed their interest in getting a piece of Busang. The list included Teck and Newmont, most likely in combination. Freeport and London-based RTZ-CRA were also thought to be interested. "It's like a fog, I can hear two fog horns out there but I don't know who they are," said Teck's chairman Norman Keevil in late January. "I'm hopeful it [the bidding] gets opened up." (Keevil's most memorable comment came in a fax to *The Globe and Mail*, in which he suggested a movie of the Bre-X saga with himself played by Sean Connery. His suggested title: "Apocalypse COW," the acronym for Contract of Work.)

A few days before the February 15 deadline, Michael Fowler of investment dealer Lévesque Beaubien Geoffrion, one of Bre-X's most enthusiastic supporters when the stock was soaring, drew up the following list of potential suitors.

"Barrick Gold – Undoubtedly well qualified. Hungry for this deal. Prepared to pay a high price.

"Placer Dome – Needs Busang to upgrade its asset quality. Busang would be very positive for the company. Main competitor to Barrick.

"Teck/Newmont – Much more of a long shot. Newmont has substantial assets in Indonesia already and Teck is not known to pay high prices.

"RTZ – Busang is typical of the assets that the company seeks. Already well entrenched in Indonesia and operates the Kelian Mine in Kalimantan. Probably has difficulty with the [high] valuation of Busang.

"Freeport Copper – Hasan is a friend of Jim Bob Moffett. Moffett met Suharto with Hasan to try and initiate an auction process for Busang. Freeport may not want to add to its already sizable Indonesian assets.

"BHP [Australia's Broken Hill Pty Co. Ltd.] – May have problems with the valuation, but fully capable.

"South African producers – Their shares do not command the same premiums as North American producers, which means that they will have trouble doing a deal – very much a longshot.

"Out of these companies, Barrick and Placer Dome are the likely candidates to win the battle for Busang . . . The upside for Bre-X shares looks good. Barrick and Placer are running neck and neck in this race, with Placer having a slight, but maybe temporary initiative."

Of course Fowler, like most observers, underestimated one of the dark-horse candidates.

Certainly the general view was that the winner of the battle for Busang would become the global king of the gold heap. However, Harry Bingham, the powerful, veteran portfolio manager with Van Eck Associates in New York, which had big holdings in Barrick and Placer, was less charitable – and more insightful. "These companies must be desperate for reserves to bid for this thing in a corrupt nation like Indonesia. They are just outbidding each other with Suharto. Why take the risk?"

Why indeed?

CHAPTER NINE

"Bob" and "Jim Bob" Cut a Deal

"Why not Freeport?" – *Bob Hasan, February 1997*

"Bre-X has been saved from a forced marriage with a gold digger." – *The* Jakarta Post, *February 1997, slams Barrick Gold Corp.*

Critics Put the Pressure On

Nationalism is never far from the surface in Indonesia, a country that suffered under long rule by the Portuguese and the Dutch, and occupation by the Japanese during the Second World War. If ever there was a saga that provided bountiful ammunition for government critics, nationalist or otherwise, the Busang drama was it. By early 1997, Indonesians had witnessed the dubious behaviour of Bre-X, the unseemly involvement of two of Suharto's children, bickering among foreign mining companies for a share of the spoils, inexplicable reversals in official policy, endless missed deadlines, and the presidential anointment of Bob Hasan as powerbroker. As the *Jakarta Post* summed up the situation on January 31, "Never before has the government's mining policy come under such scrutiny and sharp criticism by analysts and politicians, as that sparked by the battle for the control and ownership of huge gold deposits at Busang in East Kalimantan."

The critics fell into two camps. The most dangerous were the nationalists, particularly those who belonged to Muslim organizations. For years, Suharto had worked to limit their influence, out of fear that they wanted a state that was radically different from the secular state he offered. Those in the second camp took a more international approach. They believed that Indonesia depended on foreign investors and had to keep them happy; in this specific case that meant limiting government intervention and holding a western-style auction for the Busang property. Many of these critics were former mining officials who had helped to develop the Contract system that was now under attack.

Nationalists who felt that the government should ensure that Indonesians, and not just wealthy international mining companies, should receive substantial benefits from the development of Busang could muster some powerful arguments. Article 33 of the 1945 constitution, which was constantly invoked, said that "all natural resources of the country are controlled by the state and should be utilized for the greatest welfare of the people." The very first clause of the Contract of Work, a meticulously crafted ninety-two-page document, categorically states that "all mineral resources contained in the territories of the Republic of Indonesia, including the offshore areas, are the national wealth of the Indonesian nation."

One such critic, economist Rizal Ramly, argued that the Contract system was too generous to foreign companies and should be changed. Rizal singled out Freeport-McMoRan as a company that had been given too much when it was granted a thirty-year extension (with the option of two further ten-year extensions) to its Contract. "The government should have made a better deal [for Indonesia] in 1991, when the company's Contract of Work was renewed," he told the *Jakarta Post*. What the country needed were higher corporate income taxes and higher taxes on dividends and interest, larger royalties, and a greater equity stake in foreign companies. The government and Hasan each had slightly under a 10 per cent share of PT Freeport Indonesia.

Meanwhile, the government was so worried about criticisms by powerful Muslim leader Amien Rais of the constitutionality of its mining contracts and of Freeport that it forced him out of his position as head of the government-supported Association of Muslim Intellectuals.

To economist Hartojo Wignjowijoto, who has advised the World Bank, Indonesia's central bank, and various mining companies, the underlying forces of the saga were "big money and capital gains." Despite institutional problems such as corruption, he said, "the rate of return in gold mining in Indonesia is very high." And those returns should be going to "a strong mining industry owned by Indonesians," rather than to the shareholders of Bre-X, which offered neither financing nor technology. Nevertheless Hartojo argued that the government should not intervene in the dispute, "to avoid Indonesia being labelled one of the most corrupt countries in the world."

Nor were the veterans of the mines department happy. "What we old-timers are criticizing is government intervention," said Soetaryo Sigit, a retired senior mining official who designed the Contract of Work system. "Barrick used very hard lobbying to get a 75–25 split to be imposed on Bre-X. An auction was always the case in the past." Barrick didn't spend a single cent on a mine, Sigit complained. Mohammad Sadli, a former minister of mines, added his complaint, in very diplomatic language: "Foreign investors have also asked whether they have to team up with the sons or daughters or close friends of high-ranking government officials if they want to enter Indonesia for big projects. Unfortunately, there has been no firm answer given to this question."

In interviews in Jakarta in early March, several weeks before the world had heard of Michael de Guzman or the intricacies of salting, both Hartojo and Sadli questioned the evidence for the size of the deposit at Busang. "It's not a proven discovery," said Hartojo. "Even the government doesn't know" if there are 200 million ounces there, since "no one has proof. . . . I told Kuntoro to say we know nothing about this number. There is an element of dishonesty on the Bre-X side." What was needed was a feasibility study, he said.

"Certainly all the figures given have some elements of speculation," Sadli wrote in his notes on Busang. "After all, they did not come from the department of mines but from Canada." In an interview, he said that the estimates were extrapolated from a limited number of samples and that "geologists are usually crazy people."

These two veteran Indonesian mining officials seem amazingly shrewd, in retrospect; yet if these sceptics had raised their voices higher, who would have paid any attention, amid the general excitement about Busang?

That Indonesians would want a fair share for themselves was entirely predictable. "We had FIRA," commented Canadian ambassador to Indonesia Gary Smith, referring to the Foreign Investment Review Act. "The results aren't surprising in a country born out of colonialism." The colonial experience under the Dutch, which only ended in 1949 after four years of fighting, was an unpleasant one and made Indonesians wary about doing business with the West. In the run-up to the May 1997 elections, Suharto warned Indonesians not to be swayed by "a foreign frame of mind" or "foreign values."

Not surprisingly, there was much grumbling in the foreign mining community about the nationalist critics. *They don't realize the risks involved*, was the usual line, and *They only focus on the handful of successful mines that make exploration worthwhile. You need to look at a thousand sites, drill a hundred of them, and do feasibility studies on ten to end up with one operating mine.*

For its part, the *Jakarta Post* argued that the real problem was not foreign investors but the intervention of Hasan, whom it managed to refer to without naming. An editorial of January 14 referred to "misplaced and groundless" criticism of foreign contractors and went on to argue that "the criticism should have been levelled against the manner in which several politically well-connected business-people – without any mining track record to speak of – tried to bull-doze their way into mining contracts, such as the Busang concession in East Kalimantan which holds one of the world's largest gold deposits."

All these criticisms made the government look bad and put pressure on foreign contenders like Barrick. There was even some sympathy for Bre-X, which had earlier received support from the Indonesian Mining Association. In this climate, any deal would have to include the solid participation of the Indonesian government and private Indonesian interests. The man in a position to bring that about was the president's friend, Bob Hasan.

The Deal No One Predicted

Truth is indeed stranger than fiction. The deal the Indonesian government finally announced on February 17 was a surprise to everyone but a handful of insiders, when the foreign mining company that won the prize at the eleventh hour was Jim Bob Moffett's Freeport-McMoRan. Until a few days before the deal was announced, Freeport had only been mentioned a couple of times as a distant possibility. Even more ironic, given the months of struggle between Barrick and Placer, Freeport was lukewarm about its involvement in Busang, though its Indonesian staff led by David Potter, the vice-president of exploration, was – in the words of one observer – "gung ho" to begin work on the world's largest deposit. Certainly the company already had its hands full in distant Irian Jaya, where it had thousands of workers and the unruly tribes to contend with. Yet the apparently reluctant suitor had won the hand of the fairy princess.

Under the Hasan-inspired, government-approved deal, Bre-X ended up with a 45 per cent share, half what it started with but double what it would have received had the Barrick offer closed. (Shareholders learned to their dismay that they would get precisely nothing for handing over a 40 per cent position to Indonesian

Bre-X founder and president David Walsh in March 1996, when Bre-X was capturing the attention of the world. (Edward Regan/*The Globe and Mail*)

David Walsh, flanked by vice-chairman John Felderhof (left) and director Paul Kavanagh in an up-beat mood at the Bre-X annual meeting in Toronto, March 1996. (Edward Regan/ *The Globe and Mail*)

In less happy times, Walsh and another Bre-X employee stand outside the Bre-X Minerals building in Calgary during a bomb threat in May 1997. (Reuters/ Patrick Price/Archive Photos)

John Felderhof and author Douglas Goold in Felderhof's suite in the Shangri-La Hotel, Jakarta, at the end of February 1996. (Taufan Herjanto/*The Globe and Mail*)

Beneath Christmas decorations in downtown Manila, Bre-X geologist Michael de Guzman, born and raised a good Catholic, poses with Lilas, one of his four wives. (*The Globe and Mail*)

One man, two votes? The world's longest-ruling dictator after Fidel Castro, Indonesia's President Suharto about to cast his ballots in May 1997. (Canapress Photo Service/Denis Paquin)

Suharto looked relaxed at the controls of his Harley-Davidson at his palace, February 1996. (Reuters/Archive Photos)

Suharto's eldest son Sigit, Bre-X's ineffectual ally (second from left), pictured with his wife Elsye Sigi (second right), younger brother Bambang (right), and their formidable elder sister Tutut (left). October 1996. (Reuters/Enny Nuraheni/Archive Photos)

Top Indonesian mining official Kuntoro, who cancelled Bre-X's exploration permit in October 1996, precipitating the ownership crisis. (Reuters/Enny Nuraheni/Archive Photos)

Indonesia's mines minister Sudjana announces an ownership deal in February 1997. (Reuters/Supri/Archive Photos)

Failed Bre-X suitor, Barrick chairman Peter Munk was pleased to greet director Brian Mulroney at the company's annual meeting in May 1997. (Fred Lum/*The Globe and Mail*)

James R. "Jim Bob" Moffett, chairman, Freeport-McMoRan, winner in the ownership struggle for Bre-X. (Freeport-McMoRan)

John Willson, CEO of Vancouver's Placer Dome, was among the disappointed suitors for Bre-X, and had harsh words to say about Barrick's campaign. (Canapress Photo Service/Kim Stallknecht)

Among the many financial analysts who enthusiastically recommended Bre-X stock, none was more prominent than Egizio Bianchini of Nesbitt Burns.

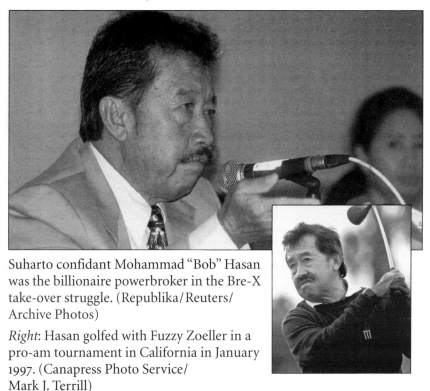

Suharto confidant Mohammad "Bob" Hasan was the billionaire powerbroker in the Bre-X take-over struggle. (Republika/Reuters/Archive Photos)

Right: Hasan golfed with Fuzzy Zoeller in a pro-am tournament in California in January 1997. (Canapress Photo Service/Mark J. Terrill)

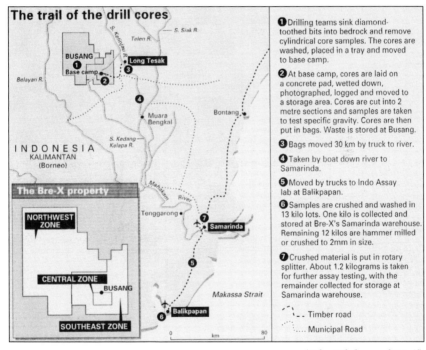

The trail of the drill cores

BUSANG
1 Base camp
2
Long Tesak
3
4
Muara Bengkal
Bontang
Belayan R.
S. Kendju R.
Telen R.
S. Siak R.

INDONESIA
KALIMANTAN
(Borneo)
S. Kedang Kelapa R.

The Bre-X property

NORTHWEST ZONE

CENTRAL ZONE
BUSANG

SOUTHEAST ZONE

Mahakam River
Tenggarong
7
Samarinda
5
Makassa Strait
6 Balikpapan

0   km   80

1 Drilling teams sink diamond-toothed bits into bedrock and remove cylindrical core samples. The cores are washed, placed in a tray and moved to base camp.

2 At base camp, cores are laid on a concrete pad, wetted down, photographed, logged and moved to a storage area. Cores are cut into 2 metre sections and samples are taken to test specific gravity. Cores are then put in bags. Waste is stored at Busang.

3 Bags moved 30 km by truck to river.

4 Taken by boat down river to Samarinda.

5 Moved by trucks to Indo Assay lab at Balikpapan.

6 Samples are crushed and washed in 13 kilo lots. One kilo is collected and stored at Bre-X's Samarinda warehouse. Remaining 12 kilos are hammer milled or crushed to 2mm in size.

7 Crushed material is put in rotary splitter. About 1.2 kilograms is taken for further assay testing, with the remainder collected for storage at Samarinda warehouse.

--.-- Timber road
.... Municipal Road

(The Globe and Mail)

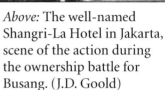

Above: The well-named Shangri-La Hotel in Jakarta, scene of the action during the ownership battle for Busang. (J.D. Goold)

Left: Jakarta, city of contrasts, where the luxurious Shangri-La Hotel towers above a shanty town. (J.D. Goold)

The local Dayak people of Mekar Baru village were those most affected by Busang. Village chief Pesalung Njuk poses in front of the long house, right. (John Stackhouse/*The Globe and Mail*)

A road through typical jungle hacked out by Bre-X to carry core drilling samples back to their main camp. (John Stackhouse/*The Globe and Mail*)

The Busang camp seen from near the main entrance. Lower left is the duck pond; above it and to the left is the VIP house where John Felderhof spent most of his time. (John Stackhouse/*The Globe and Mail*)

Bre-X Minerals spelled out in flowers on the sloping lawn in front of the hilltop storage shed. (John Stackhouse/*The Globe and Mail*)

Close up of Bre-X workers' white wooden huts at Busang.
(John Stackhouse/*The Globe and Mail*)

A drill assistant puts core samples in a box to be carried to camp.
(John Stackhouse/*The Globe and Mail*)

Bagged samples, foreground, await transportation from Busang by
Indonesia Air Transport (IAT). It was on one of these helicopters that
Michael de Guzman took his final trip. (John Stackhouse/*The Globe and Mail*)

In March 1997 Michael de Guzman (pointing) conducted a survey with his colleagues at Busang three weeks before his death. (*Gatra Magazine*)

At Michael de Guzman's funeral in Quezon City just outside Manila, his son Paul leads the procession. April 4, 1997. (Canapress Photo Service/Victoria Calaguian)

The house that Bre-X built. Bre-X Minerals headquarters in Calgary . . .
(Reuters/Patrick Price/Archive Photos)

. . . . and the
man who
brought it
down. Graham
Farquharson
of Strathcona
Mineral
Services Ltd.,
the independent
geological
consultant
whose May 3
report precisely
documented
the Bre-X fraud.
(Jay Bannister)

The start of the carefully documented test trail. Bre-X core awaiting logging and sample bagging at Busang. (Courtesy of Strathcona)

Bre-X samples after arrival at Indo Assay at Balikpapan. Two plastic bags per sample inside an outer fibreglass bag. (Courtesy of Strathcona)

Two Freeport test holes less than two metres behind a Bre-X hole. (Courtesy of Strathcona)

Strathcona drilling a hole. (Courtesy of Strathcona)

Strathcona prepares to drill another hole in deep mud. (Courtesy of Strathcona)

Strathcona's successful core recovery is stored ready for transportation. (Courtesy of Strathcona)

Armed Indonesian military policeman stands guard over core transport from drilling site back to the Busang camp. (Courtesy of Strathcona)

Helicopter prepares to transport cores from the site to the Indo Assay lab in Balikpapan. (Courtesy of Strathcona)

Core arrival in Perth, Australia, under the watchful eyes of representatives of Freeport and Nusamba, and government of Indonesia officials. (Courtesy of Strathcona)

Core in Perth after being split by a diamond saw prior to bagging half-cores for assaying in labs around the world. The results doomed Bre-X. (Courtesy of Strathcona)

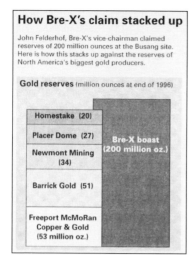

How Bre-X's claim stacked up

John Felderhof, Bre-X's vice-chairman claimed reserves of 200 million ounces at the Busang site. Here is how this stacks up against the reserves of North America's biggest gold producers.

Gold reserves (million ounces at end of 1996)

Homestake (20)

Placer Dome (27)

Newmont Mining (34)

Barrick Gold (51)

Freeport McMoRan Copper & Gold (53 million oz.)

Bre-X boast (200 million oz.)

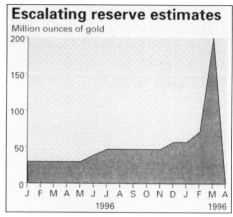

Escalating reserve estimates

Million ounces of gold

200
150
100
50
0

J F M A M J J A S O N D J F M A
1996   1996

The charts tell a literally incredible tale.
(Alexandra Eadie/*The Globe and Mail*)

The Beginning of the End. Bre-X shares re-open on the TSE at $3.50 on March 27, 1997. (*The Globe and Mail*)

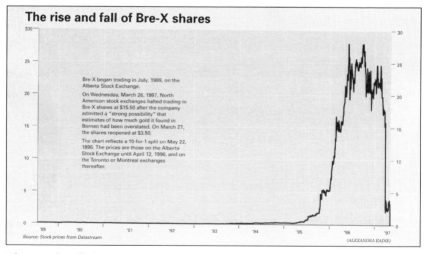

The rise and fall of Bre-X shares

Bre-X began trading in July, 1989, on the Alberta Stock Exchange.

On Wednesday, March 26, 1997, North American stock exchanges halted trading in Bre-X shares at $15.50 after the company admitted a "strong possibility" that estimates of how much gold it found in Borneo had been overstated. On March 27, the shares reopened at $3.50.

The chart reflects a 10-for-1 split on May 22, 1996. The prices are those on the Alberta Stock Exchange until April 12, 1996, and on the Toronto or Montreal exchanges thereafter.

'89 '90 '91 '92 '93 '94 '95 '96 '97

Source: Stock prices from Datastream   (ALEXANDRA EADIE)

The graph tells its own story. (Alexandra Eadie/*The Globe and Mail*)

interests; at Bre-X's current market value, that translated into a
$2-billion gift.) Next largest was the Indonesians' share, with 30 per
cent going to two Hasan-controlled private companies, Askatindo and
Amsya Lyna, and 10 per cent to the government. Freeport was given
the remaining 15 per cent. The company was to play the largest role
in the financing and developing of a mine, which it would operate.
Jim Bob Moffett agreed to finance 25 per cent of the estimated initial
cost of a mine, up to $400 million (U.S.), and arranged a $1.2-billion
(U.S.) commitment from the Chase Manhattan Bank for the remainder. (Another irony: When Felderhof was asked what he thought of
his new partner, Freeport, he replied that he had never had any relations with them, but they were "a very good company, from what I've
heard.") For its part, the government agreed to issue the long-delayed
Contracts of Work quickly.

Hasan was the originator and the chief beneficiary of the
February 17 agreement. He and the government believed Indonesia
was now in a position of control. Both knew they could effectively
control Freeport, which could operate in Indonesia only with the
government's blessing, giving them 15 per cent on top of their joint
40 per cent stake. That meant Indonesian interests would in effect
have 55 per cent of Busang.

"We are going to run it [the mine] together," Hasan said the day
after the agreement in an interview from Tokyo, where he was
meeting 500 of his forest products buyers. The timber baron said he
had been operating in Kalimantan for more than twenty years, where
he had plywood mills, a new $1.1-billion pulp mill (built by
Vancouver's Commonwealth company), and more than 15,000
employees. His companies were also familiar with building roads. "I
think our combined experience will contribute a lot to the operations" and save a lot of money, he said. Hasan expected a mine would
be in production within two years.

The Indonesian government was pleased that an agreement
with substantial Indonesian participation was finally in place. State
Minister of the Environment Sarwono Kusumaatmadja even

launched a shot across the bow of the foreign winner of the battle for Busang: "Freeport made a lot of mistakes in the past but it has shown its goodwill to repair the environmental damage," he told the *Jakarta Post*. "It is not easy, however, to change its past image among the public, particularly non-governmental organizations which deal with environmental preservation." The *Post*, which revealed that the "bulldozing businessman" it had criticized was Hasan, recanted and congratulated him for satisfying all parties, including the "owners of the natural resource – the Indonesia people."

Barrick's Principles

Peter Munk had met Hasan in early February and agreed to provide a larger stake for Bre-X's Indonesian partners, but said they could not reach a deal because Barrick refused to give up control. That certainly was the theme of Munk's remarks after an agreement was announced, alongside a very transparent sense of hurt and loss. "Obviously we are very disappointed," he admitted. "I personally am because I led the charge." He was glad, however, that he hadn't caved in and given up control. "To do that, now that it has become a game of Mr. Hasan's, and a political game, would transfer the destiny of our funds and our human resources – because it takes both of these to build this mine – outside of our control. And that is totally contrary to the founding principles of what Barrick is all about." In fact, "I think that we all feel that this was going to be a bit too messy for us. I mean we are a company of – despite what you people [at *The Globe and Mail*] wrote about Bush's letter and Mulroney's letter – we've acted totally above board. Of course we used our board members – that's what board members are there for. If they've got contacts, well, of course I'm going to make the pitch to the level of people I can make a pitch to, and rather than standing in line and get 'X' from the sub-secretary, of course I try to go to the most important people in any country."

Munk held forth on the same themes with a hint of melodrama and pathos at Barrick's annual meeting in May. He was the Iron John of Barrick's principles who did what he had to do despite "a high level of personal loss, a high level of personal embarrassment."

"I don't think I have expended, personally, more energy to secure a particular project for my company than I have on this particular Busang situation," he complained to shareholders. While some might argue Busang was an exception and Barrick should forgo its principle of control, he would have none of it. "Ego is what destroys rational decisions and I've seen it too often in my life that the greatest businesspeople have been brought down into a situation of tragedy by being driven by ego. . . . You would not want us to have a billion or a billion and a half dollars in Indonesia or anywhere else out of our control." By comparison, Placer Dome saved its verbal firepower, expressing disappointment at being shut out but saying it was still interested in a piece of Busang, if one became available.

Not everyone bought the Barrick line that it had been saved by sternly adhering to its wise principles. Rather, it had been saved by its failure to cinch the deal and, as events transpired, by blind luck. After a boilerplate presentation by executive vice-president Randall Oliphant at a high-power gold-mining conference in June 1997 held at the Noga Hilton overlooking Lake Geneva, Graham Burck, a manager for London-based Mercury Asset Management, one of the largest owners of gold shares in the world, stood up and asked whether Barrick's "lucky escape" with Bre-X would produce a "more cautious" acquisition strategy in the future. Oliphant replied that his company was not about to change its goals: "We are still determined to grow through acquisitions. It's been very successful for our company. We think that most people in our industry are honest and decent, but at the same time, we'll take our precautions and in each situation adjust our program accordingly."

Later, on the terrace overlooking the lake's famous fountain, which the Swiss sensibly turn off at night, a Denver-based mining executive whispered a typically unkind assessment of Barrick, the

800-pound gorilla of the gold-mining industry. "Oliphant must have mentioned five times that Barrick was the world's most profitable gold-mining company. There's an old Texas expression that people born on third base think they've hit a triple." Surely having the good fortune to buy the Goldstrike mine in Nevada, which threw off millions in free cash flow, was indeed like being born on third.

The Market Reacts to the Deal

Meanwhile, by the end of the week in February that the deal was announced, investors had knocked $400 million off the market value of Bre-X in heavy trading. Some investors were simply following the "buy on rumour, sell on news" dictum. Others were upset that Bre-X received no compensation for the portion of Busang that it was forced to forgo, and with the contrived way the agreement was reached. "The essence of the deal is Bre-X gets shafted," said Lévesque Beaubien analyst Michael Fowler, a former fan, as he drastically downgraded his rating to sell – a rarity in the investment business – from speculative buy. And while other firms prudently lowered their rating on Bre-X – RBC Dominion Securities to reduce, with a one-year target of $17.50, and ScotiaMcLeod to sell, though its target was still a hefty $20.58 – the thrill wasn't gone for everyone.

The Busang deposit "will become almost certainly the most profitable gold mine in the world," Kerry Smith of First Marathon Securities wrote in a speculative buy report. "Given the exploration potential and tremendous exploration success at Busang, we see no reason why Busang could not be at least a 100-million resource within six to twelve months."

While the shares of Bre-X suffered, junior mining companies with an interest in Indonesia did extremely well. Market watchers believed that the money flowing out of Bre-X shares would find a home in these companies. "It's amazing how smart the market is," Calgary-based newsletter writer Ted Carter commented the day the deal was announced. "The true speculation began about a week ago that this thing was going to get resolved." As it turned out, however, the market wasn't so smart after all.

Bre-X Hypes the Deal

There was no better illustration of Bre-X's promotional abilities – beneath the guise of caution and restraint – than the company's conference call with analysts and the media on February 19. Conference calls have been criticized for disseminating important information to investment houses, who can then contact sophisticated investors while leaving ordinary investors in the dark. The media are normally refused permission to listen in. Not in this case. This call was important because Bre-X had to placate uneasy analysts who believed that a poor agreement had been imposed on the company.

Walsh told the participants that it was the best deal available to Bre-X and was "blessed by our local partners," in other words, by Hasan and the government. In his view, the Barrick deal was so complex it was tough to evaluate, while this agreement "provides the largest direct share of ownership available to it [Bre-X], and we can certainly say with a high degree of confidence that it's in the ballpark in terms of its value compared to the other ones." Freeport, Walsh continued, was the most experienced mining company in that part of the world, "and that's a big comfort to us."

Bre-X and its backers made a number of startling statements to the call's listeners. "Some have mistakenly thought that we somehow owned 90 per cent of this property. This was never the practical reality, nor was it ever a basis for the valuation of the stock," said Walsh, directly contradicting what the company had said many times before. Only two weeks earlier, vice-president Stephen McAnulty had said, "Our legal and beneficial ownership of [Busang] has never been in question. We have a joint-venture agreement backing up our ownership, in which Bre-X has a 90 per cent stake and [our two Indonesian partners] have a 10 per cent stake." (Later, a class action suit launched by the Houston law firm Baker & Botts against Bre-X charged that during the call "defendant David Walsh admitted that Bre-X's representations concerning its ownership interest in Busang were false.")

The conference call included a telling exchange between Bre-X and Egizio Bianchini of Nesbitt Burns, one of the company's staunchest supporters during the days of its spectacular rise. But this time Bianchini was worried about lawsuits from shareholders, because Bre-X didn't hang on to its 90 per cent. Bre-X "never thought they would get 90 per cent," replied Leslie Morrison of J. P. Morgan, the company's financial adviser. "Management and we always recognized that a larger share of Busang would have to be made available to local entities." So much then, said Bianchini, for the revered Contract system – "We now know what kind of paper it's printed on" – and for the fact that "the parliament of a sovereign nation had agreed to a 90 per cent interest by Bre-X." Felderhof responded with a line that was to become one of his favourites, delivered in his tight, world-weary Dutch accent: "I think what happened here was we found too much gold, so it becomes an issue of national interest. If we found a lot less, this would have never happened." But Nesbitt's gold analyst was not persuaded: "I think we are going to have to look at Indonesia in a much different light than they have presented themselves at conferences and around the world on their road shows."

Felderhof countered with empathy and a new argument. "I guess I'm a bit disappointed, but you've got to also appreciate this is a very unique situation, and even with 45 per cent I feel that Bre-X could end up with 90 million ounces in Busang. That's my feeling, and that's a pretty good mine." His quietly expressed boast, which almost tripled to 200 million ounces the 71-million-ounce estimate for the entire deposit that the company had conveniently announced the day of the deal, went unchallenged. Now, suddenly, the concept of a 200-million-ounce deposit was in play.

It was this hype at a time when the company was under attack that was the most memorable part of the conference call. Later during the lengthy call, Felderhof made his much-repeated claim that "I feel very comfortable with 200 million ounces," which would have made the deposit worth $70 billion (U.S.), equivalent to the gross domestic product of the Philippines. Walsh casually added, "People have referred to this as the find of the century."

As the call progressed the numbers got much bigger and better on all fronts. Bre-X said it could be producing 4 million ounces a year from a single mine at Busang by 2002, at an average cost of $75 (U.S.) an ounce. It doesn't take much imagination to figure out how profitable such a venture would be even if the price of gold remained in the range of $350 (U.S.) an ounce. "If you look at the cash flow of this thing, it pays off at any reasonable gold price – or unreasonably low gold prices – in a period of time which is way, way shorter than any major project we've ever seen," argued J. P. Morgan's Morrison. "The margins are so huge it's relatively insensitive to either higher costs or lower gold prices." The powerful Wall Street bank was doing a stellar job of putting the faltering Bre-X story in its best light. "I won't provide you with a specific valuation number because that's your job," Morrison continued disarmingly when asked to value Freeport's 15 per cent, for which it was to pay $400 million (U.S.). But, he added, tantalizingly, "I will tell you that our valuation is in excess of the cash, well in excess of the cash, that Freeport will pay for the 15 per cent. . . . It's a lot higher than today's share price." This was typical of the highly enthusiastic talk that had convinced Bre-X shareholders that Busang was much bigger and better than the company allowed in its official statements.

The final issue discussed was whether Bre-X would continue as a separate company. Walsh said that it would, but added, "That is not to rule out a potential suitor if the price is right. I guess that old expression 'Everything has its price' must be taken into account here." Walsh claimed that Bre-X's 45 per cent of Busang was totally unencumbered and could be sold to the first party to come up with an attractive offer. Here he played the role of sober, reflective chief executive with considerable skill. Asked whether a suitor should propose marriage now or wait until the deal was closed and Bre-X had its

Contracts of Work, Walsh replied, "I think if I was an acquisitor, I would wait until everything is in place, [it's] just due diligence. But we have a deal."

The conference call had the desired effect. The already supportive Kerry Smith of First Marathon Securities said the call enhanced his valuation of Bre-X. Bruno Kaiser of CIBC Wood Gundy felt the same. "We share in the optimism of a 200-million-ounce (or more) reserve since a property visit we had last summer," he wrote, raising his rating – which he had briefly lowered – to a buy recommendation with a twelve-month target of $30.

Soothing the Regulators

As usual, Bre-X had left uncertainty in its wake. The Toronto Stock Exchange and the Ontario Securities Commission wanted an explanation of the company's claim that it had never said it owned 90 per cent of the Busang deposit. "There are a few things that I want to have clarified here," said Neil Winchester, the TSE's market surveillance manager. "Number one is . . . about the fact that they were saying that they had 90 per cent of this play, and then they say – whatever the wording is – people shouldn't have assumed that there was 90 per cent ownership." Bre-X was forced to backtrack, confirming that until the deal with Freeport it had said it owned 90 per cent of Busang. Ironically, that view was met with derision by Bre-X's new partner, Bob Hasan: "Ninety per cent in the air, you mean! Yeah, many birds in the air. It's better one in your pocket than nine or ten in the air."

The two regulatory bodies also wanted an explanation of Felderhof's statement that he felt "comfortable with 200 million ounces." Bre-X appeared to backtrack – but then didn't backtrack – in a press release the company generously referred to as a clarification. While Walsh piously stated that the new number shouldn't be seen as a new estimate, he didn't miss the chance to deliver a sales pitch, adding that "John Felderhof and the Bre-X technical team have been, to date, accurate in their projections." Interpretation: we haven't confirmed 200 million ounces, but we will.

Meanwhile, reports filed to the Ontario Securities Commission revealed that Walsh, his wife Jeannette, Felderhof, and Stephen McAnulty, the vice-president of investor relations, sold $37.6 million worth of Bre-X stock between August 19 and September 18, 1996. It always looks bad when insiders dump massive amounts of stock in a company they are running and are supposed to believe in, but this looked particularly bad. It was during this period that insiders knew they had lost their exploration permit, but had neglected to tell anyone. So while Bre-X had a tenuous hold on its single important asset, its main executives, the only people who knew this, were bailing out.

The solution to this embarrassing state of affairs: another "clarification," in which Walsh said he had sold only 3 per cent of his position in the company, for personal reasons, and remained Bre-X's largest shareholder.

No problem.

How the Deal Was Done: "Why Not Freeport?"

After seven months of frustrating negotiations between Bre-X and Barrick, not to mention talks with Placer and other suitors, the deal that finally emerged – without any of those suitors – was put together in a startlingly simple fashion. It was, however, the logical outcome of Suharto's frustrations, his choice of Bob Hasan as powerbroker, and the widespread demand for a strong Indonesian stake in the Busang deposit.

Hasan claimed he almost gave the much sought-after foreign stake to Norm Keevil of Vancouver's Teck Corp. "But after a lot of consideration, I thought it would save a lot of money, it would save a lot of overhead expenses, and it would save a lot of time" to look closer to home, Hasan explained. But who was there closer to home who would make sense?

Just a few days before the February 15 deadline, Hasan said he thought: "Hey, I have a friend here and he's already been here for so many years, he has his operations here. His headquarters is also here, and he is the biggest taxpayer in Indonesia. So I thought: 'Why not Freeport?'

"Their people are already here and they know the local rules and regulations. I don't have to teach them from scratch." Hasan said that until he suggested to Jim Bob Moffett the idea of becoming involved, Freeport "didn't show any interest. We actually asked them to come in."

In Hasan's view, the results were better than they would have been with anyone else. "The deal we have done is clean. There is no money involved, there is no signature, there is nothing. So I think it is a very good, clean deal." And why did his friend Moffett, "a very honest guy," accept? "Probably he just wanted to help us."

Both Munk and Walsh echoed the view that the deal was driven by Hasan. Munk said that he had not even heard of Hasan before the middle of January, when the Indonesian government ordered Bre-X and Barrick to talk to him. "Obviously, we thought we had the best offer," said Munk. "But Mr. Hasan is the boss and he though, 'Why not Freeport?' . . . So we had to bow out." Bre-X had a similar explanation. "As an exploration company, we have always acknowledged that a large, experienced partner was critical for the success of the Busang project," Walsh intoned. "Our local partner, Mr. Mohammad 'Bob' Hasan, nominated Freeport-McMoRan for this role, and Bre-X seconded this choice." For his part, Jim Bob Moffett asserted that Freeport had shown little interest in Busang because he assumed Barrick was poised to become the successful foreign suitor. He said he had not seen any assay reports until the second week of February, when Hasan offered Freeport a stake at the last minute.

Although the deal was put together at the last minute, it was not quite as casual as Hasan pretended. After all, it had been two and a half months since Suharto had ordered him to work out an agreement that would satisfy Indonesians and placate foreign investors. It is stretching credulity to believe that Hasan just happened to think of his golf buddy Moffett – who of course was at the decisive tête-à-tête at Suharto's ranch in December – at the last minute. Hasan is a cunning businessman and helpful to the president, with whom he had joint business interests through their holding company Nusamba. Hasan knew he had to choose someone the president would approve of, someone like Moffett, whom the president had known and liked for decades. And Moffett was someone whose interests in Indonesia were so great he could easily be controlled. Certainly Hasan's personal preferences were also important. Like many Indonesians, he didn't like Barrick and the way it threw its weight around. He did like Norm Keevil of Teck, but the company was too small to become involved without a partner. Hasan also liked John Willson of Placer, but the company's environmental record in the Philippines counted against it. So, why not Freeport?

Why the Canadians Failed

Corporate Canada, in the form of Bre-X, Barrick, Placer, and Teck, failed. They were beaten by an Indonesian tycoon and a Texan who understood how Indonesia's power game worked. Moffett was willing to participate in a major project when asked to do so, since he was aware that the figure controlling the shadow puppets was Suharto himself. But the Canadians also helped defeat themselves. The endless delays, the alliances with the president's unpopular offspring, and the bickering among the Busang contenders gave critics plenty of opportunity to press the government for a made-in-Indonesia solution.

The story of Bre-X was the story of a company that blundered from the moment its executives set foot on Indonesian soil. Above all, it succeeded in antagonizing the government, the key player, which led to the cancellation of its exploration permit in August 1996. Bre-X acted as though it had Contracts of Work giving it clear title to the entire Busang property in its pocket. Without keeping the Indonesian mines department fully informed, the company tactlessly made a series of increasingly buoyant announcements about drill results in Canada and relentlessly promoted its stock in Canada and the United States. Kuntoro, the senior mines ministry official, for example, first learned about Bre-X's astonishing find when he was visiting Toronto in the summer of 1996. "What a terrible way to find that your country has the biggest gold deposit in the world," commented one mining executive in Jakarta. Then Bre-X blundered by choosing Sigit, the Suharto offspring who effortlessly combined greed, a bad reputation, and ineffectiveness.

"I said to Bre-X that the way they handled it [the ownership dispute] was wrong," Beni Wahju, the widely respected head of the Indonesian Mining Association, said in early March. "Things have to be worked out in a more amicable way. I told Bre-X that the way they operated was wrong. They had no one who was responsible in Jakarta." Even though the association lobbied the mining department for a fair deal for Bre-X, Wahju said he couldn't even get a map of Busang from the company until the beginning of that month, a revelation that now appears more suspicious than it did at the time. "Bre-X, where are you?" he pleaded. And Bre-X lacked a strong, ongoing relationship with the mines department.

If Bob Hasan bulldozed his way into the Busang swamp and succeeded, Peter Munk bulldozed his way in – and failed. Much of that failure had to do with the Indonesians' dislike of what they perceived to be Barrick's arrogance, an arrogance that other mining companies had long found insufferable. Certainly Barrick was initially successful, since it persuaded the government that it could quickly resolve the ownership dilemma and that it had the financial clout and expertise to quickly bring a mine into production. The result was the announcement in November that Barrick would become the partner of Bre-X.

But unluckily for Barrick, the clearly coercive arrangement brought out the critics, and their clamour had an effect. And there was so much to attack: the back-room pressure the company put on certain mining officials; the deal with Tutut; the use of Bush and Mulroney; the lack of investment in Indonesia; and the flying in and out of Peter Munk. This was precisely how not to do business in Indonesia.

Another example: Barrick's sizable office in Jakarta was left out of the loop and was not even informed when Munk made his first trip to Jakarta on November 13, 1996, in the Barrick company jet. Over drinks in O'Reilly's Bar at the Grand Hyatt, where Munk stayed in the presidential suite on both of his *sub rosa* visits, one well-informed regular of the bar, who was familiar with the negotiations, commented that he believed the company's Jakarta office "was opposed to doing business with the Royal Family." He added that the local staff correctly anticipated that Barrick's strategy would fall short because it failed to address the consensual, highly personal way of doing business in Indonesia, and that it would leave the company open to a lot of criticism.

Barrick was also unsuccessful in completing a deal because it was negotiating with a party, Bre-X, that resented being forced into a deal. So Bre-X stonewalled until something else came along – and it did, in the form of Bob Hasan.

In the view of Indonesian economist Hartojo Wignjowijoto, Barrick misunderstood the game at which it tried to excel – the connections game. "Barrick chose the wrong strategy. They worked on the assumption that if you get the support of the senior minister [mines minister Sudjana] and the eldest daughter of Suharto, everything will be okay. But politics and business don't recognize daughters and sons" because there is only one person in the country who ultimately counts: the president.

Many of these themes were brought together in an editorial in the *Jakarta Post*. Barrick was "apparently too confident about its political backing" from Tutut and the minister, and "too strong in dictating its terms to Bre-X." Thanks to Hasan and Freeport, "Bre-X has been saved from a forced marriage with a gold digger."

Not that it was easy to negotiate with Bre-X, whose negotiations were led by executive vice-president Rollie Francisco. This lent some interesting personal background to the negotiations. Francisco, a Torontonian, was the distinguished former chief of finance at Lac Minerals. When Lac was bought by Barrick a few years earlier, Francisco was not among those who continued in their jobs. In these negotiations he was facing Barrick across the table. Bre-X made endless delays and endless demands, and even accused Barrick of breaking a confidentiality agreement. Walsh later told Dow Jones that he rejected many offers because he thought they were low-ball bids. "We got offers that were too aggressive," he explained. "I certainly believed in the resource. I was trying to cut as thorough a deal [for] shareholders as possible. . . . I was such a believer that I was standing firm." Of course, a cynic looking back would note that a quicker deal would have meant that the successful party would have carried out its due diligence, and thereby uncovered the fraud, that much sooner.

The bid by Placer was hurt by bad publicity about its environmental problems, by the vagueness of its offer, and by J. P. Morgan's unfavourable comparison of Placer with Barrick. Connections also explain why it failed to win a piece of Busang. As Placer's amiable country manager in Indonesia Ron Stewart saw it, "The government considered us carefully but didn't know us well enough to empower us. . . . It defaulted to someone [Freeport] they knew better and who had a long-term record here." Although Placer has operated in Papua New Guinea for five years, it has a minimal presence in Indonesia.

As previously noted, Hasan said that he almost picked Norm Keevil of Teck at the last minute. But in the critical few days before Hasan made his decision, Keevil was in Australia visiting mining promoter Robert Friedland, who said he had urged Teck to bid for a 15 per cent share. Keevil thought of stopping in Jakarta on the way back to Vancouver, but he called Hasan's right-hand man, Gerry White – a Canadian – who said all was well, and not to bother. Given the importance of personal contact, Keevil might have closed the deal if he had insisted on seeing Hasan just when he was about to make his decision.

Unfinished Business

After months of delay, the final deal was a hurried affair negotiated between two men, Hasan and Moffett, who trusted one another, and with the backing of the president. Indonesian interests got what they and the critics wanted. Of course, no agreement can last if it does not reflect the realities of power. Because this one did, it was widely thought it would succeed. In that sense at least, it was a good – if not a moral – deal, although not for those who were left out. "As a citizen I am satisfied," allowed director general Kuntoro. "But as an official it is not a factor."

"The appointment of Freeport McMoRan makes sense," wrote Mohammad Sadli, the former mines minister. "It has extensive experience in copper and gold mining in Indonesia. It is close to the highest echelon of the government and therefore has the government's trust. Apart from that, the company is prepared to meet all the financial requirements for the development of Busang II and III." As for Freeport's record on social and environmental matters, the Indonesian Mining Association's Beni Wahju said, "I've seen the way they operate," adding that he believed it had learned from its mistakes.

By mid-March, the main part of the story appeared to be over. However, the applicants for seventy unsigned Contracts of Work, the vast majority of which were, like Bre-X, Canadian mining companies, were growing anxious. Without the president's signature, they couldn't move beyond the exploration stage. The worry was that without a go-ahead soon, some of these companies would leave. "In the long term, geology will tell a company to come," Beni Wahju told a visitor at the beginning of March, unaware how ironic his comment would appear only a few weeks later. "Geology dictates everything."

Certainly up to this point, everyone agreed that Indonesia's geology was among the best in the world. Robert Friedland, whose Indochina Goldfields Ltd. holds two properties directly south, three big blocks straight north, and three due west of Busang in Kalimantan, said that Busang "should be in the ranks of the immortals" and that the deposit would "outlive our children." Kuntoro seconded Felderhof's comment that in five to ten years the country would be the world's second biggest gold producer after South Africa.

As for all the attention paid to Bre-X, "This has put our name in front of the Indonesian public and business community," said Canada's ambassador to Indonesia, Gary Smith, in his Jakarta office. "It has increased our profile enormously." Indeed it had, but that profile was well short of something to boast about – even apart from the events that were about to unfold.

After so much tumult, Walsh was finally triumphant and serene. "We showed the world that Canadian companies are nice guys, but we also showed we've learned how to go into the corners and come out with the prize," he said in a speech to university business students in Saint John, New Brunswick, three days before Michael de Guzman died. "It makes other people and other countries more aware of Canada."

At the end of the day, it was evident that Bre-X's discovery and story were unique. "This will not be a precedent," Kuntoro insisted. "I believe it will never happen again," he said with a laugh. And the moral? "Don't do anything before a Contract of Work has been signed because you are not protected." Bre-X had been very careless. "Be careful if you find something huge. If you do, Big Brother will interfere."

Oxtail Soup with John Felderhof: "I'm glad it's over"

Felderhof was right on at least one point when he made his cynical comment about having found "too much gold." Like those tales of huge lottery winners whose lives turn to misery, the story appeared to carry with it the curse of too much success. "I think we found almost too much, and attracted the attention of major international mining companies," he repeated only a few weeks before the world would be transfixed by the fate of Michael de Guzman. While "it's been very distracting for me," he "absolutely" did not regret the experience.

Felderhof's wide-ranging conversation with a *Globe and Mail* reporter began in his suite at the Shangri-La Hotel and was the last interview he would grant before the whole Bre-X fable came apart. The suite had been Bre-X's nerve centre during the ownership battle. For such an elegant hotel – even the elevators boasted elaborate hand-carved panels – suite 1824, with its light brown carpet, orange sofas, and prints of waterfowl and blooming water-lilies, was undistinguished. The conversation continued over dinner on the ground floor of the hotel, overlooking the glistening pool that stretches towards a white-domed mosque. Felderhof passed up the lavish buffet, ordering oxtail soup.

The Bre-X story "became political when Barrick made contact with government officials here," he explained. "I don't know how they got their foot in the door. The company just convinced officials that they were the only mining company able to mine such a huge deposit. But others were capable." In any event, "we always wanted to bring a major in; that was never a secret." Even though he believed that Barrick had broken its word when it had tried to take over Bre-X in 1994, he added primly, "I'll make no comments or accusations. I've got to work and live here." But his eyes turned fiery at the mention of Barrick director Brian Mulroney. "Aren't Canadian taxpayers still paying his bills?" he snapped, referring to his government pension.

Against the backdrop of a world-class hotel, Felderhof was an unpolished figure. In a pallid face the only remarkable features were his impressive, bushy eyebrows. He seemed tense and unhappy and anything but an adventurer, or a recently minted multimillionaire. His light blue open-neck button-down shirt did nothing to hide a modest paunch. Mercifully, there was no sign of the hulking bodyguard that Bre-X had hired for him. Tense and bristling with a sense of grievance, Felderhof answered questions in an unmistakable Dutch accent, speaking in a curt, clipped manner. He insisted that a tape recorder not be used, a rarity among those who agree to be interviewed. "Your paper is anti-Bre-X," he charged, asking sharply if the reporter was the one who had written the original story with "Robertson," a reference to mining reporter Allan Robinson. Twisting a straw as he spoke, he said he felt "badly treated" by the media. "For example, we had a fire at the Busang camp. A Vancouver paper said we tried to destroy records. That's ridiculous." He continued, as if pleading for sympathy, "We were presented wrong. We were always the bad boys. We're a small, junior mining company that has achieved a lot in the past three years." Not content to answer questions, the geologist asked them, in a petulant voice, as in "So what do you think of Bre-X, Doug?" The Bre-X vice-chairman grew angry over questions concerning the cancellation of the company's exploration permit seven months earlier. That was the reason the company had had such a rough ride, he said. "Why is it such a big issue?" And no, the company was not trying to hide the cancellation. "I believe we announced it," he said. "But you have to go through the press releases. I'm here and the boys are there [in Calgary]."

Of course, Bre-X had never announced the loss of the permit: *The Globe and Mail* had.

Felderhof was also defensive but inconclusive when asked why he had sold so much of his company's stock. "To my knowledge, I have never in my life broken the rules and regulations of a stock exchange. As a director, I have a tremendous responsibility to shareholders." As for his eye-popping 200-million-ounce estimate, "I was not trying to promote the stock." A final, full feasibility study would be completed in 1997, with production of 2 million ounces a year starting in the year 2000, building towards 4 million ounces. "It's the find of the century," he concluded, echoing Walsh and paying himself a handsome compliment. "There's no doubt in my mind."

Although many of these issues visibly caused Felderhof pain, he was happy to talk in detail about geology and his years in the bush. A good geologist needs persistence and experience, he explained. It was a tough life – years earlier he had been stranded for several days in Papua New Guinea without any food – but it was also an adventure. No one had previously found gold at Busang because no one realized "the gold is depleted in the first two to four metres." And not many geologists, he explained, are familiar with maar diatremes, the feature at the centre of his theory. Not that he was shy about his accomplishments, producing a page entitled "Bio Data." His theories, the biography said (in a memorable phrase), had been "further enhanced" by Mike de Guzman. With the assistance of geologists Cesar Puspos, a Filipino, and Jonathan Nassey, an Indonesian, the theories had led to the discovery of Busang.

Where did this adventurer consider home? For the first time, Felderhof smiled broadly – almost sheepishly. "That's hard to say," he replied. "I spend 70 per cent of my time away ... But I have a family with three kids in the Cayman Islands." And what relaxed this very unrelaxed man? "I like gardening. It relaxes me."

Looking ahead, "a takeover is always in the cards because it is such a huge deposit," he suggested. In any case, there was more to life than a single discovery, however large. "Busang has become a drilling exercise and the challenge is gone, in a sense. We have some other good properties which look exciting."

Felderhof avoided the rounds of drinks for which he was famous and raved about the oxtail soup. "It's a meal in itself," he said. "You should try it sometime." Although he didn't drink, he smoked a succession of Marlboros, despite a bone-rattling smoker's cough. "I want to try to get a few hours' sleep," he said as he stood up after dinner. "I have a wake-up call for 4:00 a.m. to catch a 6:10 helicopter back to

Busang." Now that the ownership deal was done, he was confident the spotlight would be taken off Bre-X.

"I'm glad it's over and I'm going to get on with my life," he sighed. "It's been very distracting for me. . . . [Now], we've got to move forward rapidly. Freeport McMoRan has already begun due diligence."

CHAPTER TEN

The Australian Connection

"What obviously does come to mind was that at the end of the day there simply wasn't any gold." – Warren Staude, Australian mining analyst, on gold company promotions in the 1980s

"The information available had been written by Mike [de Guzman] and basically the information was a load of baloney." – Michael Everett, de Guzman's colleague and former director of Pelsart Resources NL

Riches and Rags

When John Felderhof checked out of his light brown and orange suite at the Shangri-La hotel in March 1997, he had every reason to feel on top of the world. Sure, there was lots of work to be done. But opportunities for play were also plentiful. Felderhof had cashed in Bre-X options worth $42 million the previous year. Now he had the money to buy anything he could dream of, and there was much he desired.

Already there were houses, three of them, in the Cayman Islands in the heart of the Caribbean. History buffs may recall that the notorious British pirate Blackbeard once considered the Caymans his sanctuary. When he wasn't in Indonesia, Felderhof lived on Grand Cayman at an estate he'd bought for $2.9 million (U.S.). In contrast with his former self, the river walker who had prided himself on being jungle tough, the veteran geologist now lived a soft life. His main residence, a white stucco beach-front house with a red tile roof, sprawls inside the island's posh Vista del Mar neighbourhood, a walled community located next door to the Cayman Islands Yacht Club. There are granite waterfalls, a swimming pool and Jacuzzi, seven bathrooms, rooms with seventeen-foot ceilings, and a red-roofed gazebo overlooking the ocean. The driveway is crushed white stone, and the place screams new money. The Felderhofs also own a beach-front condominium worth $1.25 million on nearby Seven Mile Beach and a house purchased for $433,000 in an upscale neighbourhood called Snug Harbor.

On June 6, 1996, just a few months after buying, John Felderhof put all the properties in Ingrid's name.

Then there were the cars. Ingrid had just put a new one in the garage for her husband. "She just bought me a Lamborghini for Christmas," Felderhof told a reporter from *Fortune*. "It's two seats strapped to a fucking engine. I think she's trying to kill me." If he tired of the $200,000 sports car, there was a Mercedes, and a Land Rover, and a Jeep – a fair amount of horsepower on an island that measures just thirty-five kilometres by thirteen kilometres. If short dashes down the road grew tame, Felderhof could pound the waves in a $250,000, thirteen-metre Sea Ray power boat. In short, life was sweet for Bre-X's vice-chairman – as it was for many of the long-time colleagues who worked alongside him at Busang.

It hadn't always been so. The majority of the geologists who worked at Bre-X in the 1990s had come through lean years together while working on Indonesian projects from a base in Australia during the 1980s. In every school yard, there is always one gang of boys who constantly get into mischief. If that gang was to grow up and become geologists, they would be John Felderhof and his friends Jonathan Nassey, Mike Bird, and Mike de Guzman. And Indonesia would be their playground.

Peter Howe can take credit for introducing everyone to the region. In the early 1980s, the mining consultant at ACA Howe got interested in Indonesia. The privately owned, Toronto-based firm had done some work for a company called Jimbarlana Minerals in Indonesia, and Howe saw huge potential in the country. Through Jimbarlana, Howe met a young local engineer named Jonathan Nassey and hired him to set up an ACA Howe office in Jakarta.

It was one of Nassey's first jobs. Born in 1950 and educated at a Catholic mission school in his home province of Irian Jaya, he graduated from a local university with an engineering degree in 1974. Despite his inexperience and youth, Nassey had a critical role at Howe because, at the time, only Indonesian nationals could stake mining claims.

Not long after opening the Jakarta office, Howe met Michael Novotny, who'd been trekking around the country for years looking for gold. Novotny, a tough survivor, had fled to Australia in 1949 from his home in Czechoslovakia to escape the advancing Russian army. Once in Australia, Novotny immediately became involved in the mining business, which he found fascinating. Novotny was one of the first Australians to take an interest in Indonesia, exploring the country in the 1960s, long before any other foreigner. In 1978, he left an oil industry job in Australia to devote all his energy to seeking out Indonesia's riches.

"I learned the language, I got to like the people, and I was approached by so many Indonesians on the basis of 'come and take a look at what we've got here,'" he recalled. Novotny soon accumulated an impressive portfolio of properties, but he needed a financial backer to develop the sites. His search for financing led him to Kevin Parry, a flamboyant self-made millionaire who started out as a cabinet-maker in Perth. From his base in Western Australia, Parry had created a business empire that included a chain of furniture stores, shopping malls, and interests in broadcasting. Not a shy man, he once planned to make an action film with himself as the star.

Parry's manifold holdings included an oil company called Pelsart Resources NL. But Novotny was not interested in oil so he convinced Parry to get Pelsart into Indonesian gold. Once he had Parry's financial backing, Novotny needed a team of geologists to look over his prospects. He decided to hire Peter Howe's company, and Howe turned the job over to John Felderhof. The ACA Howe team he pulled together for Pelsart included none other than Michael de Guzman and another Filipino geologist named Caesar Puspos. Under the guidance of this group, Pelsart soon accumulated an interest in fifteen Indonesian properties, mostly in Borneo. Parry boasted that Indonesia would soon become the world's second largest gold producer, next to South Africa.

Parry became a pushy promoter of Pelsart. His sales pitch worked, and investors initially clamoured to join in, easily raising more than $15 million (U.S.) for Pelsart to start exploration. Howe and Felderhof could see that Australian investors were enthusiastic about Indonesia, and they obligingly decided to create more companies that could raise more money. In 1983, they set up Jason Mining NL, and Felderhof was made a director. Jason immediately became a partner with Pelsart in six of its Indonesian properties.

Mike Bird, a former colleague of Novotny's in the oil business, was hired to manage the joint ventures. Bird, an Australian geologist with years of experience in Indonesia, was also closely tied to the Indonesian military through his wife, a huge advantage in a country where both the military and family connections mattered a great deal. Felderhof and Bird became great pals, looking for deposits by working the local villages together in search of areas where the locals had panned gold from rivers. Felderhof was doing more than just prospecting, though, for he was also acquiring a large personal stake in the ventures. He was given options in Jason to buy more than 500,000 shares at 20 cents each. The options soared as Felderhof and the others pumped out news of more and more gold prospects. At the peak in 1987, Felderhof's options were worth nearly $19 million.

Peter Howe benefited as well. He received similar options in Jason, and his company was also being paid about $100,000 (Aus.) a year by Jason for the consulting services of Felderhof and other ACA Howe geologists. The lucrative relationships soon expanded. ACA Howe took ownership stakes in other mining companies involved in Indonesia, including Argonaut Mining NL and Kingstream Resources NL. Again, there were all sorts of ties between the companies – Felderhof was a part owner of Argonaut and a director of Kingstream, and ACA Howe was receiving hefty payments, up to $600 a day, for providing consulting services to the companies.

By the mid-1980s, Jason, Pelsart, and the other companies linked to ACA Howe had started an Indonesian gold rush, involving mainly Australian mining companies. In 1986, in fact, Australian companies were involved in more than twenty mining projects in Indonesia, far more than companies from any other country. The Australian Stock Market couldn't get enough of the excitement, and Jason's shares jumped from $2 in 1986 to $37 in 1987, even though it had lost $1.1 million (Aus.) in 1985 and $2.8 million (Aus.) in 1986. Many Australian analysts fuelled the fire by issuing glowing reports on the companies.

"Together with its joint venture partner Pelsart, Jason will be able to successfully and profitably mine the big gold deposits discovered," said a 1987 report by Frank Renouf Bickers Pty Ltd., an Australian investment house. "We recommend investment." Another Australian research firm, J. B. Were & Son, estimated that Jason's profit would jump to $58.8 million (Aus.) in two years.

The rosy reports were based largely on presentations made by Felderhof. "They were fairly upbeat," says Warren Staude, who was a mining analyst with a large Australian insurance company at the time. "But then again it's hard to point a stick at anybody because of what went on, because there was just so much hype and things going on at the same time. What obviously does come to mind was that at the end of the day there simply wasn't any gold."

The End of the Good Times

One property that intrigued Felderhof was a piece of dense jungle in Borneo called Busang. "John had already identified Busang as a potential acquisition for Jason," recalled Howe. "He had written a paper for one of those mining conferences where he laid out the mineralized potential. He thought he could find other mines by looking at the structure of faults. Busang is one of those faults and he suggested that Jason acquire it."

But it was too late. By 1987, the gold rush was starting to fizzle, and with it, the fortunes of all those linked to ACA Howe were declining. At the same time, Parry had become obsessed with winning the America's Cup for Australia, and he diverted $30 million that had been raised for Pelsart to yacht racing, universally acknowledged as the most expensive sport on earth, and described by one cynic as like "standing in a cold shower tearing up thousand-dollar bills." Then in October 1987, the stock market crashed, ending investors' enthusiasm for ventures like distant gold projects. Pelsart was driven to near bankruptcy, and Parry was voted off the board of his own company. "At first Parry was a pleasure to work with," said Novotny. "But when he won the challenge to the America's Cup he got too excited, and it all went to his head. Had it not been for Kevin Parry in 1987, I dare say Pelsart would still be in existence under the Australian management, and I dare say Pelsart would be producing substantial amounts of gold."

Pelsart's best prospect, Mount Muro, was sold to Aurora Gold of Australia. "I was so pissed off when we had to actually disgorge ourselves from Mount Muro," said Novotny. "I had made a deal to buy that a long time before and I was the first one to step there. And Felderhof wrote excellent supporting reports and that's why we were able to raise a substantial amount of money in Australia." In March 1988, Novotny arranged to sell Pelsart to a group of Hong Kong businessmen for $12 million. Novotny and a colleague, Laurie Whitehouse, left the company a year later. Recollections of the circumstances surrounding the departures differ. Novotny says he retired and Whitehouse says he moved on to other projects. But Michael Everett, a former director and executive at Pelsart, said the two were dismissed.

Michael de Guzman was also fired, after using Pelsart's money to buy gifts for a girlfriend; whether the fortunate recipient became one of his four simultaneously maintained wives is unknown. Everett said the offence wasn't serious but a senior manager didn't like de Guzman and fired him anyway. With their financial backing pulled out from under them, the ACA Howe team struggled to find work. None of the geologists had managed to cash in their stock options before the crash and they were now worthless. Felderhof took the hardest hit, with a paper loss of $19 million; he would not be so slow in cashing in options in the future.

De Guzman went to work for another Indonesian mining company, and at one point he tried to interest Everett in a property. However, Everett said his old colleague's work had slipped badly. "It was a very poor piece of work," he said. "The information available had been written by Mike and basically the information was a load of baloney. There weren't too many facts in it, let's put it that way."

Jonathan Nassey was hired by Toronto-based Inco in Indonesia but left to pursue his political ambitions. He tried to beef up his credentials with a mail-order engineering doctorate from the Beverly Hills School of Engineering in California, a name that did not inspire widespread confidence; the mining community in Jakarta later laughed at references to Nassey as "Dr." Nassey in Bre-X's annual reports, when, like many of Felderhof's friends, he ended up on their payroll. In addition, his political career was a disaster. When he ran for governor in his home province of Irian Jaya, he failed badly. Charitable friends ascribe the problem to the fact that he had no strong connections to the ruling Golkar party, which doles out positions based on patronage.

Faking It at Karpa Springs

Novotny and Whitehouse returned to Australia and landed in the midst of what became one of the country's biggest mining scandals, with some patterns that may interest students of Bre-X. It started in 1990. Novotny was doing some consulting work for a mining company when a colleague in the office, Leonard Ireland, told him about some prospecting he'd been doing on a property near Perth called Karpa Springs. "He said, 'I'm taking a few days off because my brother and his partner have a prospect that they are going to drill and I am going to help them,'" Novotny recalled. "I said fine. I didn't take any notice and when he came back I said, 'How did it go?' He said, 'Well, it seems we've got plenty of gold.' I said, 'Well, tell me more about it' and so this is how I met them." The trio that Novotny encountered were Leonard and his brother Dean Ireland and Clark Easterday.

Soon Novotny formed a company and offered to buy the property for $6 million. He also hired Whitehouse as head geologist, who looked over the information provided by the Irelands and was impressed. According to the report, the site had a medium-sized gold deposit with very high grade ore, with up to 13.75 grams of gold per tonne of rock (two or three grams per tonne is considered enough for a profitable mine). Whitehouse told Novotny it could be the largest gold mine in Australia.

Novotny took the information to Perilya Resources NL, a small Australian mining company. They were also impressed and immediately agreed to pay $10.2 million (Aus.) for a 50 per cent interest in the project. But the cautious Perilya also wanted to check the site before closing the deal. In July 1990, preliminary assaying began, and the results proved worrisome. They couldn't find any gold.

Naturally concerned, Perilya's geologist asked to review some core samples that the Irelands had supposedly saved from their first drilling on the site. Dean Ireland took Novotny and the geologists to the shed where the samples were kept. Ireland had secured the door with two locks. Giving Novotny the key to one lock, he refused to hand over the other until his group was paid the $6 million (Aus.) promised by Novotny. The money was handed over a few days later, and Perilya's geologists went to fetch the samples. When they got to the shed, it was empty. Dean Ireland's explanation: the samples must have been stolen. Of course.

More concerned than ever, Perilya geologists went back to the site to see if there was any gold there. When their drilling still couldn't uncover any, the company called in the police, who charged the Irelands and Clark Easterday with fraud, saying the trio had doctored the samples and laboratory results. Novotny and Whitehouse, who were not implicated in the salting scandal, later testified for the prosecution. At one point, it was discovered, the accused partners had changed a number on a lab report that showed .01 parts per million by adding a "1" before the decimal point. The police also recovered other incriminating lab data hidden, improbably, in a wildflower nursery.

The Ireland brothers and Easterday pleaded innocent and used arguments that would later be heard in Indonesia, on a much larger scale. They claimed the differences in the testing were caused by coarse gold at the deposit – which can make some samples appear extremely rich and others worthless. They also argued that the testing process used by Perilya was inadequate. As for the falsified report, their lawyers said the changes could, you never know, have been made by someone else. The jury didn't buy it and all three were sentenced to three and a half years in jail; only $4 million of the $6 million Novotny paid was recovered.

John Felderhof Does Some Arm Waving

Life for Felderhof didn't turn out much better after Pelsart, Jason, and the other gold rush companies crashed. He had never cashed stock options in ACA Howe's stable of companies, and when the Australian exploration bubble burst, he watched his $19-million paper fortune vanish. As the 1990s began, he was married to Ingrid, his second wife, and was supporting three children. However, his job prospects were bleak and he drifted from Perth to Canada and back to Indonesia looking for consulting work.

In 1991 back in Jakarta, he took a job with a new mining venture called PT Minindo Perkasasemesta. It looked like an exciting opportunity. Minindo had been created in 1989 by Armand Beaudoin, a Montreal-born mining promoter, who had picked up the properties abandoned by the fleeing Australians. Beaudoin convinced a small group of Australian investors to finance Minindo, and they later brought in a wealthy Singapore group, which soon clashed with Beaudoin. Bowing out, he sold his 52 per cent interest to them for $1 and quit.

When Felderhof joined Minindo, the managers had high hopes. The company was about to become the first Indonesian mining company to be listed on the Jakarta Stock Exchange. Felderhof was hired as an assistant to the general manager, and, naturally, he soon asked de Guzman to join the company. Not only did Minindo have interests in six properties, but, more importantly, it had a management team loaded with clout, a key ingredient for success in Indonesia. The company's president was Suharto's brother-in-law. Its chairman was a former chief of Indonesia's intelligence service, and the board of directors read like a who's who of Jakarta's political élite: the mines minister's younger brother, the foreign minister's nephew, the retired president of a state-owned mining company.

Minindo's pitch to investors demonstrated breath-taking gall, given the horrible state of the country's mining sector. The company produced a glowing assessment of each site by Normet Pty, the same Australian company that would later verify Bre-X's project. It claimed profits would soar from an expected $2.5 million (U.S.) in the first year of operation to $13.7 million by 1995 and $21.6 million by 1997. "A number of company projects [it named two] are well advanced in as much as a resource has been defined," the company said in a package of material sent to investors.

Felderhof started work on May 1, 1991, and immediately became one of the company's biggest promoters. "Being the first domestic mining company to be listed, this will provide Minindo with unlimited opportunities particularly in view of rapid decrease in mining activities by foreign mining companies since 1987 in Indonesia," Felderhof wrote in a letter to a local analyst in 1991. He also said Minindo had "unlimited opportunities" to pick up cheap mine sites. The company went public on June 30, 1992, with great fanfare and high expectations. But problems soon emerged. Minindo's shares didn't sell as quickly as the company had hoped. More importantly, it didn't sell the amount of stock that management had actually promised securities regulators. Minindo had rashly told Indonesia's Capital Market Supervisory Agency that it had orders for all of the shares. When the issue came up short, the agency began investigating the company and soon uncovered falsified reports and misrepresentations to investors.

"They lied to us," says Herwidayatmo, head of corporate finance at the Capital Market Supervisory Agency. On November 23, 1992, Minindo voluntarily suspended its shares to sort out the problems. In a bold move it also fired Suharto's brother-in-law. But the problems continued. The company couldn't pay a major creditor, and (in a soon-to-be familiar scenario) doubts emerged about the ownership of one of its key assets, a small alluvial gold mine called Waylo in Aceh, a province on the northern tip of Sumatra.

Minindo had told investors that the small mine would produce $6.8 million (U.S.) in revenue over the next three years. Beaudoin, however, said he owned the property. According to Beaudoin, Minindo had lost control of Waylo in 1991 by failing to meet filing requirements with the mines ministry. Beaudoin said he picked it up in 1992, about the same time as the disastrous public share offering. In addition, Beaudoin said Felderhof was responsible for maintaining the portfolio of properties and should have known about the ownership change. "He should have been a little more diligent when he was at Minindo," Beaudoin said, although he added, "I don't think he knew what happened. It was an Indonesian operation."

Indonesia's securities agency delisted Minindo in March 1993, stripped its lead underwriter of its licence, and ordered the underwriter's parent company to buy back all the shares. The company was taken over by its underwriter's parent company, a major Indonesian conglomerate, and the new owners shelved the mining projects.

The scandal was another blow to Felderhof. When the winter of 1992-93 set in, he hadn't been paid in six months, and he and de Guzman were desperately trying to flog Minindo's shares. "I saw John at the end of 1992 with Mike de Guzman and he said the float was under-subscribed. It was badly under-subscribed," said Colin Bryant, a mining consultant in Perth who was working for Canada's Lac Minerals at the time. Lac had been offered a piece of Minindo, but had no interest. Bryant said Felderhof appeared frustrated and eager to leave the company. "Felderhof had a bad time. He didn't get any money. He didn't get paid. I felt bad for the guy."

As 1993 began, Felderhof's career was in ruins. His mining prospects were so dim that he accepted an invitation from his old pal Jonathan Nassey to start a resort hotel in Irian Jaya that would cater to the growing trend to ecological tourism – a new dream they could sell to investors. "John was pretty desperate. He was pretty broke," said Theo van Leeuwen, who heads Rio Tinto's Indonesian operation.

Felderhof and de Guzman managed to get a brief job with a joint-venture company in Indonesia called Westralian Atan Minerals, or WAM. The company's property was called Busang, the same piece of land Felderhof and other geologists had worked over earlier. A Scottish company, Waverley Mining Financing, had taken over control of WAM and it wanted some geologists to review the properties one more time. Peter Howe sat on Waverley's board and encouraged the company to hire Felderhof and, of course, de Guzman.

WAM had been operating in Busang since 1986 when Indonesia's Syakerani family first staked the area. The Syakeranis also brought in some Australian interests and Indonesian businessman Jusuf Merukh to help with financing. Another familiar name was involved – Jonathan Nassey was a minor shareholder in the venture, and no doubt looked forward to working with his old colleagues again.

WAM had an exploration licence for the area and had drilled nineteen holes. The results appeared promising but not spectacular. But after Felderhof and de Guzman took a second look at the property, the assessment quickly changed. Felderhof, who had never lost his interest in Busang, was still convinced that the geography was perfect for gold. He immediately told WAM it was sitting on up to 2 million ounces of gold, far more than any other geologist had ever estimated.

"From the very beginning they were engaged in what we call here arm waving," said Warren Beckwith, a former WAM partner who later sued Felderhof and Bre-X over ownership of Busang. "Felderhof claimed to have reinterpreted the old [WAM] drilling results and defined the resource at 1 million ounces with a possibility of 2 million ounces, without doing any other work at all. Of course, our geologists say that was way too ambitious a statement to make at that time. To even say there was a million ounces in the first place – the [WAM] drilling didn't establish any kind of resource at all, and no geologist could say it was sufficient to establish a resource of any kind."

But Felderhof was convinced his theory was correct. When he got together with David Walsh at the famous Sari Hotel meeting in March 1993, Felderhof doubtless had Busang on his mind. With Walsh's financial backing, Felderhof could finally prove his theory about Busang and its vast riches. Felderhof brought de Guzman, Bird, and Nassey along to meet Walsh and back up his case. The old gang was back together.

CHAPTER ELEVEN

Behind the Scenes at Busang

"This is a simple mill, a simple process; it's a question of size. There's no new technology required, and there's no doubt it's do-able." – John Willson, chief executive, Placer Dome

"Before Bre-X came here, people were not so open to outside culture. We didn't know about things like paint and roofing." – Yusuf Ingan, thirty-four-year-old Bre-X drill operator

"Indonesian management was distinct from and operated virtually independently of the Canadian management." – Stephen McAnulty, Bre-X vice-president, testifying during a lawsuit

The Promise of a Gold Mine

By the summer of 1996, anyone associated with Bre-X could draw a picture of what the enormous open pit mine at Busang would look like. The dream was coming closer to reality as the company commissioned consultants at Kilborn Engineering to draw up blue-prints. Kilborn sketched the shape of the pit on a map, with digging to begin where gold concentrations were richest – the hole would rip a two-by-seven-kilometre scar across the jungle. Various designs were evaluated for the mills that would crush the ore. Dams would be built to capture the toxic tailings left over when gold is stripped from bedrock, and power would be supplied by a dam and generating station on a nearby river. The machinery and supplies would come into the camp by barges with forty-tonne capacity, then travel the last twenty-five kilometres on a gravel logging road to Busang. Helicopters could land at a pad next to the drill holes, while light planes could put down just five kilometres from the base camp. It was clear the project wouldn't be cheap – estimates of the cost ran to $1.7 billion (U.S.) – but the payoff looked enormous.

De Guzman forecast the company would start open-pit mining in the final months of the year 2000, with an annual gold output of 2 million ounces. By 2005, with teething problems worked out and the pit growing larger, de Guzman expected production to hit 2.5 million ounces a year. He talked of $400 million a year in cash coming out of the ground. At these levels, the mine would pay for itself in four years. And while most analysts said there was enough gold to last for twenty-five years, de Guzman confidently predicted fifty.

Companies such as Placer Dome were making detailed proposals for developing the mine, despite having no first-hand knowledge of what was in the ground. The proposals were meant to impress Indonesian politicians and specifically Bob Hasan, but they unwittingly had the effect of further legitimizing Busang. Placer Dome outlined a huge development, a four-year project that would involve four pits, each served by a mill that could crush 50,000 tonnes of rock per day. The company projected that 4 million ounces of gold a year could flow from this mine. Placer Dome was dreaming big. "This is a simple mill, a simple process; it's a question of size," said John Willson, Placer Dome's chief executive and the builder of several mines around the Rim of Fire. "There's no new technology [required], and there's no doubt it's do-able."

Upriver to Busang

The closest big city to Busang is Samarinda, a sleepy administrative centre before Kalimantan's resource boom took hold in the 1970s. Now the city of 100,000 lives, and dies, by the bounty brought downstream on the Mahakam River, which cuts a 100-metre-wide path through the centre of town. Were it not for the river, Samarinda's main attractions would be a Kentucky Fried Chicken outlet near the central mosque, and a suburb of brothels built on the other side of the hill from the city.

The river's role is palpable, even in the early morning, when mist has barely lifted from the Mahakam's muddy, choppy waters. Both banks brim with great thick logs that have been floated down from the highlands. Not far upstream the banks are spotted with mountains of coal, brought down river by barge. A big natural gas deposit sits near the Mahakam's mouth. And the river's many fingers reaching into the jungle lead to what many people still believe to be good gold deposits.

Just as the resource boom changed Samarinda, the transformation continues upriver, past the old royal capital of Tenggarong, where a sultan held court until the 1950s. Since then, Indonesia's authoritarian government has imposed its militaristic style on almost every aspect of life in the former sultanate. All government officers must wear uniforms and perform drills every morning in office courtyards. Further upriver, tiny villages fly flags of the ruling Golkar party, which has won every election since President Suharto seized power in the 1960s. At each stop, village elders, all on the government dole, dutifully record the names of visitors. It is hard to imagine how one of the world's greatest scams could be pulled off in one of the world's most controlled societies.

The Mahakam remains choppy until it reaches a fork in the river at a trading post called Maurakaman, only four kilometres from the spot where de Guzman's body was found. On the many banks of the Maurakaman Delta, satellite dishes point straight up, an indication that the river is about to cross the equator. From the busy Mahakam River, the South Kelinjau tributary that leads to Busang snakes its way north through the jungle, through forests of twenty-metre-tall trees and shrubs that crawl over one another till they reach the river's side. Occasionally, a tugboat passes, towing a huge rack of logs, but the timber trade that pays for so many satellite dishes and Coke bottles on the coast leaves little in its wake along the South Kelinjau. As the forest grows thicker, and the muddy river slows, the huts along the shore grow fewer, their comfort dependent on small fires and paltry herds of cattle that wander the shoreline in search of fodder.

Heading upstream, a small steamer chugs along with brand-new Japanese off-road vehicles strapped to its roof, and rows of diesel drums destined for a mining or timber camp. In the other direction, a family passes in a small dugout canoe in which all their worldly possessions are piled high for the journey to Samarinda, where they will seek a better life. In both directions, travelling salesmen paddle the river, with canoes full of shirts, shoes, pots, and pans. At each town, the number of satellite dishes grows fewer, as the number of latrines built on stilts over the river banks grows larger, until the South Kelinjau reaches a tranquil, muddy hamlet named Long Tesak, which was no more than a transit point until 1993. Then it became the gateway to Busang.

Even without a mine, Bre-X's impact on the Busang area was extraordinary. Long Tesak, a town close to the claim, became a hive of commerce. Its wood-shack shops, which once traded spices and basic foodstuffs, started to fill up with Coca-Cola, Bintang beer, Marlboro cigarettes, Milo tinned milk, and Close-Up toothpaste. Two one-room restaurants, each sporting official portraits of

President Suharto, began to serve curried fish and rice to travellers. The ramshackle wooden docks, which once catered to long boats, soon bustled with speedboats carrying fuel and supplies to Busang. Local youths played an Indonesian knock-off of Guns 'n' Roses on their boom boxes and talked for the first time about local jobs. There were jobs to transport the goods up the road to Busang, and plenty of jobs at the exploration camp for cooks, cleaners, labourers and, for the lucky ones, drillers, who could earn $450 (U.S.) a month.

Long Tesak, however, was not to be the Busang boom town. That right would go to a small tribal village deep in the forest on the banks of another river called the Atan. The Dayak people of Mekar Baru believed their lives would be transformed by the Busang deposit, and they were right. A generation ago, the Dayaks lived by slash-and-burn agriculture, cutting forests, planting rice crops on the scorched earth, and then moving on. The Indonesian government, which disdains such primitive ways because it believes they mar the nation's modernizing image, insisted the Dayaks settle down. In the 1980s they were given land along the Atan River and funds to build a small community. The Keniya Dayaks called their new home Mekar Baru, which means "new blossom." They built a neat grid of dirt roads, shops, football field, big primary school, and two churches, one Catholic and one Protestant, shaded by palm trees and the jungle that runs up to the town's edge. They planted rice and fished for survival, and found they could earn a nice cash income, too, panning for gold in the Atan River.

Then, in 1993, they were told their land – still government land, actually – bordered on a massive gold deposit. One of the first outsiders to visit the Keniya Dayaks to discuss the big gold deposit was John Felderhof. The dour Dutchman knew the importance of local support to any project. He had worked in the jungles of Southeast Asia, off and on, for nearly thirty years, so he knew the locals could lead him to possible sources of the gold. If a mine went ahead, he later told the tribal chiefs, they would see paved roads, electricity and a good share of the proposed mine's 3,000 jobs.

Boom Town

Bre-X built its first exploration camp next to a ridge about five kilometres from Mekar Baru and the Atan River, and before long, millions of dollars of exploration funds flowed into Busang. The Dayaks started to buy private power generators, satellite dishes, and glass windows. Electric wires were linked to every home in the expectation that power would be supplied by the eventual mine operator. Like the shops of Long Tesak, the tribal village's shops stocked up with canned food, beer, plastic toy boats, and insect repellents.

One of the luckiest Dayaks was Yusuf Ingan, a tall, lanky, thirty-four-year-old who quit a timber job to return to New Blossom, his home village, to work at Busang. Bre-X gave Ingan a job as a drill assistant, but within six months he was a full-fledged drill operator, tripling his income to $450 (U.S.) a month, which he could triple again in some months with performance bonuses. "Before Bre-X came here, people were not so open to outside culture," he said. "We didn't know about things like paint and roofing."

By early 1997, Bre-X was so confident of its future that it built a new residential colony, with eighty small houses and a mosque and a Catholic church for its local staff. Each house had two bedrooms and neat little flower garden and fence. Once the mine had started construction, the company said, employees would be allotted homes in the new township. Bre-X also planned to build an airstrip, water station, and 100-megawatt power plant. The locals would get a poultry farm and a fishery, both of which would sell their food to the mine. Even the government planned to build a new administrative centre at Busang. Almost everyone in Mekar Baru considered Busang to be a godsend, as welcome as the fresh spring rains. They no longer would have to send their children down river to Samarinda to boarding schools for a secondary education, and families no longer would have to migrate to the coast, or to logging camps, for work. In the interior of Borneo, this was the Indonesian dream come true.

Viewed from a helicopter, the base camp was an island of civilization in a sea of jungle. There were satellite dishes, comfortable bungalows for senior executives (and inside those bungalows were computers and refrigerators), helicopter pads, and roads bulldozed through the undergrowth. It all looked impressive. In reality, both the site and its methods were far from professionally run. Outsiders who knew what was taking place in the jungle characterized Bre-X's operations as sloppy and secretive. It started with people.

The Maverick Factor

Felderhof and de Guzman took pride in their reputations as mavericks. Felderhof seemed to live up to a Dutch stereotype, which one countryman equated with the title of a Dutch novel, *I Am Always Right*. "I don't think he would have questioned the results," the Dutchman said. "He would have seen the numbers and said, 'Yes, this proves I am right.'" Since they first worked together in the 1980s, Felderhof and de Guzman had been outsiders, even outcasts in some circles. By the early 1990s, they were both out of work and broke. Felderhof's geological record was good, but perhaps not quite as good as he liked to claim. There were rumours about his drinking habits, too, and several big firms were wary about doing business with him. Besides, no one could understand how such a feverish smoker – the locals at Busang called him "choo-choo" – had survived this long.

When Felderhof got back on his feet with Bre-X, he did not forget the way he had been shunned. Nursing those grudges, he often refused to talk to big firms like Barrick that wanted to buy out his company. He even refused entry to the site to brokerage firm analysts who did not endorse Bre-X stock, such as John Ing, president of Toronto-based investment dealer Maison Placements and a noted gold stock picker. Indeed, in December 1996, Felderhof refused to allow Barrick's drilling team to set foot on the Busang property, even though the two companies appeared to be close to a partnership. According to a Barrick official, Felderhof sent a radio message to Balikpapan, instructing his helicopter crew not to provide transport for the Barrick team. He liked to ridicule senior companies like Barrick by calling them "claim jumpers."

"The only jungle they know is the concrete jungle and the closest they get to rocks is scotch on the rocks," he said at one point, speaking with some authority on matters pertaining to drinking. "All I can say is: go find your own."

Felderhof's jealous hold on Busang didn't stop with Barrick. In 1995, David Walsh had hired a geologist he had worked with in the past named Kevin Waddell, with the intention of sending him off to Indonesia. Barry Tannock, a former Bre-X employee who worked closely with David Walsh for several years and has written a brief memoir about the time, said Felderhof refused to use Waddell. "Whether it was actually Felderhof's objection or just conveyed through him, I don't know," said Tannock. "In hindsight, one wonders if it was a case of not wanting a strange camel's nose under the tent." All the while, Felderhof and de Guzman refused to bring in experienced geologists to help Busang reach its next stage of exploration – they preferred to hire recent university graduates with virtually no experience. Yet both men began spending less time at the site.

By 1996, Felderhof was off much of the time enjoying his new wealth in the Cayman Islands, and even when he was in Indonesia, he preferred a suite at the Shangri-La to a bunk at Busang. He was busy with other projects, too. In 1995, when Busang should have had a senior geologist on site at all times, Bre-X's chief geologist teamed up with his old friend Mike Bird, who kept an office on the same floor as Bre-X's main office in downtown Jakarta, to buy into an old tin project on a small Indonesian island called Bilitung.

De Guzman had his own distractions. Besides Busang, he was responsible for three other Bre-X exploration sites in different corners of Indonesia, requiring him to spend much of his time in small aircraft and jungle boats. In de Guzman's absence, a group of young Filipino geologists and mining engineers – Cesar Puspos, Bobby Ramirez, Jerry Alo, and later Rudy Vega – were left to run one of the world's most important exploration camps. None had ever managed anything big before, and all were beholden to de Guzman and Felderhof for their jobs. Even de Guzman had run only a few small exploration camps in Indonesia. The bulk of his experience came from the Benguet Corp. mine, a decent sized operation in the Philippines, but he had been only an order-taker there. This was very different.

Two Solitudes at Busang

The Filipinos have their own culture in the mining world. They are well-educated and often have trained at big U.S.-owned mines in the Philippines. They are fun-loving, attuned to western tastes and sensibilities, yet Asian. "If you tell them what to do, they go out and do it," said an Australian geologist who employs several Filipinos in Indonesia. For much of the 1980s, mining was kind to Filipino geologists. Indonesia was emerging as one of the world's great new mining centres but there was a dearth of indigenous talent in the country. In the neighbouring Philippines, however, there was no shortage of geologists in search of U.S.-dollar salaries and bonuses.

At Busang, the Filipinos mostly stayed to themselves. They lived in the VIP guest-house, with comforts such as air-conditioning, steaks, beer, and satellite TV, rather than in the Indonesian bunk houses, where rice, vegetables, and river fish were the nightly fare. After work, most of the Indonesians played volleyball. The Filipinos used to wait for the game to finish so they could play a half-court game of basketball. Even de Guzman, who'd had a severe limp since his teenage years, liked to join in, relying on his perimeter shots, which he could sink with pinpoint accuracy. While the Filipinos played for half an hour under a spotlight that attracted legions of bugs from the jungle, the Indonesians would retreat to their bunk houses or stroll down the road, past the police check-point, to the makeshift night-clubs.

Although the two cultures – one Catholic, the other Muslim; one gregarious, the other reticent – did not mix, they did not clash either, even though work at Busang reached a feverish pace. By 1995, Busang had four drilling rigs working around the clock, producing eighty boxes of core samples a day. By 1997, with six rigs running, Bre-X had produced 35,000 core samples, weighing more than 600 tonnes. When the drilling program took off in 1995, it was run by only two geologists – one Canadian and one Filipino, Cesar Puspos, both young and relatively inexperienced. Oddly, right through 1996, in a change from normal practices, de Guzman refused to let his Indonesian geologists handle the core samples; he also refused to hire more outsiders.

The young Canadian eventually quit Bre-X, and Busang was put in the hands of an all-Filipino team headed by Puspos, described by some colleagues as a run-of-the-mill geologist who suddenly found himself in daily charge of the world's most celebrated exploration program. Only two years earlier, in 1993, a desperate, unemployed Puspos had written to a former employer asking for any kind of work. Before Busang ran its course, Puspos would gain notoriety for showing off a rock studded with visible gold, which he said he found on the ground at Busang.

Like the other Filipinos, Puspos was so eager for work he accepted most of his compensation in the form of stock options. Had Bre-X turned to gold, each would have been a multimillion-aire. Instead, the Filipinos wound up with nothing. When the Bre-X dream collapsed, Jerry Alo still had 150,000 options. Bobby Ramirez had 75,000. De Guzman died with 250,000 options to his name; he had cashed another 150,000 earlier in the year, bringing him $4 million. They also heard rumblings about Felderhof's rich life after the chief geologist sold $42 million worth of his Bre-X shares in 1996 and bought into the good life in the Cayman Islands.

Understandably, they were not happy when the stock price began a rapid descent in 1997.

Storm Warnings

By early 1997, doubts about Busang were growing, even though Bre-X remained a favourite of brokers in Canada. In fact, many veteran geologists in Jakarta had doubted the find for a long time. Theo van Leeuwen, head of Rio Tinto's Indonesia operation and a pioneer of the big Kelian gold mine not far from Busang, was a sceptic from the start. Barrick's Jakarta staff also had reservations and warned Peter Munk to stay clear of Bre-X. Many Freeport people wanted nothing to do with it, either, until President Suharto persuaded their boss, Jim Bob Moffett, to intervene.

The old Indonesia hands couldn't figure out who the brains was behind Busang. There was Felderhof, to be sure, but he was best known for his past failures. If people knew de Guzman, they knew him for his hard work, not for any geological brilliance. In an earlier job, at another Kalimantan site called Mirah, de Guzman had missed a 90,000-ounce gold deposit. David Walsh, who was hailed as the luckiest man of the century in Canada, was an enigma in Indonesia. He checked into the Shangri-La Hotel seven times between 1995 and February 1997, but spent little time with other mining executives, even though many were eager to learn about Bre-X and could have told him a lot about Indonesia's unique culture.

Felderhof, who did not have much time for financial types except when they were writing cheques, preferred to keep Walsh informed by fax. The fourteen-hour time difference between Jakarta and Calgary did not help communications, either. Felderhof, according to one colleague, "used the KISS method" – Keep It Sweet and Simple. Walsh seemed to prefer leaving Felderhof free to run Indonesian operations his own way, with almost no oversight from head office in Calgary. "I'm no geologist," Walsh once told CBC's "As It Happens" radio show. "We gave our geologists the freedom to develop their theories, and one of Mike de Guzman's theories was the nature of the Busang deposit."

Employees at head office were willing to testify under oath about their ignorance. In a 1996 lawsuit over the ownership of Busang launched by Indonesian businessman Jusuf Merukh, Bre-X vice-president Stephen McAnulty told the lawyers, "Indonesian management was distinct from and operated virtually independently of the Canadian management, whose function was largely the funding of the Indonesian operation."

During his visits to the country, Walsh showed a total lack of regard for Indonesian sensitivities. He went to the mines department only when there were problems – a serious cultural *faux pas* in Indonesia, where courtesy calls are one of the most important aspects of business. Mining officials were even more disturbed that Bre-X did not share information with them. The Indonesian government considers itself a partner in any resource project and expects to be kept informed about developments, big or small.

Back in Canada, however, no one – not least the big brokerage houses touting Bre-X – dared to suggest the whole operation was run by rank amateurs. Moreover, no one in Canada had bothered to do a thorough check of Bre-X's Busang operation. If they had, they would have found some startling information.

Geologists and mining engineers in Indonesia who knew Bre-X operations well questioned Felderhof's refusal to split the core samples. Normally, one portion is kept as a physical record while the other was crushed and assayed. Felderhof's explanation of why he crushed the entire core went back to his unconventional theories that Busang's rich gold was found in nuggets laced haphazardly through the rock. If half the core was left behind, it would be easy to miss a great deal of the gold, he said. Felderhof's stubborn streak made him a man few dared cross. When assay results from the labs began to support his theory, who was going to argue? One investment banker who knew Felderhof described his role at Busang this way to *Maclean's* magazine: "You're talking about God here. You're asking God to bring in outsiders to double-check results."

Felderhof also ran into criticism over his choice of the assay methods he ordered up from the labs, but came out fighting. When Busang rock finally reached the Indo Assay labs, it was crushed into a powder. To be tested for gold, no piece of rock could be longer than six millimetres – the size of a large snowflake. The idea was to free the gold from the surrounding bedrock. Indo Assay soaked the rock powder in a cyanide solution that leached the gold out of the rock, a messy process, but one that recovered all the gold in the rock. However, the assaying process destroyed the samples. When the lab finished its work, there was nothing left of the rock Bre-X had extracted from Busang's hills.

Felderhof could have instructed Indo Assay to use another testing method, fire assays, which many companies use when initially checking samples for gold. It's more expensive but is considered more reliable, and preserves some of the original samples. At the time, some experts questioned Bre-X's reliance on cyanide leaching, but Felderhof dismissed their concerns. "A little knowledge can be more dangerous than none at all on any subject," he said. "I strongly suggest that those individuals commenting on the reliability of the cyanide leach assay method go back to school. I do not have the time to educate them on the various grade determination methods for gold commonly used on a global basis in the mining industry."

Outside experts would have looked on in horror at the transportation of those core samples from Busang to Indo Assay's facility in Balikpapan, the big oil town on the Kalimantan coast. Cores were labelled in the field, then carried back to the base camp by truck and stacked in one-metre sections on wooden racks. De Guzman supervised the building of a prep lab at the base camp that crushed the cores into more manageable chunks that ranged from dust to bits the size of a child's fist. The crushed rock went into plastic bags, then two bags each weighing seven kilograms went into a tough fibreglass sack. The fourteen-kilogram sacks began the journey to the lab with a thirty-hour ride on a barge, then floated 210 kilometres down the Kelinjau and Mahakam Rivers to Samarinda.

In the early days of the Busang drilling program, in late 1993 and early 1994, the samples had moved quickly by truck from Samarinda to Balikpapan, a two-hour drive away. But as Bre-X drilled more samples in an effort to expand the size of the deposit, the piles of rock samples grew and grew. Indo Assay could not handle the flow. Overwhelmed, Bre-X stored the samples at its Loa Duri warehouse on the Mahakam River and in an open courtyard in its Samarinda office. Bre-X did not tell investors about the Loa Duri warehouse, and visitors to the Samarinda office frequently were chased away by private security guards. Although a flower garden spelling the name Bre-X seemed friendly, the sign was barely visible behind the large guardhouse and wall, topped with barbed wire.

If a visitor had gained access to the Samarinda office, he or she would have seen a disorganized mess. The office was located in a small house on the northern outskirts of the town, next to a neatly manicured university campus known for its indoor boxing stadium. The office, the size of a large suburban home, provided administrative support, a radio room with constant contact to Busang, and guest quarters for Indonesian and Filipino staff in transit. Felderhof and other senior Bre-X staff preferred to stay in a comfortable hotel downtown or drive two hours to Balikpapan, where they could stay in the Dusit Hotel's beach-side resort and frequent a better grade of karaoke bar. But the locals did not mind the Samarinda quarters. For entertainment, there was a half-court for basketball, and in the back office, there was a pool table.

With so much activity and so many people flowing through Samarinda, the only place for the Busang core samples – the most important rocks in the mining world – was an open courtyard separating the radio room and guest quarters. At any time of day or night, Bre-X employees wandering into the office could gain access to sacks of core samples that contained the clues to Busang's true worth. Guests sleeping at the office could open the bags at night as frequently as they wished – there was no special guard, and there appeared to be no marking system. Only when the order came from Busang, from de Guzman or Puspos, would the bags be loaded on to a truck and shipped to the Balikpapan lab.

Bre-X's allure, however, was fading quickly by the last few months of 1996. The more closely the mining world looked at Busang and Bre-X, the more problems it saw. One of the strongest warnings came early in 1997, although some of the world's biggest mining companies were too consumed by their battle for Busang to realize what was going on. On January 23, 1997, long after the great struggle for Busang had begun, a mysterious fire on site destroyed the camp's administrative building, which housed a small computer system and many of Bre-X's most important geological records – records that could have detailed who knew what, and when, about the drilling results. Jerry Alo, the site manager, blamed the fire on the camp's hasty construction. He said the fire started when a computer short-circuited in the office – an odd explanation, since the fire began at about 5 a.m. Busang did not even have a fire truck, and the fire was put out quickly only because local employees happened to be up before dawn to eat an early breakfast in observance of daylight fasting during the Muslim holy month of Ramadan.

It would take another two months for most observers to question the Bre-X miracle, but dispelling a myth would not be easy. The investment world had bought into the Bre-X dream. No one had questioned the pasts of Felderhof, Walsh, and de Guzman. No one had seriously doubted the Busang operation. Now, the mysterious fire began to change that view. It began to show that something was critically wrong in the jungle.

CHAPTER TWELVE

Death of a Ladies' Man

"He had all these wives but I bet none of them loved him. I don't think Mike was a happy man. I don't think he had a real friend in the world." – A geologist who worked with Michael de Guzman

The End of a Career

Ever since he was a teenager, Mike de Guzman had not been able to walk properly. He hobbled up hills and, on downhill jungle trails, allowed others to walk in front of him. He never relied on a cane; he was too proud for that. He did not even like to tell people about his bad left knee, let alone what caused it. De Guzman's hobble was the result of a horrific high school experience. Quite short but possessing a smooth basketball shot and all the right quick moves, young Mike had been a high school star in Manila in the early 1970s and was almost assured of a spot on the Philippines national team. Then, one night, a gang of ruffians mugged him and smashed his knee to a pulp with sticks. Michael de Guzman would never play serious basketball again.

The young Filipino was crushed. In a nation that adores things American – the Philippines once was a U.S. colony – basketball was meant to earn de Guzman fame, if not fortune, and lots of female adoration, which he loved. He had to switch his sights, and, being a bright student, he opted for a geology degree at Manila's Adamson University; at least a mining job would get him far away from sweltering Manila. De Guzman was a frustrated man when he left Adamson and the local mining community. His radical theories on how gold ended up collecting along fault lines was never accepted by contemporaries in Manila.

Physical pain came to define de Guzman's life, and his death. In the aftermath of his fall from the chopper, many who thought they knew him were surprised to learn the full extent of his health problems. He endured no fewer than fourteen bouts of malaria, a run of typhoid fever, and an excruciating ordeal with hepatitis B, which seizes the liver and pounds through it like a drill hammer through bedrock. One of his wives said he sometimes lay awake at night crying in pain. Thirty-six hours before his death on March 19, 1997, de Guzman uncharacteristically confided to a dinner partner in Jakarta that he could endure the pain no longer. Not only had a visit to Singapore's Mount Elizabeth Hospital the previous day confirmed he had hepatitis B, but a doctor had also advised the philandering de Guzman to avoid direct sexual contact with others, whom he would put at risk. This was sobering advice to a man married to four different women – sometimes mistaken for mistresses – in two countries; two of them bore him children. How, de Guzman asked his dinner partner, would he explain all this to the women he already had cheated so badly?

A consummate liar, de Guzman could perhaps have found a way out of this mess, but by mid-March there were many other problems in his life that he could not escape. At forty-one, he was bone-tired, having run four exploration camps across Indonesia for the past two years. He had been on the road almost interminably, flying, boating, and painfully hiking to the far corners of Indonesia's out-lying islands. His four wives were each secret from the others, and his polygamy was unknown to his six young children back in his home town of Manila. He had made a mockery of his Catholic upbringing by marrying in Protestant and Muslim ceremonies in the past two years. Moreover, his first wife in Manila was growing deeply suspicious. She had been left behind to raise their six chil-dren when he moved to Indonesia in 1987 for a $2,200 (U.S.) a month job; now the media were reporting that her husband was worth at least $8 million (U.S.), thanks to Bre-X's success. So where was all the money?

That could be explained away, but even de Guzman's fertile, romantic mind could not mask the news emerging from the Busang exploration camp. While de Guzman was in Toronto in early March with the rest of the Bre-X team, being fêted at the annual Prospectors and Developers Association of Canada convention, a team of geol-ogists at Busang had found something very wrong indeed. Experts from Freeport McMoRan Copper & Gold had drilled seven test holes next to holes bored by de Guzman's team. The Bre-X holes had pointed to a huge deposit. Freeport found nothing.

With his health deteriorating and his personal life falling apart, de Guzman received a telephone call from Freeport's exploration chief, David Potter, who had set up camp at Busang. Potter told de Guzman to get back to Busang as soon as possible. He had some very serious questions to answer.

During the previous week in Toronto, de Guzman had been the talk of the mining world. Using slides and jokes, he roused and excited one of the mining world's most sophisticated crowds. He regaled them with tales of how he once hiked thirty kilometres along a jungle path to Busang. He told them how he lived off the land, and he lured them with outrageous hyperbole. Busang, he suggested to the unquestioning audience, could have more than 100 million ounces of gold. Two hundred million, maybe.

But as he had packed his bags in Toronto and prepared to return to Busang, de Guzman, physically ailing and emotionally troubled, must have realized his career was over. Even if he could prove he was not part of a salting operation, he would be the laughing stock of the mining world. Overnight, his name would turn from gold to mud. His career was over; Busang might even jeopardize his life, so humiliating would the revelation be to Indonesia's all-powerful president, Suharto, who had a large personal stake in Busang, along with Bob Hasan, through their holding company Nusamba. "He was devastated," one of de Guzman's closest friends said later. "There was nothing left for him." The newspapers that had treated him like a hero – perhaps even a legend – would soon ridicule his name. Thoughts of disgrace no doubt swirled through his mind, but de Guzman, typically, kept his feelings to himself. "He had all these wives but I bet none of them loved him," said one geologist who knew him well. "I don't think Mike was a happy man. I don't think he had a real friend in the world."

The Last Flight of Michael de Guzman

De Guzman's final journey started in Toronto at the Royal York Hotel, where he sent Lilas, one of his four wives, a birthday card to express his enduring love. To most of the people travelling with him, he seemed in good spirits – in fact, he seemed that way right up to the end. On the gruelling Cathay Pacific flight to the Far East, he cracked jokes and drank with his Filipino buddies, who also were returning from the Toronto convention, and were unaware that things were quickly falling apart at Busang. At a refuelling stop in Anchorage, de Guzman got off the plane to stretch his legs and buy a shirt at a duty-free shop. In Hong Kong, he made a phone call and then changed planes to fly to Singapore for his medical check-up at Mount Elizabeth Hospital. The check-up, which was to monitor his malaria, was not unusual. Almost any expatriate in Indonesia who fell seriously ill flew to Singapore for medical treatment, and Mount Elizabeth is the city-state's best hospital.

Stopping by for this final check-up, de Guzman was not an everyday malaria patient. In 1994, his fevers had been so severe he was taken by boat from a mining camp in Aceh, at the northern end of Sumatra, to be hospitalized in Jakarta for a month. When the Jakarta hospital put him next to the hepatitis ward, his friends knew something was wrong. Over the next two years, de Guzman's liver swelled like a balloon and became excruciatingly painful. His colleagues were astonished at how much weight he put on. He looked nothing like his 1989 passport photo, which showed a slim and fit black-haired man, weighing seventy kilograms. By 1996, he was overweight and tired, carrying ninety kilograms, with plump cheeks and a rolling chin. In January 1997, he had been hospitalized again for a week with flu and high fever.

"He told me he had problems with malaria but he said he could handle it," said Beawiharta, an Indonesian magazine photographer who had travelled with de Guzman to Busang on March 1 for four days, in what would be the Filipino geologist's last trip to the camp that made, and then destroyed, his name.

Two weeks later, as de Guzman slowly made his way from Singapore back to Busang, he kept to himself. During his one night in Jakarta, he stayed in Bre-X's guest-house, with its pool table, satellite television, and staff cook, located on the southern fringe of Jakarta's urban sprawl. The large house is built on a private street, a few minutes' drive from the Cilandak Commercial Estate, where most of Indonesia's mining companies have their headquarters. Bre-X employees preferred the privacy of hanging around the compound, and few, if any, ever visited the Cilandak bar, which was the industry's most frequented watering hole. And Bre-X people were never seen at the industry's monthly pub night arranged by Barrick's Indonesian office, a get-together hosted by the Society of St. Barbara, the patron saint of miners and firemen and held on the last Friday of every month at the Smuggler's Arms. In time the company's secrecy – and the near reclusiveness of its employees, at least in Jakarta circles – became legendary.

On his final trip to Jakarta, de Guzman did not want to see anyone other than his closest friends. The next day, March 18, tired and ill, he boarded another airplane to take him one step closer to the grim realities that awaited him in Busang. It was a trip he had taken dozens of times – a two-hour afternoon flight from Jakarta to Balikpapan, the oil town and commercial centre on the east coast of Borneo. From Balikpapan, it would be another two hours by car to the provincial capital Samarinda, where Bre-X kept a small office in a converted bungalow on the outskirts of town. One of his four wives lived in Samarinda so he could stay with her, and he could catch a morning helicopter from there to Busang.

While he waited in Jakarta for a plane of Garuda Airlines, the national carrier, de Guzman made his usual arrangements. He telephoned the Samarinda office and asked the staff to send a car to meet him in Balikpapan that evening. He also asked Rudy Vega, a Filipino metallurgist who worked in the Samarinda office and who had joined Bre-X only ten months earlier, to come to Balikpapan. De Guzman told Vega they needed to talk about a few things in the car from the airport to Samarinda.

The sun had just set over the Borneo jungle when de Guzman's plane touched down on Balikpapan's big new airstrip next to the beach. Twenty years ago, Balikpapan was a dirt-strewn outpost but two decades of oil, timber, coal, and mining wealth had transformed it into a boom town. The seaside town enjoys direct air connections to Singapore and a big luxury hotel run by Thailand's Dusit chain. (The Dusit enjoyed so much Bre-X business that its airport transfer staff actually wept when they heard the news of de Guzman's death; he was one of their best customers and most generous tippers.)

That evening, as electrical storms filled the equatorial sky over Balikpapan, de Guzman whisked through the modern airport terminal. He greeted the Dusit's liaison officer but said he would not need a room that night. He planned to head straight to Samarinda.

Once through the sliding doors, however, de Guzman's plans changed abruptly. He met Rudy Vega and the Bre-X driver, and told them he wanted to have dinner in Balikpapan. As they entered town, motoring up a lazy hill, he announced to Vega that he wanted to stay overnight in Balikpapan, and Vega should stay, too. Vega did not have a change of clothes or toothbrush, but de Guzman said not to worry; he would buy him and the driver whatever they needed.

"Whatever you say, boss," Vega said. He always called de Guzman "boss." Vega, a nervous middle-aged newcomer to Bre-X, figured everyone did the same. Among the Filipino and Indonesian staff at Busang, the big tubby geologist was almost a cult figure. He had given these people their jobs and created a fever of excitement around the camp. Nevertheless, de Guzman was extremely hard on his staff. He rarely said thank you, and at events like the Toronto convention, he made sure the limelight focused on him, not the team.

On this night, however, the famed geologist seemed to be in high spirits. He laughed and joked as the Bre-X pick-up truck made its way up the hill from the seaside airport and into the bright lights of Balikpapan. He then suggested they check into a cheap small hotel rather than the $100-a-night (U.S.) Dusit and enjoy an evening on the town. Perhaps dinner and karaoke. Many Filipinos love to sing, and de Guzman was no exception. He kept a karaoke singing machine at his wife Lilas's house in Samarinda and often belted out mushy American tunes for her.

De Guzman asked the driver to stop at a store before they got to the hotel so he could buy some clothes. Why, Vega asked later, would a man on the verge of committing suicide buy new clothes? He didn't know what to make of his boss's mood. At the hotel, de Guzman showered and changed, chose a small, middle-class Indonesian chain restaurant for dinner, and then picked a little karaoke bar for drinks afterwards. There was no mention of the business problems de Guzman had said on the telephone he wanted to discuss urgently. Vega knew there were concerns about a backlog in Bre-X's ore samples. Piles of bags were mounting at the Samarinda office, and they needed to find ways to speed up the process of getting them crushed and assayed to determine their gold value.

At dinner, Vega kept waiting for de Guzman to raise his concerns, but his boss's mind seemed to be elsewhere. Throughout the meal, de Guzman spoke to Vega in Indonesian, even though Vega spoke only a few words of Bahasa Indonesian, the national language, and although the Filipinos normally spoke to one another in English. "Boss, I can't understand you," Vega kept saying. De Guzman would revert to English but soon slip back to Indonesian.

By the time they reached the karaoke bar, Vega knew his boss had no interest in talking business, in any language. They ordered the local beer, Bintang, and de Guzman hobbled up to the stage to sing a few of his favourites: Frank Sinatra's "My Way," the Bee-Gees' "Words," an Indonesian pop song. The two did not return to their hotel until after midnight, when de Guzman announced they should catch the regular early morning helicopter to Busang via Samarinda. Vega could get off the helicopter in Samarinda when it stopped for fuel and supplies from the Bre-X office there.

In the morning, they reached the Balikpapan airport half an hour late, but the helicopter charter company had waited for them anyway. Bre-X was one of Indonesia Air Transport's best clients; the Calgary company paid $35,000 (U.S.) a month to charter the Alouette III helicopter, plus $400 (U.S.) an hour of flying time. IAT, a private company, kept half a dozen or so helicopters at Balikpapan airport for oil and mining companies and often hired Indonesian air force officers to pilot them on their days off. One of the moonlighters was Edi Tursono, a lieutenant based in Jakarta who, like many men in the Indonesian military, could not make ends meet on his salary. During his occasional leaves, Tursono would catch a flight to Balikpapan and pick up some work from IAT. Although

Tursono was new to the Busang route, neither de Guzman nor Vega showed concern. They climbed in the back seat and quickly fell asleep, still a bit hung over from the karaoke bar. When the helicopter touched down twenty minutes later at Samarinda's tiny airport, in the middle of a residential neighbourhood, de Guzman got out to stretch his legs and say goodbye to Vega. They never did discuss the assay problems that de Guzman had raised the previous day from Jakarta.

More strangely, de Guzman made no effort to contact Lilas, his fourth wife, who lived only five minutes by car from the Samarinda airport. He could have called her during the ten-minute stopover or asked her earlier to meet him there. They had not seen each other in two weeks, after all. De Guzman, however, made no mention of the Samarinda stopover when he called Lilas that morning from his Balikpapan hotel. He only mentioned their first wedding anniversary, which coincided with her March 22 birthday, and suggested she make dinner reservations for them. He would be back from Busang by then, he told her.

When de Guzman said farewell to Vega, he showed no emotion, no hint of what was to come, even though back in the helicopter, in his three bags, there were packed a suicide note, a notarized will, and instructions to Rudy Vega to deliver his gold Rolex watch to wife No. 2, in Bogor near Jakarta. Dressed in dark jeans and an orange Bali shirt, with strings dangling from its short sleeves, de Guzman walked back to the waiting helicopter and climbed into the back seat. Normally, a passenger would choose the front seat, which gives a stunning view of the jungle and rivers below. Instead, he sat next to the back left door, piled his bags between him and the mechanic in the front seat, and put on a headset to muffle the noise.

Seventeen minutes later, around 11:00 while the Alouette III was cruising at 150 kilometres an hour, the left door of the craft slid open and de Guzman plunged 240 metres into the thick forest below. Edi Tursono, the pilot, and Adrian Milan, the flight mechanic, reported that they felt a gust of wind from the back seat and turned around to see their only passenger gone, the headset ripped from its socket. They frantically circled back around the forest but saw nothing. When it became clear that they were wasting their time searching over the solid pattern of green below, Tursono noted the co-ordinates and returned to Samarinda. The IAT staff and local police knew the case promised big trouble because of Suharto's interest in Busang.

A Body in the Jungle

The spot where Mike de Guzman fell to his death is a thick swatch of new forest planted a couple of decades ago to cover hillsides that Indonesia's coal industry had left barren. A set of rolling hills blocks the forest from the river, but there was enough timber and coal business in the district for the government to have paved a one-lane road through the forest. Even that road, however, could not help police and de Guzman's colleagues find his body. For four days, two rescue teams combed the jungle in 37-degree equatorial heat looking for the body, which lay only about 500 metres from the road. In the end, two of Bre-X's Indonesian workers tracked down de Guzman's remains by following the horrible stench emanating from a swamp. They radioed for help to a helicopter circling overhead but the forest cover was so thick that the pilot and Jerry Alo, Bre-X's camp manager who led the search operation, could not see them. One of the Indonesians had to climb thirty metres to a treetop to tie a red jerry can to signal the helicopter pilot and Alo.

When the helicopter removed de Guzman's body from the jungle, his corpse was so badly disfigured and decayed that even his closest friends could recognize only parts of it. The geologist's buttocks had been eaten by wild boar and much of the rest of his body was infested by maggots. His arms and legs were broken in several places, his nose was pushed in through his head, and most of the rest of his face had decayed. His hair had fallen out. The sight was so gruesome the Philippines authorities decided not to let the de Guzman family see his remains. Alo, who accompanied the body to a morgue, identified it by de Guzman's pronounced chin. De Guzman's body was then flown to Jakarta for an autopsy and a small memorial service, and on to Manila, where a second autopsy confirmed the identity.

After the Death

When the news of de Guzman's death reached Busang, the Indonesian staff wept openly. A few weeks later, one young Indonesian geologist said he could not sleep at night because of all the nightmares he had about his former boss, the man he called his "teacher." De Guzman had been good to the local staff. He knew what it was like to be a local hire for a big project, having spent all those years at a Philippines mine working for American bosses. But away from the Indonesian canteen, de Guzman was seen very differently. At the memorial service in Jakarta, only thirty or so people showed up – not much for a man credited with the biggest mining discovery in Indonesian history. Only one of his four wives, Theresa, from Manila, attended. There was a stoic John Felderhof, of course, and his gregarious wife Ingrid, who was dressed in a black miniskirt, top, and hat and seemed to weep every time the Indonesian television cameras turned her way. No one from the mines department was there, and many of Bre-X's office staff stayed away as well.

Those familiar with Bre-X knew why. De Guzman, courteous to strangers and as fun-loving as any Filipino, was a ruthless boss. He once sent a fax to an employee stating he would be fired if he made one more mistake. He forced other employees to sign undated resignation letters. And he demanded that everyone work around the clock, seven days a week, when he was in camp. Some of the Indonesian workers had not seen their families in a year, but when they asked de Guzman for leave, he responded, "I don't take vacations, why should you?"

"We were completely royally understaffed," said one geologist who quit Busang in 1995. "I was getting four hours of sleep a night. One reason I left was I would have died of exhaustion."

Cold-hearted to some, de Guzman also was insatiably romantic. His polygamy was not uncommon; many geologists, working in lonely, remote postings, have what they call "project wives," local women with whom they live while on site and then usually abandon. De Guzman was different. Sentimental to the core, he agreed to marry each woman in an elaborate ceremony and then kept it secret from the others. His first marriage, in Manila, was in the Catholic church and produced six children. He then married another woman in Bogor, a tranquil hillside academic town near Jakarta, where he found some work in the early 1990s. In 1995, he told a young woman, Susani Mawengkang, working in Bre-X's office in Manado, a town on the northern tip of Sulawesi island, that he would convert to Islam for her if she married him. She agreed, and they had a baby the following year.

In March 1996, he married another young woman working in Bre-X's office in Samarinda, this time in a Protestant church. He wore a brown suit and white gloves; his bride, Lilas, wore a full white wedding gown. Their reception, at a local restaurant, attracted close to 300 guests, none of them de Guzman's friends. "He said his family and friends were difficult to contact," Lilas said after his death. It was only then, through the media, that she learned of the other wives, a revelation she met with a shrug. Lilas, young and naïve when she met de Guzman in 1995, came from a middle-class family in Samarinda with enough money to get her a standard education and a clerical job in the Bre-X office. She is tall and bone-thin and possesses the deep, dark eyes de Guzman preferred. He promised her the moon, flying her to the Busang camp and three times to Singapore on shopping sprees. He bought her ceramic Mickey and Minnie Mouses, brought her father airplane liquor bottles, and gave the family cash on every visit. He sang sappy love songs to her on a karaoke machine and wrote her letters that sounded like puppy love. For a young woman who had always lived with her parents and had never been out of Kalimantan, his marriage proposal seemed too good to be true. De Guzman told Lilas he planned to stay in Samarinda "forever."

De Guzman's Byzantine personal life had consumed much of his dwindling energy. At Christmas 1996, when he should have been back in Manila with his six children, he attended a party in Jakarta with his Bogor wife, said goodbye, and flew to Manila with Lilas. They spent a few days at the downtown Shangri-La Hotel, shopped and dined, and avoided his extended family. De Guzman explained to Lilas that his Manila marriage had fallen apart. He said he was separated (divorce is not allowed in the predominantly Catholic Philippines) and his ex-wife and children had moved to the United States. In fact, Tess, as de Guzman often called his first wife Teresa, was not in the United States. She was across town in Manila and growing impatient with her supposedly wealthy husband who had left her alone to raise five girls and a boy.

In ten pages of suicide notes – one to Tess, the other to friends – de Guzman wrote in his large circular handwriting about his illnesses, but he made no effort to explain his affairs to his wives, nor did he beg for forgiveness. In one of his two suicide notes, de Guzman referred to the "shame" of hepatitis and said he did not want to give it to "loved ones." He already had bought a white villa and sporty Suzuki jeep for Lilas. He left a gold Rolex and gemstone ring to his Bogor wife. He left nothing for the Minado wife and baby son, whom he had not seen in seven months.

There could be no doubt a storm had been brewing in de Guzman's soul, however. When he had reached Toronto in early March for the mining convention, he sent a packet to Lilas. It contained a free hotel postcard, and cards for her twenty-second birthday and their first wedding anniversary, which would coincide on

CHAPTER THIRTEEN

What Freeport Found

"Once we drilled our initial holes, we had information that was dynamite. We had a good idea where this bastard was headed." – James R. "Jim Bob" Moffett, chief executive officer, Freeport-McMoRan Copper & Gold Inc.

"I told my wife she might want to take careful notes. I knew this one phone call was going to cost the company billions." – Graham Farquharson, president, Strathcona Mineral Services Ltd.

"There appears to be a strong possibility that the potential gold reserves on the Busang project have been overstated." – David Walsh, chief executive officer, Bre-X Minerals Ltd.

A Rumour on the Internet

In a different era, it would have taken several days or even weeks for rumours of Bre-X's problems in the Indonesian jungle to reach North American markets. In an age of electronic commerce and the Internet, it took minutes.

It was early Wednesday, March 19 in North America when the news broke that Michael de Guzman had taken a 240-metre plunge from an Alouette helicopter, near Busang. Two days later, on Friday, March 21, an obscure Indonesian business newspaper called *Harian Ekonomi Neraca* published a story that recounted an incredible rumour. The paper revealed that Freeport had drilled seven holes and had not turned up any gold. According to an unnamed source at one of Bre-X's local partners, PT Askatindo Karya Mineral, "It is possible that the deposit is not as big as mentioned before. It could be that it is not viable to mine the deposit."

Harian Ekonomi Neraca filed its stories electronically to news services, which made them available to an Internet audience. That audience spread the story like wildfire. "Copyright – sloppy right: Here's the article. It's too important for people not to know about it," wrote Internet contributor "Gerald Lampton." He proceeded to post the entire Indonesian story on a Bre-X chat page. At the end of the ten-paragraph article, Lampton added, "I signed up for this service specifically so I could read this article. I don't know how reliable the source is, because the article won't identify it, which is why I am doing nothing until I hear further developments from Bre-X and/or Freeport."

The Internet was the medium of choice for moving the news and the stock, and lots of people were happy to break copyright laws by taking a look. Many of them showed no reluctance to act on what they read. On a normally busy day, a million Bre-X shares had been changing hands. On Friday, Bre-X stock fell rapidly, dropping $2.25 to $15.20 a share in an extremely heavy volume of 9 million shares. In that session, investors trimmed $880 million off the company's market value. As usual in these cases, the Toronto Stock Exchange halted trading briefly to give Bre-X officials a chance to comment.

Experts, as well as Bre-X, dismissed the rumour. Until the following Wednesday, many mining analysts continued to praise the company. Lévesque Beaubien Geoffrion's Michael Fowler reiterated his buy recommendation on the stock, writing about the technical competence of Bre-X's geological team and the due diligence done by Kilborn and Barrick Gold. He also wrote from the heart. "The death of Mike de Guzman is a huge tragedy," said Fowler in a report that Bre-X promptly posted on the Internet. "He was a very skilled geologist and a very nice person. He will be missed, but now that Freeport is becoming the operator, we do not see any material effect on the stock price from his shocking event." Fowler concluded, "The bottom line is that we believe that given all the engineers and testing that has been done at Busang we would be surprised if there would be any huge discrepancy to what has been stated."

Once again, Nesbitt Burns' Egizio Bianchini was even more definitive. "We are of the view that if indeed an assay discrepancy exists it will be resolved within a short period of time," he told clients. Repeating a phrase that became his mantra, Bianchini said, "The gold is there! Therefore we continue to recommend the purchase of Bre-X shares. Our target is $29 a share." That was almost twice the price of Bre-X at the time.

Long-time shareholders also kept the faith. Roughly 100 residents of St. Paul, Alberta, population 5,000, had bought into Bre-X early in its rise, acting on the advice of John Kutyn, a loans officer at the local credit union and an amateur gold bug. "De Guzman was a pretty big person in the organization to take out and maybe people think that will affect the company, but that's not the case at all," said Ollie Drouin, a Bre-X shareholder and part-owner of the local newspaper, the *St. Paul Journal*. "As for the newspaper story from Jakarta, that was just a bunch of bull," Drouin told the *Calgary Sun*. "It really ticks us off. It was written without any facts or substantiation at all. It was typical irresponsible journalism."

Fellow junior mining executives in Indonesia also lent their support. "Bre-X is being sabotaged, having stories made up about them by people with political motivations," said Anwari Arowo, who ran the Indonesian operations of Borneo Gold Corp. "The Bre-X find is very legitimate and it can be mined without any problems."

From its head office in New Orleans, Freeport issued a qualified denial. Chief financial officer Richard Adkerson told reporters Freeport had not commented on its drilling at Busang and that the article was "wrong" and the result of "miscommunication."

Bre-X fought to put out the fires started by the rumour. Walsh fired off a press release on March 21 stating that Freeport was still hard at work and hadn't announced any drilling results. He threatened to sue the mudslingers who were making "unsubstantiated claims" about his company and made vague references to "smear campaigns" against Bre-X. "It's obvious that there were very heavy and strong forces trying to discredit us," he said. "I won't name names, I won't play that game." Walsh even took time to joke that his detractors would one day complain about the colour of the gold that he was going to turn out at Busang. Felderhof chipped in from Jakarta, "I'm 110 per cent confident the gold is there."

Walsh and Felderhof were bluffing. Both had known for several days that Freeport had found almost no gold. In March, while the Bre-X executives were in Toronto, Freeport had confronted Bre-X with the fact that its assays yielded "insignificant gold values."

On March 19, after learning that de Guzman was dead, Walsh had his executive vice-president Rollie Francisco hire a top Toronto-based mining consulting firm, Strathcona Mineral Services Ltd., to investigate the discrepancy. On March 26, the rest of the world officially learned what Freeport found.

Freeport's "Remarkable Investigative Work"

The first outsiders with unrestricted access to Busang were Freeport McMoRan's vice-president of exploration, David Potter, and his team of professional geologists. Potter's boss, Jim Bob Moffett, had struck a deal with Walsh and Bob Hasan on Monday February 17. Within days, Potter left Jakarta for Busang on what he thought would be a routine job. He expected quickly to verify Bre-X's results, then move on to the more difficult task of designing a mine. Potter was well qualified for the job; he had run Freeport's extensive Indonesian operations for years, and his credits included bringing the huge Grasberg open-pit mine on the island of Irian Jaya into production.

Potter set his crews to work on seven drill sites in the southeast zone. First he picked four holes where Bre-X had found rich concentrations of gold and "twinned" or duplicated the company's work with his own rigs. In each case, Freeport was drilling within two metres of where Bre-X had sunk holes and was going down 250 metres. That was only half as deep as Bre-X had gone in its tests, but was more than enough to prove the gold was there. Then Potter sank two "scissors holes," so called because they cut on an angle across four Bre-X holes. Finally, the Freeport team drilled between two lines that Bre-X had worked in order to check the continuity of the deposit. When Potter finished, he had collected 1,757 metres of rock core, broken it into two-metre sections, and packed it into wooden boxes, ready for the trip to the assay lab.

Then Potter turned to the Bre-X geologists at the Busang base camp for help. They gave Freeport four samples of core, each two metres long, that Bre-X had pulled from the ground. Several weeks before his death, de Guzman had predicted these cores would likely contain gold. These samples were sitting in open crates at Busang, waiting to be crushed, bagged, and sent off to the Indo Assay laboratory.

The last samples Potter tested came from bags that Bre-X had stored at its office in Samarinda, on the coast of Kalimantan. These crushed rocks were leftovers, stored in ten-kilogram plastic sacks after Bre-X's geologists had extracted the 1.25 kilograms of material needed for Indo Assay's tests. Potter helped himself to a total of 497 samples, which he selected at random from the bags casually stacked up in the yard and the back room of the office.

Freeport sent all these samples to four different labs. One was Indo Assay in Balikpapan, which Bre-X had used. Two more labs were in Jakarta and the final centre, Crescent Technology Inc., was in New Orleans. The results came back quickly – and they were devastating. Freeport's labs found only trace amounts of gold.

Worse news came when Freeport's lab workers started to examine the metal. Using a scanning electron microscope on the new samples drilled by Freeport, the Crescent Technology lab found gold grains that were extremely small and angular in shape. They measured 34 to 85 microns in length, or less than the thickness of a human hair. The tiny grains were what one would expect from the hills of Busang. Then Crescent looked at the test results from the rocks culled from Bre-X's reject bags in Samarinda. Here, they found much more gold. But the grains were far larger, ranging anywhere from 100 to 2,000 microns. Crescent described what it found as "coarse grains, rounded, abraded and pitted." When slipped under the microscope, they were found to be a gold-silver mix, with a gold-rich rim around each edge. The geologists had seen this type of grain many times before. It is typical of alluvial gold, or gold that is found in rivers and streams. When he saw these results, Potter knew that the grains didn't come from Busang but had to have been introduced into the Bre-X samples. He knew he was looking at tampering. But securities laws and agreements with Bre-X would prevent him from releasing details of his findings for another four weeks.

In a review of Freeport's work at Busang several weeks later, mining consultant Graham Farquharson, the president of Strathcona, wrote: "The due diligence program carried out by Freeport has been very thorough and of a highly professional standard in all respects." Farquharson went on to praise the Freeport geologists for "remarkable investigative work."

Potter called his boss in New Orleans with the news in the second week of March. Later, Moffett talked to *Fortune* magazine about that period in mid-March when the information wasn't yet public. "I didn't talk to anyone, because once we had drilled our initial holes, we had information that was dynamite," he said. "We had a good idea where this bastard was headed. We were doing due diligence and we had to get the Bre-X people to come and see the data. We couldn't get anyone to show up!"

At the time, the Bre-X brains trust was enjoying the limelight at the Prospectors and Developers Association convention in Toronto, where Felderhof was honoured as prospector of the year. "They send de Guzman, and the poor sumbitch disappears – whatever happened to him. I was so pissed off I could eat dirt," Moffett said. "I'd had it with these guys."

Enter Strathcona

Graham Farquharson practically grew up underground. His father was a mining engineer in Timmins and he took his son down into the mines when the boy was only a few years old. By age nineteen, Farquharson was working in a gold mine; at twenty-four, he had a mining engineering degree from the University of Alberta. Five years later, in 1969, he added an MBA from Queen's University in Kingston, Ontario. Over the next three decades, he worked as a consultant for mines around the globe, including pioneering work on mines in the high Arctic.

The first thing you see when you walk into Strathcona's office is a huge framed cartoon that pokes fun at mining promoters who mislead little old ladies into investing in properties that don't contain any gold. Farquharson hung the cartoon more than a decade ago. In the wake of Bre-X, it's a striking bit of irony.

Strathcona's offices are located close to the heart of Toronto's financial district; the elegantly restored nineteenth-century headquarters of media baron Conrad Black's Hollinger Inc. is right next door. Farquharson dryly observes, "We look down on Conrad all day," knowing the appeal of the thought of this slight, soft-spoken mining engineer, with his sensible short-sleeved white shirt and tartan tie, looking down on a captain of industry. Farquharson's corner office is decorated with a stone-carved little miner smoking a pipe and a collection of tasteful Inuit art: narwhals carved from soapstone adorn the president's coffee table and a soft water-colour of the Nanisivik zinc mine on northern Baffin Island faces his desk. The print is signed by everyone who worked at the first mine built in the high Arctic, which Strathcona developed and ran for more than twenty years.

Somewhere along the line, a junior mining executive pinned the nickname "Dr. Death" on Farquharson because the consultant's prudent approach had nixed a proposed mine. It's not a nickname that this modest executive enjoys or that really suits him, but in one respect, it fits. Farquharson and his partners are quick death to sloppy methods in mining.

Like many specialized professions, the upper ranks of mining executives in Canada make a relatively small club, in which everyone important knows everyone else. So it was no surprise for Farquharson to get a call at 3:30 on Wednesday, March 19 from Bryan Coates, Bre-X's corporate controller. Farquharson is on the board of directors of Cambior Inc., a Montreal-based gold mining company, and Coates had been its CFO until Bre-X had lured him away a few months earlier, as the company expanded.

Coates's request was something of a surprise. The Bre-X executive phoned from the Toronto office of Bre-X's law firm, Bennett Jones Verchere. "Bryan asked if I could come over and see them, soon," Farquharson said. Curious, he grabbed a blazer and headed out the door. A few minutes later he was in First Canadian Place, sitting with Coates in the law firm's main meeting room, along with two lawyers, John Sabine and Mike Melanson, and Rollie Francisco, Bre-X's executive vice-president and chief financial officer. Francisco, who had done the bulk of the negotiating for Bre-X during the ownership battle for Busang, was also a familiar face. He had been the CFO at Lac Minerals, which fought a bitter battle for the rich Page-Williams gold mine in northern Ontario during the 1980s. While the lawyers argued, Farquharson had spent more than three years as the neutral outsider who headed a committee that was asked to run the mine. In the end, Lac lost Page-Williams. The fact the two men were still on good terms was a testimony to Farquharson's even-handedness.

Francisco took control of the meeting. Results from Freeport McMoRan's initial Busang tests had just come in. An angry Jim Bob Moffett had shouted the news over the long-distance lines and his geologists had also given their prospective partners at Bre-X an earful. In four holes, each drilled just 1.5 metres from holes where Bre-X struck it rich, Freeport had come up empty. No gold. Oh, yes, and geologist Michael de Guzman was dead in what looked like a suicide. Was Strathcona free to figure out what was going on?

Farquharson was intrigued. Mining was a passion as well as a profession, and Bre-X was apparently on the verge of developing the biggest gold mine on earth. It would be an incredible project to work on. Farquharson had followed Bre-X from a distance, keeping up with the company through the newspapers. He knew it claimed to have found an elephant deposit in Borneo and had greeted the recent mind-boggling rise in claims, to more than 200 million ounces, with a shake of his head. Although he knew the relative newcomers like Rollie Francisco and Bryan Coates and Paul Kavanagh on the board of directors, he didn't know David Walsh or John Felderhof. Yes, said Farquharson, Strathcona was free. "What we had in mind was a short visit, two or three days, that would see us talk to a few people, visit the site and write up a report," said Farquharson. He would be away for almost a month.

In that first meeting, it was Coates who raised the possibility of fraud. He asked Farquharson if tampering with core samples could explain the discrepancy between the Freeport and Bre-X results. "I told Bryan I didn't believe it was possible," Farquharson remembers. The reply drew on thirty-eight years of mining experience in which the Strathcona president had seen a half-dozen examples of salting. The frauds were always small scale and relatively easy to detect. Bre-X was a big company with a huge following in mining and financial circles and it had tested thousands of core samples over three years of drilling. How could it be a scam?

The following day, Farquharson and his team, Strathcona geologists Henrik Thalenhorst and Reinhard von Guttenberg, met in Toronto with Bre-X's Kavanagh. The former Barrick gold executive had visited Busang four times and his head was stuffed with technical knowledge. He briefed Strathcona on Busang's geology and the work done to date. Kavanagh gave Felderhof and the Bre-X geologists a vote of confidence. He was certain there was gold in the ground and that Freeport's findings were the result of a ghastly mistake. After the briefing, Farquharson and his colleagues packed their bags and began the twenty-hour flight to Indonesia.

In Indonesia: "A Number of Red Flags"

The first stop in Jakarta was Bre-X's offices, run by Greg MacDonald, a young Canadian geologist. It was here that Farquharson got his first taste of John Felderhof. Bre-X's chief geologist phoned from Jakarta's Shangri-La hotel. He was angry at being questioned by Freeport, furious at the arrival of the Strathcona team, and annoyed at head office in Calgary for imposing all these outsiders on him. It was not an endearing first impression, and it was not one that was going to change over their future encounters. Farquharson recalled, "Felderhof felt he had the situation under control, so he didn't know why we were there." The hostile tone would flavour all of Farquharson's conversations with Bre-X's guiding light in Indonesia.

Farquharson and his team went to the Regent Hotel, intentionally steering clear of Felderhof and other Bre-X executives who might influence their investigation. Their first priority was to assemble the paperwork. At the Bre-X office, Farquharson had met with local officials from the geological consulting firm Kilborn, which had verified Bre-X's drilling results and signed off on estimates of a 71-million-ounce reserve. They gave Kilborn's files to the Strathcona team, including all of Bre-X's drilling and assay results.

Doug MacIntosh, an investment banker with J. P. Morgan who was working for Bre-X, also gave the Strathcona team something to read. A mining engineer by training, MacIntosh had been through the tangled discussions with Barrick Gold and Placer Dome and then helped negotiate the deal with Freeport. Now he was a very worried man. MacIntosh had the assay results from the four Freeport holes tucked in his briefcase. He handed them over. "It was the first hard numbers we'd seen. We took everything back to the hotel and worked until after midnight," said Farquharson, who had finished a long and tiring flight the previous day. "We quickly picked up on a number of red flags. We started to become concerned that there was a real problem."

By the next morning, Tuesday, March 25, Kavanagh had arrived in Jakarta, and he met again with the Strathcona team to discuss what they'd found. Despite the warning signs the Strathcona experts had already picked up, Kavanagh continued to believe that the gold was there – he would maintain this faith until the end, as would Felderhof and Walsh. At 10:00, Freeport's two top geologists in Indonesia – David Potter and Steve Van Nort, who ran the tests at Busang – arrived at the Regent Hotel. More than any other briefing, this session signalled the end of Bre-X's fairy-tale run. "I admired the way Potter and Van Nort did it. We didn't know what to expect, they could have been quite hostile," Farquharson recalled. "They didn't imply there was any hanky-panky. They said there must be gold somewhere, but they couldn't find it."

Potter and Van Nort spent two hours going over their findings. They explained how they took core samples. The logic behind the holes Freeport drilled was to give the maximum chance of finding gold and the maximum chance of proving the size of the deposit. Yet they had found only trace amounts of gold. Freeport's geologists also laid out what they found when they peeked through the electron microscope, focusing on the difference between the relatively large, rounded gold grains Bre-X discovered and the tiny grains that Freeport would expect to see in this kind of deposit. The Strathcona team was impressed by the professionalism of Potter and Van Nort.

After lunch and a long discussion with his colleagues, Farquharson sat down with Kavanagh and MacIntosh. His tone was grim. He explained that Strathcona suspected a major problem, most likely tampering, and that its findings should be made public. Until this point, there had been only rumours and the Indonesian newspaper article on March 21 that suggested Freeport hadn't found enough gold to justify a mine. Farquharson wanted to confirm that rumour and tell the world he was quite certain there was no gold.

If Strathcona dropped this bombshell, everyone in the room understood what would follow. Bre-X was Busang. If the deposit was worthless, so was the company. Kavanagh objected strenuously. He tried to argue that the consultant was jumping to conclusions and should visit Busang before making any concerns public. The Bre-X director was overruled. "We didn't want to have widows buying the stock while we were sitting on this kind of news," Farquharson said. "I explained that I thought we were going to give a very negative report, and we better shut down the stock." It was late afternoon in Jakarta, twelve time zones ahead of Toronto.

The Three-Billion-Dollar Phone Call

At 5:30 on the morning of March 26, Rollie Francisco got a multi-billion-dollar wake-up call. He'd told Farquharson to call any time, day or night, and was taken at his word. Now, lying in bed at his home in a Toronto suburb, a groggy Francisco was astounded by what he heard from the other side of the world. "I told him the initial indications were not good. I told him I didn't think there was any gold," Farquharson said. "He kept saying, 'I can't believe it, are you sure?' At one point, he said the company had been nothing but trouble since the day he'd joined."

Clearly shaken, Francisco told Farquharson to do whatever was necessary. He agreed to make an announcement through the Toronto Stock Exchange and authorized a $900,000 budget for Strathcona's drilling and assaying at Busang. Farquharson estimated the new tests would take about four weeks to complete. Francisco asked to be kept informed.

Farquharson then called Toronto and got his wife out of bed. For eighteen years, she had been his secretary at Strathcona. She knew how to take dictation and she could be counted on to keep Bre-X's dark secret in the family for a few hours. "I told her she was about to write the most significant letter of her career," Farquharson recalled. "I told my wife she might want to take careful notes. I knew this one phone call was going to cost the company billions." Farquharson dictated a two-page memo that described what Strathcona had found and what they intended to do next in Indonesia. Half-way through the letter was the line that spelled Bre-X's doom. "Based on the work done by Freeport and our own review and observations to date," Farquharson dictated, "there appears to be a strong possibility that the potential gold resources of the Busang property have been over-stated because of invalid samples and assaying."

Farquharson's wife drove to the Strathcona office, typed the letter, and faxed a copy to Jakarta, where her husband was standing over the fax machine at the Regent, waiting to check the spelling and con-tents of a note that would close down forever a company then valued at $3 billion. By 9:00 in the morning, Bre-X's lawyers in Toronto had a copy of the letter and had asked the TSE to halt trading in the stock. Strathcona's letter was sent to Calgary, where a stunned David Walsh and equally bewildered colleagues read it, then prepared a brief press release. At 10:30, the news went out.

A One-Two Punch for Bre-X

David Walsh hit the stock market with a one-two punch. Early on March 26, he faxed the Ontario Securities Commission and the Toronto Stock Exchange a terse, three-paragraph note on what Bre-X was hearing from Indonesia. Shortly after, he made the note public. Walsh said Strathcona found that "there appears to be a strong pos-sibility that the potential gold resources on the Busang project in

East Kalimantan, Indonesia have been overstated because of invalid samples and assaying of those samples." He added that Bre-X had hired Strathcona to review its own drilling and the product of Freeport's due diligence.

The TSE kept Bre-X from trading right through Wednesday to give time for this devastating news to sink in. Walsh said the company would soon announce more details. The next day, he unleashed the second shot in the form of even more damning information. Bre-X detailed Freeport's drilling and explained the problems. Freeport's assays, Walsh stated, "have indicated insignificant amounts of gold" in samples drilled right next to Bre-X's holes. In addition, he said Freeport geologists "noticed visual differences in gold particles contained in samples from core holes drilled by Freeport and core holes drilled by Bre-X."

The reference to visual differences in the grains tipped off anyone who understood mining to the strong possibility of a salt job. Walsh, however, tried to put a positive spin on the news. He said Strathcona was hard at work assessing what was wrong, and should know what the problem was within four weeks. And, Walsh noted, "Freeport has indicated to Bre-X that its findings are preliminary and incomplete and that Freeport will provide Bre-X with additional information as it continues with its work."

The CEO took to the steps in front of Bre-X's head office to explain his case to a throng of reporters. Not surprisingly, he looked dreadful; his face was puffed and pasty, and he slumped as he spoke. "Like all the other trials and tribulations that we've gone through since discovering this project, we'll be exonerated and the property will stand as we've indicated," Walsh announced. "I talked to John Felderhof in Jakarta this morning, who just came back from Busang, and he's of the same opinion. What's going on here is just inconceivable – boggles the mind."

Walsh finished up by addressing the question that was on everyone's mind: was Busang a fraud? "It's physically impossible in our mind that the core could have been tampered with," Walsh asserted. "You would have to have an army of people involved."

Knowing the market would wreak havoc on his company's stock price, Walsh engaged in a frantic but ultimately fruitless phone campaign with TSE officials to keep the stock halted until Strathcona completed its work. He took the issue all the way to Rowland Fleming, the exchange's chief executive officer. It was a brief conversation. Fleming, who prides himself on being tough, told Walsh the matter was "not up for discussion."

On Thursday, March 27, at 3:00 p.m., the TSE opened the gates to a flood of orders to sell Bre-X. In the first trade, the stock dropped to $2.50: it last traded at $15.80 before the halt went into effect on Wednesday. By the end of the day, Bre-X had lost close to $3 billion in market value. In the first thirty minutes, 7.9 million shares changed hands. Then the huge volume of trades exposed a software glitch that overloaded the exchange's computers, and the system crashed. The computers were to go down four times over the next two days as a result of Bre-X trading, a showing that left the stock exchange open to ridicule. The TSE had never seen anything like it.

Late in the evening, Farquharson was alone in his hotel room with a chance to reflect on the news he had helped make that day. "I remember thinking, how can this be, could this really have happened, and how can so many other people not have seen this?" he said. "I don't want to give the impression we were that smart, though. We were armed with Freeport's results and we went in there looking for trouble." In the next few weeks, during twelve-hour shifts supervising drill rigs on Busang, Farquharson said he kept mulling over the same issue. How was the Busang fraud effected, and how did the whole world come to believe it?

CHAPTER FOURTEEN

Plots, Conspiracies, and Rumours

"You want to know why people like me are buying Bre-X? Because the trash the media continues to spew out has beaten thousands of people out of their personal fortunes, allowing people like me to scoop up my own share of the world's largest gold deposit at bargain basement prices." – Internet contributor "Lenis B. Warren"

Bre-X Has Left the Building

Bre-X's cute rags-to-riches story had already given way to a fight over a rich gold deposit; now the very foundation of the fable was in ruins. Was the buried treasure really there? Or was this the scam of the century? The question of who dunnit occupied conversations on the job, at parties, on radio talk shows. There was even a hint of sex as details of de Guzman's four marriages emerged. At dinner tables across the country, people wondered if the women knew of each other's existence and were shocked to find they did not. How did he get away with it, they wondered, with a varying mixture of awe and disgust, depending on gender.

Because so many small investors held Bre-X stock, virtually everyone knew someone who had won or lost money. Their stories, often exaggerated, played out across the country. In this environment, any rumour had legs. Poor Brian Mulroney, a Barrick director, saw his name being bandied about as part of the conspiracy, even though the widely disliked former prime minister's role had absolutely no bearing on how much gold was in the Borneo jungle.

People who had never bought stock before had decided to take a chance on Bre-X. These newcomers compared it to spending a day at the track. For a few hundred dollars, or a few thousand, anyone could be a player in the tale. "Call me a sucker, call me greedy, call me a Bre-X shareholder," said Alec Ross, a Kingston, Ontario, writer, in a letter to *The Globe and Mail*. The first-time stock buyer (the son of a former financial journalist) waxed on about the lottery-ticket excitement that came with holding twenty-five Bre-X shares purchased for $3.79 each. "By entering the Bre-X sweepstakes, I've linked myself spiritually to every person, past and present, who has ever dreamed of a better and more prosperous life around the corner. I've become part of a historical continuum, a weensy drop in the roiling well of greed, fear, imagination and hope that nourishes capitalism and makes the world I know go around."

Bre-X's head office in Calgary is an unassuming three-storey red brick building with a futon shop next door and a Chicken-On-The-Way restaurant across the street. In the final week of March, the fast-food joint got a work-out as hordes of reporters, camera crews, and a few anxious shareholders camped out on the sidewalk in front of the building. Comments from Bre-X were infrequent. Walsh had spoken briefly from the steps the day it was revealed that Freeport found insignificant gold. His son Brett distinguished himself by getting in a scuffle with a camera crew; criminal charges were later filed and the case is before the courts.

The media circus reflected an international preoccupation with Bre-X. Night after night, television networks made Bre-X, its supporters, and its detractors their lead news item. The normally unflappable Peter Mansbridge seemed shocked as he told the country about Bre-X's crash on Thursday night. The cover of *Maclean's* magazine trumpeted "The Bre-X Bust."

Foreign newspapers went to town on the story; Bre-X was front-page news in North America, Europe, Asia, and Australia. The prestigious *New York Times* lamented, "Oh, Canada" in a page-one article that noted the country is home to more stock scams per capita than any other. "Dubious stock promotions have been a common export across the United States' lightly defended northern border," the American paper said. Canada was not the only country on the rack. Hong Kong's *South China Morning Post* reported, "Indonesia could be acutely embarrassed by the Busang report, particularly with top-level involvement after a messy fight for control of the property." Australia's top paper, the *Sydney Morning Herald*, stated, "Australia's gold mining industry is suffering the full brunt of Indonesia's Busang scandal, as its most ready source of funds has dried up because of fraud on the North American market." Meanwhile the home-town *Calgary Herald* ran reams of articles and started a popular Internet Web site called "Fortune or Folly? A golden story of greed and fear." As the media cranked out revelations and speculation, investors found more and more to talk about.

Then there was the matter of de Guzman's death. Did he jump, was he pushed, or did he happen to fall, people wondered. His murder would eliminate a key player in a huge fraud, while his suicide would help explain who was at the centre of the scam, the conspiracy theorists reasoned. Talents honed on the Kennedy assassination and Elvis's death were now brought to bear on Bre-X. Maybe the crafty de Guzman was still alive. Although two autopsies were done, one in Indonesia and a second in the Philippines, complete results were not released. Perhaps de Guzman had slipped away and, with the benefit of plastic surgery, was anonymously enjoying the proceeds of Bre-X stock sales on a tropical island retreat.

Bre-X became fertile ground for conspiracy theories and wild rumours. The stock traded from $2.17 to $3.80, bounced about by hope, rumour, or despair. Huge numbers of shares changed hands, mostly among small investors caught up in the rich story. Over the month that passed until release of the Strathcona report, all these speculative threads came together on the Internet.

Caught in the Web

Electronic bulletin boards had been full of Bre-X rumours for months, and some of the chatter proved incredibly insightful. The day after de Guzman's death, but prior to release of suicide notes and the Freeport revelations, a contributor named "Big Dude" explained how it was impossible to accidentally fall out of a helicopter flying at more than 150 kilometres an hour. Wind pressure, he explained, would keep the forward-opening doors from popping open. Big Dude suggested something was seriously amiss at Busang and sold his shares, advising others to do the same.

With the Freeport revelation, everyone had a view on Bre-X, and the Internet traffic divided into two camps: those who believed it was a scam, and a larger, more vocal constituency that was still convinced the gold was there, dammit. Most of the postings were simply gossip. Occasionally, there would be meaty discussions on topics such as assay methods or how to profit and hedge your bets by playing off Bre-X's common shares and options.

One staunch defender went by the name of Lenis B. Warren; it is impossible to verify names on the Internet. Warren bragged that he bought shares every time the price dipped. In an electronic interview, he was asked to explain his logic.

"You want to know why people like me are buying Bre-X?" he replied. "Because the trash the media continues to spew has beaten thousands of people out of their personal fortunes, allowing people like me to scoop up my own share of the world's largest gold deposit at bargain basement prices."

A more polite view came from a contributor named Patrick Laflamme Duval. He first bought Bre-X in April 1996 at about $24, taking a small loss when he sold six months later for $21 because he was concerned about the terms of the proposed deal with Barrick Gold. Now Laflamme Duval was back, buying shares in Bresea, David Walsh's holding company, at prices much lower than before. In an E-mail interview, he said he intended to keep the shares until the Strathcona report was out. "The downside is a 100 per cent loss," explained Laflamme Duval. "The upside is a 600 per cent gain. I like these odds.

"Besides, if they were able to salt samples for three years, I would be impressed enough that I would not mind losing the money," he explained. "I have read almost everything about Bre-X, I have talked to brokers, I have talked to geologists and even to a good friend of Michael de Guzman's, but I still don't have a clue if there is 71 million ounces in Busang or not!"

Shooting the Messenger

Many of those who believed in Bre-X and had been stung by its fall laid the blame on Freeport McMoRan. "Everybody's been wanting to shoot me, the messenger, ever since I made my announcement," Jim Bob Moffett told *Fortune* magazine. "Fucking Canadian press said I was doin' it to take over Bre-X, and I was trying to discredit the Canadian mining industry, and that I had de Guzman killed. People did not want to believe this even when we gave them the information." Moffett missed several of the criticisms levelled at his company. Analysts such as Lévesque Beaubien Geoffrion's Fowler and Bre-X boosters on the Internet suggested Freeport had botched the assays because the company didn't understand the type of gold that Bre-X had discovered. In Calgary, Bre-X's spin doctor, Stephen McAnulty, fed this speculation by insisting that Busang contained not one, but three different types of gold. When pressed by reporters, the former T-bill trader was unable to describe just what these types were. In reaching for an explanation, Internet contributors suggested outright incompetence on Freeport's part, alleging exploration chief Potter screwed up by testing for copper, not gold.

Then people really began to reach. They spread unsubstantiated allegations that Freeport was part of a larger Indonesian plot to discredit Bre-X and squeeze it out of Busang. Then an Internet rumour made the rounds suggesting that Freeport itself was being scammed. Some Bre-X investors theorized that the New Orleans company's core samples had been hijacked on the way to the labs and replaced with worthless ore. The presumed motive was to drive Freeport out and let in another partner.

Some wanted to blame bad luck for Bre-X's woes. Perhaps, they suggested, Freeport missed the mother lode by a few centimetres every time it drilled, and there was gold there after all. Maybe Felderhof just got a bit carried away in his estimates. Bre-X didn't need to find 71 million ounces to impress these believers. Proof of a smaller deposit would still lift the share price and restore the happy ending to the fairy-tale.

Waiting for Strathcona

Reporters began an investigation of Busang's history while waiting on the Strathcona report. On April 7, the *Northern Miner* published an article that revealed the gold found at Busang wasn't the type normally associated with hard-rock deposits. This finding echoed Freeport's disclosure that there were "visual differences" between the gold its drills found and what Bre-X had sent to the labs. But the *Northern Miner* based its story on assays done back in July 1996 by Normet Pty Ltd., an Australian consulting firm. Normet had noted the same large, rounded, coarse gold grains that caught Freeport's attention and had sent its findings to Walsh in Calgary. Bre-X kept the report secret over the next ten months. The *Northern Miner*'s revelations appeared on the Internet late on Friday, April 4, the night before the weekly newspaper was published. Over that weekend, the influential Dow Jones magazine, *Barron's*, published an article that quoted a U.S. gold analyst, John Doody, stating that Busang was a fraud. The following Monday, after the news had a chance to make the rounds, investors once again dumped Bre-X stock. It fell 66 cents to $2.52 in a stunning volume of almost 15.5 million shares.

There were now two different drilling programs going on at Busang, one by Strathcona and the other by Freeport. On April 22, Freeport said its tests continued to find insignificant amounts of gold. By now factions were so fixed in their opinions on Bre-X that the stock barely moved on the news.

However, a rumour on the afternoon of April 23 saying that Freeport's Jim Bob Moffett had resigned sent Bre-X rocketing upwards. Brokers in Toronto spun a story that Moffett had quit in disgrace because Freeport had screwed up and there was actually gold in the ground. Bre-X flew from $2.60 to $5.75 on the rumour, but when officials in New Orleans dismissed the story, the stock price promptly slipped back to $2.80. This was the state of the market leading up to Strathcona's report.

Back in Indonesia, the government had a bit of good news for the beleaguered mining sector, where every company was feeling the fallout of doubts about Bre-X. Mining and Energy Minister Sudjana finally signed sixty-eight contracts of work on March 25, flourishing his pen on behalf of President Suharto. Among the companies picking up contracts of work were Placer Pacific, a subsidiary of Placer Dome, and units of Barrick Gold and Broken Hill Pty Co. of Australia. The fiasco surrounding Busang delayed the contracts, but as the paperwork was approved, executives were in a forgiving mood. "It is our view that the Indonesian mines department was faced with a difficult situation not of its own making," said Kenneth McKechnie, chief executive at Indomin Resources, which was blessed by Suharto. "It is not surprising that it's taken some time for them to be resolved."

On-Site Protection

The last leg of Strathcona's trip to Busang began on Thursday, March 27, with a flight to Balikpapan and a tour of Indo Assay's labs, where all Bre-X's samples had been tested. Farquharson and his colleagues found nothing amiss. In fact, they decided to use Indo Assay as one of three labs that would test the core samples Strathcona planned to gather at Busang.

Then they had lunch with Felderhof, who was just coming out of Busang with most of his team on the way to a memorial service in Jakarta for Michael de Guzman. It was the first face-to-face meeting between the Strathcona consultants and the man who ran Bre-X's Indonesian operation, and it went poorly. Felderhof was angry and made no attempt to hide it. He ranted at the Strathcona team right through the meal and Farquharson barely got a word in. "He objected to our questions about his credibility," Farquharson said. Felderhof and his colleagues were to spend three days away at de Guzman's memorial service, but promised to be back at Busang by Sunday to assist Strathcona if required.

On Friday, March 28, the Strathcona team arrived by helicopter at a nearly deserted Busang mining camp. Although there were still workers around, the only geologist was a young Canadian who had just graduated from the University of Alberta. The Strathcona team spent the day inspecting the site by chopper, making sure the places they wanted to drill were accessible. Another Strathcona partner flew in from Toronto to make sure that the twenty-four-hour-a-day drilling program was always supervised. Each man would sit for twelve hours at a time with the rigs, watching the local crews extract the core samples.

Busang didn't stay deserted for long. First came Freeport geologists. Under direct instruction from an anxious Moffett back in New Orleans, a Freeport employee stood watch over every bit of core that was extracted. Felderhof had also insisted that a Bre-X geologist be present at all times. Then, two days after the drilling began, the

Indonesian government arrived. Officials from the Ministry of Mines hovered around Strathcona, accompanied by a detachment of military police. Every core that the Indonesian drill crews pulled out of the ground was watched by four interested parties, all guarded by soldiers toting M-16 assault rifles.

On Sunday, March 30, Felderhof and the rest of the Bre-X team returned to Busang. The chief geologist brought his wife, Ingrid, along; it was the first time she had visited. Felderhof introduced another first-time visitor to Busang: his bodyguard. Walsh had ordered protection after receiving bomb threats in Calgary. Felderhof's shadow was a massive but friendly British Army veteran whose services were provided to Bre-X by Defence Systems Ltd., a London-based security firm.

Walsh ordered two more security guards sent to Indonesia to ensure the Strathcona team's well-being. The guards helped ensure Farquharson's safety, but the likely source of any threat may not have been what Walsh expected. "The only time I felt threatened was dealing with Felderhof," Farquharson recalled. "We had heated discussions about our methods. He wanted us to go back to the fundamental geology. We just wanted to run a quick program that would verify if the gold was there. He is a volatile guy, and at times, he flew into a rage.

"His wife also let me know just what she thought of me," Farquharson said with a slight smile. "She said they were going to sue us for everything we were worth and she hoped we had lots of money because they were going to take every bit of it."

Other members of Bre-X's geological team were more helpful. When asked, Filipino metallurgist Jerry Alo aided the Strathcona consultants by scaring up equipment and explaining how Bre-X had done things. The same co-operation came from Bobby Ramirez, who had supervised much of the drilling program.

It took a week to complete the drilling. Strathcona employees would pull out the drill core and, with the soldiers looking on, seal the rock in a metal box that was covered with a wooden lid. This case was enclosed with steel strapping and painted, to make sure that any attempt to break into the boxes would show. The crates went into a locked container that was watched around the clock by an armed guard. There could not have been a greater contrast to the lax security measures that used to be in place at Busang. Felderhof and de Guzman had left crates full of cores open and unwatched, while bags of crushed material were left unattended for weeks at a time when they were travelling to the Indo Assay lab. Like Freeport, Strathcona helped itself to crushed rock samples left over from bags that the Bre-X geologists had sent to Indo Assay. Sixteen of these one-kilogram samples were picked up in Samarinda from the office that Michael de Guzman used to run.

Farquharson and the rest of the Strathcona team left Busang on April 8 to begin the journey to labs in Indonesia, Australia, and Canada. An Australian Airlines Boeing 727 was chartered for $90,000 (U.S.) to carry thirteen tonnes of rock samples to Perth, where they were taken to a lab. Again, there was a procession of onlookers in tow. The day after Strathcona's 727 touched down, Freeport's Gulfstream corporate jet was on the Perth runway with Potter and a colleague on board. They wanted to keep an eye on procedures. Indonesian officials also made the trip, and so did Felderhof and his wife.

Farquharson decided to give everyone limited access to the lab each morning; after a maximum of an hour, the outsiders were shooed away and work could start again. Felderhof never showed up, sending instead a consultant from Normet to check up on Strathcona. Felderhof also sent over a representative from Kilborn to present more of their findings on the Busang site, including additional details on the report done several months earlier that stated Busang held 71 million ounces of gold. Farquharson later said the Strathcona geologists didn't bother to look at it, since they suspected that Kilborn's conclusions were all based on doctored samples.

Potter and the Indonesians made use of the inspection opportunities. In Perth, the core was split in half with a diamond-tipped saw, with 50 per cent of the rock set aside as a permanent record. The rest was crushed and sent to three labs, Analabs Pty Ltd. in Perth; Research Ltd. in Lakefield, Ontario; and Indo Assay, back in Kalimantan. It took six days of tough work to turn about 20 per cent of the cores Strathcona had drilled into powdered rock, ready for the labs. Farquharson decided this sample would be enough. He said, "If there was no gold in this, there was no gold in any of it."

On Saturday, April 19, boxes filled with crushed rocks left Perth's airport for Indonesia and Canada, and the Strathcona team headed back to Toronto. Farquharson didn't get much time to shake his jet lag. He arrived home April 22 and flew to Calgary the next day to tell Bre-X about what Strathcona had found. The meeting on April 23 included Bre-X's legal advisers. It was Farquharson's first encounter with David Walsh, and it lasted two hours. Walsh was co-operative, asked insightful questions, and clearly still believed that there was gold in Busang. "He didn't try to confront us the way Felderhof did," Farquharson said. The Strathcona consultant tried to manage expectations of lab results that were a week away, telling the Bre-X crew they were not optimistic.

On Thursday, April 24, back in Ontario, the regulators – for reasons that no doubt made sense to them – took a crack at Farquharson. He was invited in for a chat with Jack Geller, acting chairman of the Ontario Securities Commission, and Ralph Shay and Robert Cook, lawyers who worked at the Toronto Stock Exchange. They wanted to know why Farquharson had put out the letter he did on March 26, which first raised the possibility that the assays were inaccurate. Farquharson laid out his logic, citing his fears that uninformed investors would buy the stock. The regulators were satisfied with what they heard. The OSC and TSE also wanted to know if they should force disclosure of assay work done by Placer Dome and Barrick Gold. The two companies were sitting on test results from rock samples they were given by Bre-X after signing confidentiality agreements. Farquharson strongly advised against disclosure. He suspected the two senior gold companies were handed salted samples and disclosure would simply mislead the markets. As a result, the Barrick and Placer samples stayed secret.

As for questions on the timing of the first letter Farquharson had dictated to his wife, stating Strathcona's suspicions, Farquharson simply explained he was acting in what he saw as a prudent manner. "I never lost a wink of sleep from the day we sent that letter to the day we got the assay reports."

"Without Precedent in the History of Mining"

The three labs finished their tests by Thursday, May 1, and sent the results to Strathcona's Toronto office. Once again, Farquharson and his partners at Strathcona found themselves guarding the fax machine to limit the number of people who knew what the labs found. Although they trusted their employees, Bre-X was still a publicly traded company with a rabid following. The stock was down to $3.23, well off the $24 highs seen the previous summer, but that still put a price tag of more than $600 million on the company. Strathcona's findings would either wipe out what remained of the company or send the stock skyrocketing if gold was found.

Through Friday and Saturday, the Strathcona partners wrote up what they'd found. They finished the job around midnight on Saturday and then began making copies of their report. They caught the first flight to Calgary on Sunday morning. At lunch time, Strathcona president Graham Farquharson and two colleagues arrived at Bre-X's head office carrying two duffel bags filled with copies of their fifty-three-page summary. They were brought into the building through an underground garage to avoid reporters assembled outside and were ushered to the boardroom.

Just about everyone connected to Bre-X was assembled; David and Jeannette Walsh, Kavanagh, Coates, Francisco, McAnulty, the lawyers – about twenty-five people in all. The only person missing was John Felderhof. He and Ingrid had left for the Cayman Islands the previous week, but as interested parties they kept in touch by phone and fax machine. Despite all Farquharson's warnings about fraud, the Bre-X executives apparently anticipated relatively good news. To the end, Farquharson said Bre-X's head office team expected to hear that although there weren't 70 million ounces of gold, Busang was still an elephant deposit of 10 or 20 million ounces. Farquharson got out only a few sentences, leading with "There's nothing there" and explaining that a massive tampering job had taken place. Then, around him, the tears started.

"It was very emotional," said Farquharson. There was a scramble to get the Strathcona report from the duffel bags, then most of those present started to read. "We decided everyone needed time to come to grips with the news. We left and went for a walk down along the Bow River. We were gone for about two hours. By then, it had started to sink in." Pizzas and Cokes were delivered to the head office in the middle of the afternoon as the executives absorbed the news, but no one had much of an appetite. If any of the Bre-X directors and the rest of the crowd had missed the bad news in his short speech, Farquharson had put it right up front in his report, in a twelve-line note to David Walsh.

"We very much regret having to express the firm opinion that an economic gold deposit has not been identified in the Southeast Zone of the Busang property, and is unlikely to be," Farquharson wrote.

"We realize that the conclusions reached in this interim report will be a great disappointment to the many investors, employees, suppliers and the joint-venture partners associated with Bre-X, to the Government of Indonesia and to the mining industry everywhere.

"However, the magnitude of tampering with core samples that we believe has occurred and the resulting falsification of assay values at Busang, is of a scale and over a period of time and with a precision that, to our knowledge, is without precedent in the history of mining anywhere in the world."

CHAPTER FIFTEEN

The Blame Game

"It now appears that a multi-billion-dollar fraud may have been perpetrated on the investing public." – Paul Yetter, Houston-based lawyer for a class-action lawsuit against Bre-X

"The way someone put it to me was that Bre-X was a $5-million scam by some worn-out geologists that somehow got hyped into a $3.5-billion promotion." – Jack Geller, Acting Chairman, Ontario Securities Commission

"Redeem your Bre-X shares for a free table or couch dance." – Sign outside Filmores Hotel, a Toronto strip club, in early April

"We're Toast"

Bre-X released the Strathcona report late on a Sunday night, and details of the massive fraud were instantly posted on the Internet. Within moments, an Internet investor who had believed there was gold at Busang posted a succinct message: "We're toast."

Toast indeed. The three stock markets that listed Bre-X – Toronto, Alberta, and the NASDAQ market in the United States – jointly elected not to allow trading on Monday, May 5, to give investors a chance to digest the devastating news. The TSE lifted the trading halt on Tuesday at 10 a.m. The last Bre-X trade on Friday, May 2, ahead of the Strathcona report, had been completed at $3.23. On May 6, the first sale to go through was at 6 cents. By the end of the day, 58.3 million shares had changed hands on the TSE, a record volume for any one stock in a single session; an additional 11 million shares traded on the other two exchanges. Bre-X finished the day at 9 cents.

As trading closed on Tuesday, May 6, officials at the NASDAQ market gave Bre-X a final kick. David Walsh had been delighted to gain membership in the U.S. market just nine months before. Now NASDAQ officials announced they felt no obligation to carry a company that was obviously based on fraud, and did not allow Bre-X to trade on Wednesday. Bre-X traded on the Toronto and Alberta exchanges for one more session, but at the end of the day on May 7, market regulators in Toronto and Calgary reached the same conclusion and stopped listing the stock. However, it remained possible to find buyers and sellers on the dealer-run, over-the-counter market for three more weeks. Then the Ontario Securities Commission put an end to the misery by ordering trading halted because the company had not filed financial statements. Bre-X traded on a public stock exchange for the last time at 9 cents a share, finishing a run that had started in 1988 at 30 cents and peaked in May 1996 at $286.50, adjusting for a ten-for-one stock split.

The huge volumes of Bre-X shares changing hands meant thousands of investors wanted out of the stock, though many were buying in for a few cents a share. Why was anyone still interested in owning Bre-X? Part of the activity came from short sellers, the vultures of the stock market. They love bad news, because they are betting that the price of a stock will go down, not up. The smart ones borrowed Bre-X shares from their brokers when the stock was soaring and quickly sold the shares, hoping to profit by buying them back later at a lower price. One such investor was a New York-based investment bank, Oppenheimer & Co., bought by the Canadian Imperial Bank of Commerce in the summer of 1997. Its money managers began aggressively short-selling Bre-X when the stock was at $22. They doubted the strength of the company's ownership claim and reasoned, correctly as it turned out, that the Indonesian government would be unable to resist cutting itself in. It was a terrific bet. Eventually, the firm sold short more than 500,000 shares, which it bought back when Bre-X traded for pennies. Oppenheimer made more than $10 million on Bre-X's woes. Many other investors went along for the same profitable ride. When the stock started its final plunge in early May 1997, TSE records show that more than 5.5 million Bre-X shares had been sold short.

At 9 cents a share, Bre-X was no longer an investment, it was cheap wallpaper – and not very attractive wallpaper, at that. Curio collectors were among the buyers, though they were often shocked when they learned that investment dealers charge a flat fee of $125 for stock certificates, however worthless.

The question now was how did this incredible fraud happen, and who was to blame? Canadian Bre-X shareholders looked to market regulators for answers – the Toronto Stock Exchange and securities commissions in Alberta and Ontario. Burned American investors turned to their lawyers. It was a time for tears, a few laughs, and lots of lawsuits.

Bre-X Jokes and Puzzles

As Farquharson and his crew from Strathcona left Calgary on Monday, May 6, a booth went up on the sidewalk outside Bre-X's headquarters. "Kool-Aid for sale," said the sign. "Twenty-five cents or a Bre-X share." The Kool-Aid vendor was one of many people making light of the fraud. Filmores strip bar, for example, has long entertained patrons from Toronto's financial district. The week after the Strathcona report, the marquee outside the bar ran an eight-foot-high advertisement: "Redeem your Bre-X shares for a free table or couch dance." And on a ramp leading to a Toronto highway, three teenagers cleaning car windows with squeegees for pocket change ran up a sign: "Invested in Bre-X, lost everything. Please help!"

Stockbrokers, always a quick source of jokes even when they are at their own expense, began showing their wit. Question: *How many Bre-X executives does it take to change a light bulb?* Answer: *There is no light bulb.* Others claimed Mike de Guzman didn't jump from a helicopter at 240 metres. He simply stepped out and miscalculated the distance to the ground. At a mining convention in Geneva, the tasteless challenge posed over beers was: *What would you call a movie starring Michael de Guzman?* That would be *"The Fall Guy"* or *"Four Weddings and a Funeral."* Another joke: *Two old men are sitting on a park bench. One turns to the other and asks, "What's worse than finding out you have syphilis at sixty-five?" His companion replies, "Having Bre-X at twenty-four."*

In Oakville, Ontario, furniture maker Murray Farncombe bought a Bre-X share, sprinkled gold sparkles and dirt on it and added a big red sucker. He put a joke name as the owner of the share, Mr. Jack Wazburned, of 1997 Tall Tale Drive, Trustmee, Ontario. The postal code was IOA LOT. Farncombe photographed his creation and turned it into a 500-piece jigsaw puzzle, price tag $19.95. He added little helicopters to the artwork on the box and claimed the Bre-X jigsaw was "worth its weight in gold." He printed up 1,600 of the puzzles and sold sixty in the first two weeks.

Lawyers Mine for Gold

There's nothing remarkable about John Quick. From a lawyer's point of view, that makes him a perfect victim. He lives in Del Rio County, Texas, near Houston, and in May 1996, when Bre-X was trading at around $22, he purchased 1,800 shares. Quick bought into the story of the largest gold deposit in the world. Within days of Freeport McMoRan's announcement that there was no gold at Busang, he became one of the horses that Texas lawyers would ride as they pulled together a sweeping class-action lawsuit against Bre-X. The Texans were the first in a wave of U.S. lawyers pushing seven lawsuits in five states; litigators in New York, Georgia, California, and Washington also got in on the action. At the head of the pack was Houston attorney Paul Yetter, who has a string of successful class-action suits on behalf of investors to his credit.

In nine concise pages, Yetter and his colleagues laid out their version of one of the greatest hoaxes in stock market history and began to cast a net to capture those responsible. The first suit was brought on behalf of all investors by five Texas residents, John Quick and four others, who together owned a total of 7,575 Bre-X shares. "A class action is superior to all other available methods for fair and efficient adjudication of this controversy," claimed the lawsuit.

The lawyers planned to collect damages from wealthy individuals who had worked at Bre-X, including David Walsh, his wife, Jeannette, John Felderhof, and as many of the company's deep-pocketed advisers as possible. In Yetter's case, that meant going after geological consultants. "Beginning in 1994, the defendants convinced the world that Bre-X owned 90 per cent of a massive gold deposit, perhaps the largest ever discovered, located in the Busang area of East Kalimantan, Indonesia," Yetter wrote. "This was false. Indeed, it now appears that a multi-billion-dollar fraud may have been perpetrated on the investing public." He went after Bre-X over its ownership problems, the promotion of the company's reserves, and the sale of shares by company executives during the stock's glory days.

The lawsuits soon spread to Canada and ensnared investment bankers, analysts, and stock exchanges. Canadian class-action lawsuits are in their infancy. Legislation permitting this form of suing is just a few years old and exists only in Quebec, Ontario, and British Columbia. However, Bre-X looked like the perfect way to test the new laws. In Windsor, Ontario, lawyer Harvey Strosberg started a claim on behalf of an investor who lost more than $200,000. He named much the same cast of characters as his colleagues in Texas but added Canadian content. Strosberg went after Nesbitt Burns and its star analyst, Egizio Bianchini, as well as the corporate parent, the Bank of Montreal. Meanwhile, back in the U.S.A., another Texas law firm went after Bre-X's U.S. investment bank adviser, J.P. Morgan, and Lehman Brothers Inc., which had advised clients to buy the stock. Executives from both U.S. brokerages houses had visited Busang but, like everyone else, had failed to detect the scam.

In Vancouver, lawyers added in the names of First Marathon Securities and its gold analyst, Kerry Smith. "The whole point of this thing is accountability," said Terry Chalmers, a North Vancouver real estate agent who is one of two investors leading the B.C. suit. Chalmers bought 800 Bre-X shares at $15.35 through a broker who used First Marathon research. In an interview with the *Financial Post*, she said she didn't hold out much hope of collecting damages, but wanted to make a statement. "If I get something back, fine, but it's accountability, kind of a slap. These guys have been getting away with this for years and I don't think it's right."

Montreal law firm Lauzon Bélanger cited Nesbitt Burns and the largest Quebec-based brokerage firm, Lévesque Beaubien Geoffrion, in its class-action suit. Dermod Travis, a spokesman for the Quebec lawyers, said the strategy was to attack the "information they [brokers] provided both to their clients and allowed to be disseminated to the public. Was that information as comprehensive, as independent and as impartial as it should be?" The brokerage firms are vigorously defending their actions and their analysts. Bianchini and his colleagues weren't talking, but through its lawyers Nesbitt stated it had "acted appropriately" and has itself been "victimized" by the fraud. Loewen Ondaatje McCutcheon's gold analyst Robert Van Doorn, who helped arrange Bre-X's first financing, said he was embarrassed and shocked by the revelations of tampering and noted that a well-organized deception is difficult to detect. "It's not as if we can walk around the jungle with our own drill rig on our backs, sinking holes wherever they do," he complained.

"In retrospect, we all should have been a lot smarter," said Peter Ward, a New York-based analyst for Lehman Brothers. "But what are we to do next time – take our own drill rig to the site and pull out cores? We have to rely to a certain extent on the integrity of the company."

Beating Up on the TSE

Rowland Fleming can't be blamed for wishing he'd never heard of Bre-X and David Walsh. The Toronto Stock Exchange faced harsh criticism for its handling of Bre-X on two levels: the frequent trading halts and, more seriously, the decision to list Bre-X on both the exchange and its coveted indexes, the TSE 300 and TSE 100. As the exchange's chief executive officer, Fleming was at the centre of the controversy. He is a precise, deliberate executive known for using his iron will to steamroll over those who oppose him. There's an icy edge to his voice when he responds to criticism, and in late March and early April of 1997, that edge was in daily use.

The stakes were high. The TSE was a target of the British Columbia class-action suit, which pointed out that investors bought Bre-X partly because it had "an exclusive blue-chip TSE 300 listing after only eight months, thereby giving Bre-X enormous credibility in the eyes of the public." Individual investors were also furious with the exchange. In the days following the Freeport revelations, many Bre-X shareholders held the exchange responsible for their woes. One typical point of view came from Jeffery Frketich, who blasted the exchange over the Internet. "The TSE totally dropped the ball with Bre-X," said Frketich in an interview. "Putting a junior gold company that did not have one cent of revenue on the TSE 300 Index was absolutely ridiculous. It gave Bre-X credibility it did not deserve."

The TSE's decision to open Bre-X for trading late in the day on Thursday, March 27, ahead of the Easter long weekend (which produced a flood of orders to sell), caught many investors off guard, including Frketich. "What upset me was the appearance that lobbying by several large brokerage firms influenced the TSE into permitting Bre-X trading in very unusual circumstances," he said. "It appears that Bre-X was opened so that these guys could do some damage control for their own portfolios."

Fleming took great offence at the idea that Bre-X should not have been listed on the TSE, and that the exchange should have stopped trading the stock while Strathcona did its detective work. "The grey market was a factor," he said. "You had institutions able to trade in Bre-X while individuals could not." The TSE chief executive was referring to the unsupervised but legal trading of stock that takes place between large funds and investment dealers. "Regulators are not here to protect investors from losses, they're here to make sure securities regulations are not broken," he noted, with perhaps a hint of irritation in his phrasing.

"Bre-X met all listing requirements and continues to do so," he said in a meeting on March 27 in the TSE's elegant boardroom, a session interrupted by a call reporting that Bre-X trading volume had gone through 3.5 million shares in the first hour without a technical glitch. "Outstanding," said Fleming crisply before hanging up. Then he continued, "Whether there is fraud involved is another question, and that hasn't been determined."

In defending the exchange, Fleming pointed to statistics showing that of 110 mining companies that applied for membership in 1996, the TSE admitted only 56. But he is also making changes in the wake of the Bre-X fiasco. He has promised to review the admission standards to the TSE indexes, and the exchange and the Ontario Securities Commission launched the Mining Standards Task Force, which will draw on investment bankers, analysts, lawyers, and investors who had dealt with Bre-X. The task force expected to produce in the fall of 1997 new rules on how mining companies report information. But given a chance to look back, Fleming offers no apologies. In a speech just after the Strathcona report was issued, he said, "Even in hindsight, I can assure you we would have done little differently than we did." Few critics of the TSE's performance found this reassuring.

TSE officials had even more difficulty defending the exchange's technical performance. The whole idea of a stock exchange is to allow trading. Yet in the spring of 1997, Bre-X, the hottest stock in the market, seemed halted more often than downtown traffic at rush hour. The problem was a computer glitch that had lain dormant for twenty years. The TSE's systems, which were being replaced when the Bre-X storm broke, store in a temporary memory buy and sell orders that are not dealt with immediately. The flood of Bre-X trading overloaded the memory banks and crashed the entire exchange on four occasions in March and April, 1997. On Friday, May 2, just ahead of the Strathcona report, the TSE put special rules in place to make sure the computers worked and trading was uninterrupted. The TSE's fears proved well-founded. On Tuesday, May 6, when more than 58 million Bre-X shares changed hands, the system did lock up for thirty minutes, but was quickly rebooted and went on to carry near-record volumes of trading.

Bre-X's unsurpassed flair for dramatic corporate revelations also meant frequent trading halts at the company's request. The TSE's own guidelines call for a "continuous auction market." If the exchange is open, buyers and sellers expect to be able to do business. Halts are granted when material changes are announced, but trading is expected to resume within an hour. A twenty-four-hour halt is highly irregular, but the TSE's by-laws state halts can go on indefinitely "where the exchange determines that resumption of trading would have a significant impact on the integrity of the market." Bre-X's soap-opera run of suicide, deceit, and double-dealing, which market regulators dryly label "material changes in the company," tested the trading halt rules. There were tense discussions between TSE officials such as Fleming, who wanted the stock to trade, and Bre-X's Walsh, who wanted time to sort out his company's tangled affairs. Since

Fleming controlled the switch that turned trading on and off, he won these battles.

Police investigations into the Bre-X fraud began days after release of the Strathcona report, when the Royal Canadian Mounted Police sent a team of investigators to Indonesia. Even before Bre-X crashed, the Ontario Securities Commission and the TSE were taking a look at stock trading and disclosure of information by the company's senior executives. The OSC first launched an investigation in December 1996, when the company was negotiating its future with Barrick Gold and the Indonesian government. There were two central issues: whether Bre-X executives had followed the requirement to release important corporate news in a timely manner, and whether they had sold shares based on information that was not available to the public, which is known as insider trading. Both are serious breaches of securities laws, though all the OSC can do if rules are broken is take away a person's or a company's right to trade securities in Ontario.

Even in its early days, the OSC investigation of Bre-X promised to be epic in scope. Jack Geller, acting chairman of the OSC, said more than 200,000 trades were being examined. No previous probe in the regulator's history had reviewed more than 35,000 trades. The regulators shared a clear view on what they could and could not prevent. While his people were still working on the file, Geller said, "Nothing we have turned up so far indicates that additional or different regulation would have made any difference." Speaking prior to the release of the Strathcona report, Geller maintained, "If there was fraud, no additional regulation would have prevented it. If people choose to break the law, the state can punish them, but history does not provide evidence that it can prevent them from doing so."

However, even Geller, a veteran securities lawyer, admitted he was captivated by the Bre-X story. During an interview months before details of the scam were revealed, Geller leaned forward and shared his theory. "The way someone put it to me was that Bre-X was a $5-million scam by some worn-out geologists that somehow got hyped into a $3-billion promotion." Then he leaned back and shook his head in amazement.

From Heroes to Outcasts

In the mining community, Felderhof had become a pariah. On May 8, David Walsh sacked his vice-chairman and chief geologist, who had not left Grand Cayman and had applied for permanent residency on the islands. In interviews, Walsh refused to elaborate on a statement that said, "In response to a request from the companies, John Felderhof has resigned from the board of directors of Bre-X ... effective immediately." Felderhof's reply to Walsh, which severed a highly profitable four-year relationship, read in part, "I understand the company's need to conserve its financial resources at this time. In light of the decision not to proceed with our business projects, there is very little for me to do as Senior Vice President of Exploration.

"I have greatly appreciated the opportunity to work with you and our fellow Bre-X employees over the last few years, many of whom I understand will be leaving the company shortly," Felderhof wrote. Then, well aware of the blizzard of lawsuits that was starting, he added, "Please be advised however that I am reserving all of my legal rights and entitlements." A few days later, Walsh took shelter from the lawsuits by putting Bre-X in court-administered creditor protection, and the accounting firm Price Waterhouse was appointed to monitor the company.

A few short weeks earlier, in March, Bre-X's chief geologist had been named Prospector of the Year by the Prospectors and Developers Association of Canada, accepting the award before a crowd of several hundred applauding peers with a heart-felt speech. With Busang a fraud, the award was an embarrassment. In late May, Felderhof agreed to "voluntarily surrender" the most prestigious award in the Canadian mining industry. "The award was given for the discovery of a major deposit," said Ed Thompson, chairman of the association's awards committee. "But unfortunately, we now know the deposit is not there."

Mike de Guzman also had a prestigious award pulled, posthumously. The Geological Society of the Philippines was preparing to honour him at a special ceremony, but cancelled when it learned what Freeport found. Had he been alive, the cancellation would have been a stinging rebuke for de Guzman. He always craved recognition in his own country, since his geological theories had not been accepted there in the 1970s. Filipino geologists with no connection to Busang feared they would face a backlash when it became clear that de Guzman had been at the heart of the crime. "We shouldn't be looked upon as a group, but as individuals with many skills and achievements," said James Zafra, a geologist who worked in Indonesia and now heads a Manila-based mining company. "If Filipinos are part of the scam, it is a big loss for all of us." The fear was echoed by Manila-based geologist Maximo Sara, who told *The Wall Street Journal*, "Busang could put into question the credibility of all Philippine geologists. We hope the truth of the scandal is revealed soon."

Tough Times for Junior Mining Companies

Bre-X's misfortunes cast a shadow on every Canadian mining company doing business in Indonesia. Victor Bradley was about to raise $40 million for his junior mining company when Freeport's revelations hit the stock market. The president of Yamana Resources Inc., a Spokane, Washington-based company that works with Barrick Gold, needed the money to fund exploration of properties near Busang. When the world still thought there was gold at Busang, he had struck a deal with CIBC Wood Gundy Securities and expected to raise the money in the Toronto market. Two weeks before the financing closed, the market knocked $3 billion off the price of Bre-X stock, and Bradley's plans went down with Busang. "We are a casualty of the Bre-X fall-out," he told the *Financial Times*. "For us to have continued with that financing would have been just like

whistling Dixie." Another junior company with Indonesian properties, Sur American Co., dropped a planned $8.5-million deal. "The
investment institutions at the moment are undoubtedly gun-shy,"
said Rennie Blair, president of the Vancouver-based company. "An
awful lot of money has been lost."

In the wake of Bre-X's melt-down, no major money manager
wanted to appear before supervisors or investors with Indonesian
companies in the portfolio. "There's the credibility issue," said John
Embry, who manages Royal Bank of Canada's precious metals mutual
fund. "If a company of the stature of Bre-X can't be relied on, how
many other companies can be trusted?" He said Bre-X represented
a major change in market sentiment. "It has changed the market for
some time to come," Embry said. "Instead of greed dominating
people's views, fear is."

The larger issue, of course, is the reputation of the Canadian
mining industry. The previous high-water mark for scandal was the
1964 collapse of Windfall Oils and Mines Ltd. Mining consultant
Patrick Mars described Bre-X's saga as "the most incredibly bad thing
ever to happen to the Canadian mining industry. It makes Windfall
look like a ladies' tea party," Mars added. "Canada was the mine
finance capital of the world. Now it's the laughing-stock."

In the weeks after Bre-X crashed, junior companies recognized
that to raise money from the public, they had to adopt higher standards. One example of the new approach was Goldstake Explorations Inc. At one time, the Toronto-based junior mining company
highlighted its proximity to Bre-X's Indonesian claims. But in July
1997, it took pains to set itself apart. In a press release issued two
months after Strathcona's report, the company painstakingly laid
out its methods. Its drilling in Java was being supervised by an
independent consultant, while core samples were going to both
an independent lab and the Indonesian mines department, which
would run its own tests on samples. The press release pointedly
noted, "Goldstake will retain 50 per cent of each core sample for
audit purposes."

There are still mines producing gold in Indonesia, and still junior mining companies searching the jungle for new deposits. "Twenty years ago a lot of people called the mining juniors the penny dreadfuls," said Bob Parsons, head of the mining group at Price Waterhouse. "Today they're world beaters and all the pieces are in place for that to remain the case." Despite Bre-X, mining executives remain an optimistic lot. "We are committed to Indonesia because of the fabulous gold opportunities that existed pre-Bre-X and that will continue to exist no matter how the Bre-X saga plays out," said Ranjeet Sundher, president of Vancouver-based Indogold Explorations Services. "Although the market doesn't reflect it today, the potential in Indonesia is as good as ever."

Great Historic Scams: With a Pinch of Salting

Bre-X was an incredible scam, but the Indonesian fraud differed from past stock swindles only in its size and audacity. In the late 1960s, Ontario strengthened regulations on mining stocks after the spectacular fifteen-day rise and fall of Windfall Oils and Mines. In 1964, the 31-cent stock had rocketed to more than $5 in just over two weeks as promoters spread word of a fabulous find. The stock crashed when assay results revealed little of value in the claims. The company's colourful promoter, the late Viola MacMillan, had stashed the worthless drill cores in the trunk of her Cadillac to keep them from prying eyes; she served time in jail for her actions. The stricter listing requirements in Ontario resulted in an exodus of junior mining companies for the more adventurous Vancouver Stock Exchange, which soon earned a spicy reputation. There's a postscript to the Windfall story. In 1984, stock promoter Guy LaMarche was shot and killed while attending the Prospectors and Developers Convention at the Royal York Hotel in Toronto. The motive for the killing was rumoured to be rooted in the Windfall scandal, an event that had occurred twenty years previously. It seemed grudges lasted well beyond the headlines of the day.

The 1980s began with a salting scam in Vancouver that had the mining world buzzing. New Cinch Uranium Mines Ltd. claimed a rich gold strike in New Mexico. Assay results were terrific and propelled shares in the Vancouver-based company from $2.50 to $29.50 in the last five months of 1980. Early in 1981, the stock came crashing down to 20 cents on news that the assays had been doctored in the lab. A raft of lawsuits ensued. Like Bre-X, the New Cinch fiasco came complete with a grisly death. Michael Opp was an employee at the lab where the New Cinch samples were salted, and he kept notes on what he saw taking place. On the night of November 14, 1982, someone knocked on the door of Opp's apartment in Phoenix. When Opp answered, the visitor fired a single shot into his temple, killing him instantly. Opp's father later found a journal hidden under a rug in his son's apartment that contained wild theories on the salt job. No one was ever convicted of the killing.

In the New Cinch lawsuits, one of those who testified was Albert Applegath, a Canadian mining promoter who was working in New Mexico. "It's a travesty beyond description," Applegath observed in court at the time. "It will go down as one of the most infamous cases ever to come to court, and every lawyer, and that's part of what I call the tragedy or travesty, perhaps will become famous, while the rest of us are all fighting for our lives. Perhaps the greatest tragedy of all, other than human frailty, is that none of us in this room might ever know who concocted this whole damn thing."

In 1986, Oliver Reese told the mining world that he had rediscovered King Solomon's mine in Mali, an impoverished west African nation. His venture, called Mali American, claimed the backing of playboy arms dealer Adnan Khashoggi and film star Elizabeth Taylor, both of whom attended a road show for the Denver-based company in a New York hotel. Sadly, Reese's claim never got very far. He returned, undeterred, ten years later with the splendidly named Timbuktu Gold Corp., an Alberta Stock Exchange-listed junior mining company that went from pennies to $24.90 on the strength of great drill results from Mali. Then details of Reese's promotional past came out, along with suspicions about the assay results. The ASE halted Timbuktu for months until an investigation showed that the samples had been crudely salted with bits of ground-up South African krugerrand coins. Timbuktu crashed to $1.75, down $23.15 in one day, one of the largest single-day drops in the exchange's history.

The list of hypes and flops goes on, with Canadian companies continuing to play a prominent role. In a story that demonstrated greed and stupidity rather than fraud, Pickering, Ontario-based Cartaway Resources Corp. leapt from pennies to $23 by the summer of 1996. The company's geologists said they had spotted high-grade iron in core samples drilled in Labrador. The property was close to Diamond Fields Resource's fabulously rich Voisey's Bay deposit and investors were ready to believe that the magic could happen again. Unfortunately, lab tests showed that what looked like iron ore was in fact worthless iron pyrite, or – another Bre-X touch – fool's gold. Cartaway crashed back to earth, with stock trading at $2 the day after the error was revealed.

In the weeks that followed Bre-X's fall, other companies reported salting scandals. In February 1997, Delgratia Mining Corp. of Vancouver announced strong results from three drill holes on the Josh deposit in Nevada. Stock in the NASDAQ-listed company jumped from $10 (U.S.) to more than $34. When Nevada mining officials pressed for more details on the claim, the stock fell back to $12, the level at which it traded in late May when it was halted for doleful news that echoed Bre-X's releases. "We conclude that there is insignificant gold contained in the Josh deposit," stated independent consultants hired by the company. "Any gold detected beyond background amounts was introduced into the samples after they had been collected at the drill." The stock crashed and class-action suits were launched. As the *Financial Times* phrased it, "When punters and prospectors sniff gold, they forget history."

CHAPTER SIXTEEN

Winners and Losers

"When Brian Mulroney and those big boys appeared on the scene, I knew it was time for a little guy like me to head out."
– Retired General Motors worker Charlie Harper

"I'm revisiting my investment strategy." – Karl Zetmeir, retired Kansas City advertising executive, after losing $5.2-million on Bre-X

Saying Goodbye to the GM Assembly Line

Bre-X was more than stock. For several years, it was a winning lottery ticket, a dream come true. It meant General Motors assembly-line workers in Oshawa, Ontario, could beat the big money boys in Toronto at their own game. So satisfying. Bre-X meant early retirement and a new snowmobile. It meant that capitalism worked. Buy Bre-X and take a short cut to the good life. A student at McGill saw an $8,000 bet, made with credit card advances, as a way to pay off his loans. It seemed a sure thing, and it was fun for him. One in fifty residents of St. Paul, Alberta, population 5,000, became millionaires.

235

They faced jealousy and envy from neighbours who missed out. Buying Bre-X felt like getting religion. It meant reaping earthly rewards bestowed by the god at Busang. The blessed compared notes. *What price did you buy in? What will you do with the money? Isn't this divine?* Stock owners tossed out assay results and merger partner possibilities at curling rinks, at the hairdresser's, over coffee, over computers. Bre-X shareholders kept the faith, often at a dreadful price.

First, the happy story of four friends who had worked together for thirty years on the Oshawa assembly line, putting together the pieces of an endless stream of General Motors cars. They owe their comfortable golden years, not to the auto maker, but to Bre-X. Before being tipped off to the Calgary company, Bob Jones's retirement was shaping up as safe but spartan. In his late fifties, he was the only one among a gang of assembly-line veterans who played the stock market. His friends Sterling McGill and the Harper brothers, Charlie and Bill, were counting on their GM pension plan and a few Canada Savings Bonds to pay the bills.

Jones's stockbroker was Brian Cropper at the Richardson Greenshields of Canada Ltd. office in Oshawa (during the period Jones and his friends invested in Bre-X, the investment dealer was bought by rival RBC Dominion Securities Ltd.). Cropper first mentioned Bre-X to Jones in 1994, when it was trading at $1.70 a share on the Alberta Stock Exchange. The broker didn't have any research to go on; Richardson Greenshields' mining analyst didn't begin to cover the stock for another two years, because it was deemed too speculative. All the broker had was a tip or two from colleagues: *Watch this one. Bre-X is hot. Bre-X is going places.* If it all sounded like tips at the race-track, it's because playing penny gold stocks is not much different from picking ponies.

Cropper knew Bre-X's theory on gold left behind by erupting volcanoes and about promising drilling results, and was impressed. He didn't recommend betting the house, but told Jones that a few thousand dollars of his portfolio might be well spent on the stock. It was mad money, an investment that Jones had to be prepared to lose completely. Jones said, "I listen to my broker and nobody else. He's never steered me wrong." He bought the shares early in 1994.

As Bre-X began to move, Jones talked about the company with his three friends. They respected Bob's investing advice. The guys knew he was a cautious individual. They also knew that Cropper, his broker, was a decent fellow. In 1995, the story changed slightly. Jones sold Bre-X, making a tidy profit. Now his broker had a new idea. Buy Bresea, parent company to Bre-X. Here was Cropper's logic. David Walsh controlled Bresea, a holding company based in Calgary but listed on the Montreal Stock Exchange. Bresea controlled 24 per cent of Bre-X. Cropper did the math and found the value of its stake in Bre-X wasn't reflected in Bresea. It's a common situation. The market put a higher price on a company with a solid asset, a pure play such as Bre-X, than a holding company such as Bresea. Jones first bought Bresea at $7. Over the next few months, Sterling McGill came in, then Bill Harper jumped. Charlie Harper was the last one into the pool, a few days after his brother, buying at $10.70.

Other investors soon picked up on the Bresea story. They began to view it as a cheaper way to own Busang, and the difference between the value of the two stocks narrowed, raising the price of Bresea. At the same time, Bresea rode the increasing size of the Borneo gold deposit to staggering new heights. Taking into account a ten-for-one stock split, Bresea peaked at $170 in May 1996.

As shareholders, the four GM workers were part owners of Bresea, and they took the obligation seriously. The four friends began to get statements from Bresea and independent research reports from their broker. They learned to interpret drilling hole results, to understand what constituted an exciting concentration of gold, and what was considered a dud. They learned the difference between the two techniques used to test rock for gold: fire assay and cyanide leaching. Busang, Bre-X, and Bresea were the dominant topics of conversation during the summer of 1995 when the four visited one another at their cottages on Georgian Bay and blasted around on Jet Skis. In the winter, the Jet Skis gave way to weekend runs on high-powered

Polaris snowmobiles but the focus of conversation stayed the same. Friends found the preoccupation a bit tedious.

On the advice of Jones's stockbroker, the four held tight through the first hints of Busang's ownership problems in the fall of 1996. Their attitude changed in November, when Barrick Gold arrived on the scene and locked up control of the Indonesian deposit. Newspaper accounts of the bid mentioned that former prime minister Brian Mulroney, a Barrick director, was part of the lobbying effort. Former U.S. president George Bush was in there, pushing Barrick as well. Charlie Harper said Mulroney's presence made everyone nervous, including their broker at Richardson Greenshields. The game was changing in Indonesia and they didn't know the new rules. When Cropper told his clients it was time to sell, he had no trouble convincing the GM workers. "When Brian Mulroney and those big boys appeared on the scene," said Charlie Harper, "I knew it was time for a little guy like me to head out."

Brian Cropper was the most successful broker at RBC Dominion Securities in 1996, no small feat at an investment dealers with 1,600 stock salesman. He had clients who parlayed $4,000 investments in Bre-X into $4 million. Charlie Harper checked out of Bresea with a gain of just over $100,000. Bill Harper made a little more. Sterling McGill clocked in at more than $200,000. They all say Bob Jones made much more than the rest of them – he was in earlier and had built a bigger stake – but Jones prefers not to talk about just how much he made on Bresea's run. During an interview, his wife playfully yelled, "Stop bragging" from the next room when Jones's winnings were discussed. But Jones would allow, with an enormous grin and considerable pride, that his gain was "substantial."

An Extraordinary Stock for the Ordinary Investor

More than most stocks, Bre-X was a company owned by ordinary investors like the GM workers. For that reason, its rise and fall played out in extraordinary ways. A typical large Canadian company such as Inco or Canadian Pacific is primarily owned by institutional investors: pension funds, insurance companies, and mutual funds. In its early days, Bre-X was too risky for these investors. Government regulations and internal rules prevented them from buying a small, Alberta-listed junior mining stock. For the most part, the institutions became involved only in the end of Bre-X's run, when there was money to be lost, not made – as millions of unsuspecting Canadians found when they discovered that their RRSPs were not making as much money as usual, for some reason. Bre-X didn't become a member of the Toronto Stock Exchange 300 index until December 1996. It took membership in the club of TSE-listed companies to turn the junior mining company into a stock that conservative institutions could add to their portfolios.

At its peak in May 1996, 70 per cent of Bre-X's 240 million shares were in the hands of individual investors, according to statistics kept by pension fund consultant SEI Financial Services Inc. Ordinarily, individuals would own about 30 per cent of a large Canadian company, with the remainder in the hands of money managers.

Bre-X took root in many individual portfolios in part because it bloomed when the rest of the investment garden was barren. In 1995, North American interest rates were at thirty-year lows. A conservative investment such as a bank savings account offered just 2 per cent annual interest. Boring but safe guaranteed income certificates paid 5 per cent interest. Where was the fun in that? Bre-X went up 5 per cent in a dull *week*. It was a stock on steroids. In 1996, it rose 316.5 per cent, making it the hottest thing in Canadian markets, a stock that captured world-wide attention. The deposit Felderhof described as a monster gave quite a ride to those who got on early. It also ate up those who stayed on too long.

Kimberley Sparenberg and Brent Edgson were a happily married couple in January 1994 when they opened up a joint account at the Edmonton office of brokerage house ScotiaMcLeod. Edgson made one of the couple's first investments. He bought 2,000 shares in Bre-X at $1.38 each. Both agreed that the investment was a flyer, pure and simple. What they couldn't agree on in July 1996, when their marriage broke down, was who got the Bre-X shares. It was an important question, as by then the stake in the junior mining stock was worth $477,000.

When their divorce got its day in Northwest Territories Supreme Court in the summer of 1996, Edgson argued that the brokerage account was meant for each individual's investments, and profits and losses would not be shared. Sparenberg replied that if they meant to do it that way, they would have set up separate accounts. She wanted to sell the Bre-X shares, arguing through lawyers that "this investment is a highly speculative one that could drop in value just as dramatically as it increased in value." He wanted to hold; his lawyer said, "There is no evidence that the stock is at risk and any fluctuations in stock price are minor." The judge showed the wisdom of King Solomon and superb market timing, ordering 1,000 of the shares sold just as Bre-X was peaking, with the proceeds to be set aside and split between the parties. Lawyers for the two have declined to comment on what ever happened to the other 1,000 shares.

The citizens of St. Paul, Alberta, are now known for two things. The forward-looking town used to be famous for building the world's first landing pad for flying saucers (to date, unused). Now it can also claim more Bre-X millionaires and victims per capita than anywhere else on earth. For this, about 5,000 citizens can thank John Kutyn, a loans officer at the local credit union who always kept an eye on junior gold stocks. Kutyn cottoned on to Bre-X when it was still a penny stock in 1993, trading for less than $3, and told his clients all about it. About fifty people bought in early on and participated in Bre-X's spectacular run. Kutyn invested everything he owned, then cashed out when the stock hit $170, making enough to retire early and move to New Zealand as a wealthy man. But as word of what Bre-X was doing for some people's retirement savings spread through the small town, and when Bre-X peaked, estimates put the number of local investors as high as 200 people, or one in 25 St. Paul residents. Many of these individuals hung in with the company as its fortunes unravelled. "The original investors are probably laughing because most of them pulled out," said Rhea Labrie, general manager of St. Paul's Chamber of Commerce after Freeport's news had pushed the stock to $3 levels. "If they have stock in there, it's play money," she said in an interview with the *Toronto Star*. "It is those people who have taken out retirement funds or loans to invest that are crying. They are the ones you might find on the fifth floor of the provincial building," she joked, referring to the tallest building in town.

St. Paul yielded small-town wisdom on speculative investing. Local jeweller Réal Michaud rode Bre-X for a time but cashed out before the Freeport revelations; however, many family members still held the stock when it plunged. "If the whole thing crashed, I would still have my health and I would still have my family and I would do just fine. It's not a big deal. Many, many people lose sight of what is important and it sure isn't money."

The Horror of Margin Calls

When Bre-X crashed, Karl Zetmeir lost $5.2 million.

The Kansas City advertising executive took early retirement at age fifty-three, a relatively wealthy man and a savvy investor in junior mining stocks who was passionate about Bre-X. He wrote about his investment on the Internet, and in the four crazy weeks that followed Freeport McMoRan's revelation that it had found little gold at Busang, he frequently fired off a few lines giving his views on what was happening. Just hours after David Walsh had released the report from the Strathcona geological consultants that exposed the fraud, Zetmeir was relaxing at home when he took a phone call from a reporter.

Stock was at 8 cents, wallpaper levels. Did he want to talk about Bre-X? Heavy sigh. "Sure. Sure, I'd like to talk about it. I'm not thinking about much else." We know what happened, said the reporter.

How are you doing? "Well, the fat lady's sung. That's for sure. I'm pretty upset. What Walsh said means it is actually all over."

People say you had $5 million in shares. You didn't sell any? You didn't see this coming? "I believed. I'm really close to the company. I talked to Walsh a lot. I got to know him well."

How does it all feel? "This has been like watching a dear old friend die a lingering death."

Back in June 1995, Zetmeir bought 30,000 Bre-X shares after reading about the junior mining stock on an Internet investor forum run by Compuserve, an Internet service provider. The stock was trading at $6. At that time, few people had heard of the company, and few analysts followed it. The hype, the frenzy, were months away. Bre-X consisted of John Felderhof pushing out drill results and reserve estimates in Indonesia and David Walsh and a few others in head office chatting with anyone who cared to call Calgary. Zetmeir called.

The $180,000 bet on Bre-X was typical of Zetmeir's style. He operated by getting to know a few small resource companies well and putting a big chunk of his savings behind each, then hoping for a big score, the kind of win that would let a guy retire early. He borrowed money from his stockbroker's firm to back his picks. It was a high-risk strategy that went after big potential returns. Back then, he still worked full-time at a Kansas City advertising agency.

The first conversation between Walsh and Zetmeir was short. The two got along, and Walsh told Zetmeir to call any time. He took Walsh up on the offer. Soon they were talking once or twice a week. Walsh enjoyed meeting the people he made rich, Zeitmer said. "David took great pride in what the company had done for investors, in the number of small investors who had made money. He had his family in deep. Cousins, all his relatives, they were mortgaged to the hilt."

Zetmeir said Walsh had been misrepresented. "What you guys [in the media] have done to him is unspeakably cruel. Printing all that stuff about his bankruptcy, about how he had all these credit cards.

It hurt him and his family. You have no idea. He's devastated by what's happened. I'm convinced he had no idea. Absolutely none. He feels totally cheated."

When Bre-X stock cruised through $18, Zetmeir covered his original bet. He sold 10,000 shares, banking $180,000. Everything else he made from Bre-X would be pure profit. It didn't take long for profits to mount. In May 1996, when Bre-X shares split ten-for-one, Zetmeir owned 200,000 shares worth $5 million.

Religious people often preach to friends, hoping to convert them. Bre-X investors were the same. Zetmeir said he talked ten or twelve good friends into buying Bre-X. A few got out before disaster struck, but most stayed invested until the bitter end. "I felt terribly embarrassed over what had happened and what I had done, really sick about it," Zetmeir said. "My friends have been really good, though. They've all called me up and said, 'We were all big boys, motivated by the same thing.'"

Part of Zetmeir's strategy was to borrow money against his stock portfolio. The loan, known in the business as margin investing, meant Zetmeir could put down 30 cents towards a dollar's worth of Bre-X stock, and his investment broker would lend the remaining 70 cents. Zetmeir used margin investing to increase the size of his Bre-X bet. When his holding hit $5 million, Zetmeir had borrowed $1.4 million (U.S.) against the stock and invested it in other small mining plays.

Margin investing played out among many individual Bre-X shareholders across North America. The tactic was terrific as long as the price kept going up. When Bre-X crashed, the risk of margin investing became horribly apparent. When brokerage firms called in their loans, investors were forced to pay back money used to buy a stock that had just plummeted in value. Investment industry executives estimate that about 12,000 investors received margin calls demanding repayment of $500 million in loans used to buy Bre-X stock. All these calls went out the day after Freeport McMoRan's revelations of insignificant gold at Busang knocked $3 billion off the value of Bre-X.

Some investors simply walked away from their debts. Nesbitt Burns, an investment dealer that had pushed Bre-X hard, lost $4 million on clients who simply refused to pay their Bre-X bills. Others borrowed money on credit cards or lines of credit to buy Bre-X, and saw that cash vanish. A graduate student at McGill University used his meagre savings and his Visa card to raise $8,000, which he put into Bre-X at around $3 just after Freeport's release. He participated in Internet chat groups and enjoyed being part of the story for three weeks, but was wiped out on Strathcona's news. "I feel so stupid, I can't believe how caught up in this I became," he said, then pleaded that his name not be disclosed, as he had not told his wife what he'd done.

When shares in Bre-X fell on Freeport McMoRan's announcement, Zetmeir got a call from his broker. No more $1.4-million loan. The investment dealer wanted its cash back. Zetmeir had four days to comply and his collateral, Bre-X shares, had vaporized. "It was grim," he recalled, his voice still reflecting shock and disbelief. "I worked four days, twelve hours a day, to raise the cash. I completely rebuilt my portfolio. I had 100,000 shares of one junior stock, Manhattan Minerals. My broker wanted to sell it all at once. It would have killed the market. I sold it in lots of 5,000 and 10,000 shares at a time. The last thing you want to do is let your broker take out your positions when you face a margin call. They're brutal." Zetmeir added that in the wake of everything that had happened, "I'm revisiting my investment strategy."

Was Zetmeir depressed by what had happened? "I'm back to where I was two years ago. I'll likely go back to work, which I wasn't planning on," he said. "I'll be all right in the end. I'm still relatively affluent. I've talked to people who are devastated. People who honestly bet the house, who took out mortgages to buy stock. One family I know has seven kids. That gives you some perspective. Those people are ruined."

Four days after his sixty-second birthday, retired criminal lawyer Lawrence Beadle took a pistol from the drawer of the desk in his home office in New Westminster, British Columbia, and fired a single shot into his head. He died instantly. It was April 7 – one week after Freeport's revelations knocked the stuffing out of Bre-X. Beadle, who had just retired a few months earlier, had invested about $3 million. A police report said the stock was bought on margin. Beadle and his wife had just taken out additional loans to meet the margin call on their Bre-X borrowings.

In a statement to police, the widow, Davida Beadle, said, "It was not his fault." She found her husband's body in his office when she went in to pick up a ringing phone. She said she had tried to console her husband, telling him that Bre-X's fall was "just fate, bad luck and we would make everything right again by working together."

Bre-X Executives Cash In

While some small investors were banking a small fortune as Bre-X stock rose, executives in the company were reaping enormous gains. It was a sensitive subject. When reporters questioned him about sales of his Bre-X stock, David Walsh lashed out. He wasn't losing faith, he insisted. He was just being prudent. In late 1996, Walsh said, he'd sold less than 3 per cent of his Bre-X stock. Sure, his wife, Jeannette, had sold a bit more – about 5 per cent of her holdings. But, Walsh asked, can you blame us? Our whole net worth is tied up in this company. Those who knew Calgary's latest millionaires were aware the Walsh household was being uprooted from the city's suburbs to $1.9-million digs in an exclusive part of Nassau in the Bahamas.

From the company's founding through to the day it collapsed, the Walsh family remained Bre-X's biggest shareholders. What got people talking was the amount of money the family and other senior executives made by selling Bre-X stock, and the manner in which they did it. The options to buy stock at well below the market price had been approved (with no laughter or whooping recorded in the minutes) by the Bre-X board of directors. Options are meant to reward employees for their service to a company, and to align the interests of employees with those of shareholders. Bre-X's incredible run on stock markets threw that theory out of whack, especially when, in fact, the insiders had been given practically free stock options that made them fabulously rich. So rich, a cynic might observe, that far from binding them to the company it made the company's future welfare unimportant to them.

For example, in January 1996, Walsh and his wife and chief geologist John Felderhof used the option plan to buy a total of 2.6 million Bre-X shares for one cent each. The stock was trading for $16 at the time. Shortly after, David Walsh used the option plan to buy 240,000 Bre-X shares for a whopping 40 cents each at a time when Bre-X traded at $65 on the Alberta Stock Exchange. Such trading is entirely legal, as long as it is reported to provincial securities commissions. The Bre-X executives always carefully complied with these disclosure laws.

The pace of their trading was furious through the summer of 1996; it's a wonder the executives had time to focus on Bre-X business when they were so busy selling shares. Felderhof was the busiest of the lot, selling up to $2 million of shares in a single day in as many as a dozen trades during some sessions. At the same time, he was steadily expanding his public estimates of how much gold was at Busang.

In all, Felderhof banked $42.4 million by selling Bre-X shares in 1996. Just behind the geologist on the gravy train were David and Jeannette Walsh: they made $34.9 million. Stephen McAnulty, the company's vice-president for investor relations and the Web enthusiast, took home $22.2 million, and even the quiet treasurer, John Thorpe, made $6.1 million. Options could also make employees working in Busang rich. The head of the site, Michael de Guzman, had a $9-million stake when he fell to his death from a helicopter. His second in command, fellow Filipino Cesar Puspos, was worth $3 million and tooled about the dirt roads of Kalimantan in a new BMW.

Short Cuts to Fame

Chatter in Joseph's Hairstyling, a barber shop on Toronto's Yonge Street, often turned to Bre-X Minerals or horse racing. When he wasn't giving $14-dollar trims, Joseph, the owner, dabbled in the stock market. The not-yet-wealthy barber sat tight as Bre-X reserves grew and his shares soared. But the day the Indonesian government proposed a deal that saw Barrick Gold Corp. – for whom former prime minister Brian Mulroney was a director – take a majority position in Busang, the barber decided he'd had enough. "Too much politics," Joseph said. He sold the whole whack of shares for a $50,000 profit. Many similar investors seem to owe Mulroney a note of thanks for saving their bacon.

Little but Bre-X was discussed at Joseph's the day David Walsh admitted the Busang find was an enormous scam. The talk wasn't pretty. "This has been a terrible thing for some people. I had a woman come in this morning who lost $50,000. She was devastated, just devastated. Who would have believed that there was no gold?"

Why not believe? At the end of 1996, Bre-X held twenty-first place among Canada's largest companies, measured by stock market value. At $4.2 billion, it was just behind Bombardier and ahead of Nova, Falconbridge, and Petro-Canada – all real companies with real products.

The lionization of Bre-X executives made it even easier to trust this crew. Beyond the rags-to-riches story, there were awards and distinctions. In March 1997, John Felderhof had walked away with the prestigious Prospector of the Year award – the rock hounds' equivalent of an Oscar – at a black-tie ceremony just weeks before Felderhof's discovery was proven a fraud. Walsh and Felderhof celebrated the award with the head of the convention by dining at Toronto's expensive Mercer Street Grill. The newly minted millionaires showed a taste for inexpensive wine. In a restaurant where the average bar bill is $60, they spent just $29 on a bottle of Macon Village. Significantly, even in reticent Toronto, throughout the meal the two Bre-X executives were asked for autographs by admiring fellow diners.

The fame continued to spread. The international executive search firm Heidrick & Struggles Canada, Inc., made David Walsh its "High Impact CEO of the Year" for 1996. The award reflected Walsh's ability to ramp up the value of his company's shares. "Increasingly, CEOs are being held directly accountable for their company's results," said David Pasahow, managing partner for Heidrick & Struggles. "We believe this survey highlights some truly outstanding performances by CEOs whose companies created real value this year for their shareholders."

The Big Players Take a Hit

The biggest pool of money in Canada is Quebec's public pension and insurance fund, the $57-billion Caisse de dépot et placement. Not surprisingly, it attracts some of the smartest money managers in the country. The Caisse's stock pickers began to buy Bre-X when stock went for more than $150, just before it was listed on the TSE in April 1996 and then split ten-for-one. Over the next seven months, the fund bought shares steadily, until it was one of the company's single largest shareholders. It still held the stake when Bre-X crashed. In early April 1997, the Caisse announced it had lost $70 million on Bre-X. The fund noted in a terse, defensive press release: "Caisse managers decided to invest in the company based on the recommendations issued by the 10 largest brokerage firms."

The Quebec fund was not alone in missing the scam at Bre-X. The country's second largest pension fund, the Ontario Teachers Pension Plan Board, took a $100-million hit. The Teachers' fund didn't even make an active decision to buy Bre-X. The stock was simply purchased because it was part of the TSE 300 index. Teachers and many other funds make a point of owning the entire index, and count on the exchange to make sure that only worthy companies are awarded membership. The Caisse recommended, "Canadian stock exchanges should consider demanding a valuation be performed by an entity that is totally independent from mining companies. Such valuation should begin with core sampling, which is already being done in Australia."

"Many fund managers have been buying speculative stocks like Bre-X for these past few years, instead of the established companies," warned Patrick McKeough, editor of *The Success Investors* newsletter in Toronto. "Following the Bre-X collapse, some fund managers will be even more careful about the quality of stocks they buy. But others will gamble more aggressively than ever to win back their Bre-X losses."

Other stock market experts also ran aground on Bre-X. Robert Disbrow invests his company's money at First Marathon Securities Ltd., a leading investment dealer based in Toronto. He is acknowledged as one of Canada's most aggressive and savvy investors. In a good year, his prowess can earn the brokerage $20 million, while Disbrow can take home $7-million paycheques. Bre-X turned 1997 into a bad year for Disbrow and First Marathon. The company's gold analyst, Kerry Smith, backed Bre-X from its early days, and Disbrow took his analyst's recommendation. The brokerage lost $4.8 million buying Bre-X for its own account, giving it something in common with clients who lost money acting on the same advice.

Stock brokerage firms encourage their employees to play the market; they believe it aligns the analysts' interests with investors'. However, there are rules to make sure that clients are given priority over brokerage insiders. When analysts change their view on a stock – switching from a buy to a sell recommendation, for example – they must wait a number of days to let clients react before acting with their own money.

Egizio Bianchini of Nesbitt Burns pushed Bre-X with a passion. Indeed, his faith extended into his personal holdings. Although he has refused to be interviewed, co-workers speculated that Bianchini and his family held Bre-X stock worth $3 million at the company's peak. The analyst kept recommending Busang to the end, telling clients, "The gold is there!" right up to the day before Freeport McMoRan revealed the opposite. Bianchini's hands were tied when Bre-X dropped. Company rules forbade him from selling until two days after his recommendation was changed. It is entirely likely that the all-star analyst lost his whole investment.

A Nesbitt Burns broker in Ottawa, Michel Mendenhall, attained legendary status by purchasing Bre-X for pennies and holding tight until his holding was worth $70 million. Nesbitt Burns refused to let the broker be interviewed, but talk in the brokerage house was that Mendenhall upgraded his lifestyle substantially with these new riches. Bre-X shares were used to back bank loans, a mortgage on an $500,000 brownstone along the Rideau Canal, several condominiums at the base of the Mont Tremblant ski resort, and a new $200,000 turbo-charged Porsche. Mendenhall's superiors do acknowledge the broker never sold his shares, and when Bre-X crashed, he was left with a lot of pretty stock certificates and millions in debt.

The many investors who profited from their encounter with Bre-X were content to let the stock fade away as a pleasant memory. But because so many were hurt by Bre-X's crash, holding shares either directly or through their mutual funds and pension plans, and because public interest in the story was so high, the search for those responsible for the fraud became a priority for both the Royal Canadian Mounted Police and private investigators hired by Bre-X.

CHAPTER SEVENTEEN

The Scam

"The pool table was de Guzman's passion. He was the champion and everyone was afraid of him." – Warjimin, housekeeper at Bre-X's Samarinda office

"It took about $21,000 (U.S.) in gold to create a company worth $6 billion." – Graham Farquharson, president, Strathcona Minerals Services Ltd.

"This should go about four grams, yes, about four grams." – Michael de Guzman, Bre-X geologist, eyeballing rich core samples in a video shot by Nesbitt Burns analyst Egizio Bianchini

The Dayak Tribesman Who Sold the Gold

His name is Salin. He's thirty-five years old, a member of the Dayak tribe, and a familiar face to anyone who pans gold from the rivers near Busang. Salin buys river gold grains from the locals, many of whom are also Dayak. He buys them behind the counter in the store he runs in the village of Mekar Baru, five kilometres from Busang base camp, where he also sells beer, cigarettes, plastic toys, and mosquito repellent and provides a pool table. Salin is the quintessential middleman. He buys river gold at a hefty discount to the official rate and occasionally travels 200 kilometres to Samarinda and sells it for close to the market price.

Early in 1995, Salin started to have fewer reasons to make that trek.

When work began at Busang in 1994, Salin ran the store closest to the base camp and it rapidly became a popular haunt. "Most of the boys would go in there and spend their wages," said Jim Rush, who managed drilling rigs at Busang for PT Drillinti Tiko, the Jakarta company contracted to do Bre-X's drilling. Rush said everyone knew that Salin was a gold buyer and, at the right price, a seller. In fact, Rush bought a tiny nugget from the store owner and took it home to Australia as a souvenir. "If he could sell it there, it saved him a trip to Samarinda to sell it," he said.

For almost three years, Michael de Guzman was a regular customer of Salin's. He spent somewhere around $21,000 (U.S.) to buy roughly sixty ounces of river gold. It was enough to make the equivalent of a few hundred wedding rings. With a skill that rivalled Rumpelstiltskin's, de Guzman spun that gold into a $6-billion company.

A ten-page academic article laid the groundwork for de Guzman's scam. He produced the piece on Busang in 1994 with help from his old pals and fellow geologists John Felderhof, Cesar Puspos, and Jonathan Nassey. The group contended that an uncommon geological formation, a "maar diatreme" or plug of gold-rich rock left behind by an extinct volcano, explained the presence of gold. The paper, which de Guzman frequently delivered, was based on sound science. "The Busang geological setting is such that there is no doubt that it was a valid exploration target for gold," said the Strathcona report. In a discussion of the fraud, Graham Farquharson added, "This whole plan was well-organized and thoroughly thought out ahead of time. They had the right site, the right geology."

Looking back, Farquharson is confident the tampering began when Bre-X recorded poor results in the central zone, where it first began drilling in the fall of 1993. Others had drilled the site with little success. After failing to hit gold in his first few tries, de Guzman knew it was possible that the site would be shut down and that Felderhof was ready to take the tough decision. Then, on December 12, 1993, Bre-X revealed the numbers from four cores. Two were duds, one was no use because the drill broke, but the last one showed a terrific six grams of gold per tonne. Just over a month later, on January 19, the company announced testing on six new holes, all better than those reported in December. These results gave Bre-X the initial credibility needed to raise the money and keep de Guzman in business. The drilling that came soon after was from the "rich" southeast zone. By early 1994, Bre-X was devoting part of its exploration to the new zone and it was recording incredible results. But as the size of Busang mushroomed, the science behind the deposit also had to expand.

Over five months of drilling in the southeast zone, Bre-X recorded consistent, high gold concentrations. The monster, as Felderhof liked to call it, was getting even larger. Of course, de Guzman knew that the monster was make-believe. So, like a Hollywood scriptwriter, he needed a story that would get audiences to set aside common sense. He spent months coming up with it. De Guzman painted a totally convincing picture of a brilliant geologist coming up with a credible new theory, and he did it in a way that made you want to believe. He told the *Far Eastern Economic Review* that while working alone at three o'clock in the morning in January 1995, it all fell into place. Busang lay at the crossroads of several fault lines. That allowed for even greater volcanic action than experts previously assumed and the largest deposit ever seen on the Rim of Fire. De Guzman said he bounded downstairs and woke up Puspos to explain the concept. The two spent the next eight hours in "non-stop technical brainstorming." Then they went to Felderhof, who took four hours and four strong cups of coffee to accept what they were presenting him with. "It was like presenting my thesis to a professor," said de Guzman. Not quite. When de Guzman brought similar concepts to his professors at Manila's Adamson University in the 1970s, he'd been snubbed. This time, he found a receptive audience.

De Guzman would tell complete strangers that he possessed a near-genius IQ, and he liked to air his ideas whenever he got an audience. In a speech and slide show for the 1996 Prospectors and Developers conference in Toronto, he sketched out the huge geological formation, and described taking samples at Busang in 1993, just before Bre-X bought the claim. He told the audience that five of the samples contained gold concentrations of more than two grams per tonne, which wasn't unreasonable, and one that yielded 110 grams per tonne, which was beyond anything seen on the planet.

De Guzman took enormous personal pride in Busang, and liked to portray it as his own personal discovery. The last image screened for the prospectors' convention showed a group of men walking down a red dirt path in the jungle. "The successful history of Bre-X Minerals in relation to our Busang gold deposit is manifested by this slide," De Guzman solemnly told a rapt audience. "John Felderhof is leading the group of senior managers. John would always miss the bush. He would always be there any time new information came in. Beside him is Cesar Puspos. At the background is David Walsh and Paul Kavanagh. It's unfortunate I was the photographer. I should have been there."

New Uses for a Pool Table

Tampering started at Busang the moment the drill sample came out of the ground. Like any exploratory mining company, Bre-X kept detailed logbooks of its core samples. These records were its major asset in negotiations with senior mining houses, and would be even more important when it came time to bring a mine into production. They detailed the rock formations that stretched out under the ground. To make the scam work, de Guzman had to match descriptions of potentially gold-bearing ore in the log with salted samples. If the results didn't match, gold would start showing up in rocks that geologists knew couldn't possibly contain the metal.

Even now, it's possible to watch de Guzman spin the tale. Nesbitt Burns' Egizio Bianchini took a video camera along during a visit to Busang in June 1996. At one point, the gold analyst filmed an Indonesian drilling crew pulling out core samples the length of baseball bats under de Guzman's supervision. There was a carnival atmosphere to the work, despite the sweltering heat and the gooey red mud that coated everyone. "Here we go, core, straight out of the oven," Bianchini narrated. "Mike, eyeball this for us. What do you think this type of rock will grade?"

Bianchini wanted to record the geologist's best guess at the concentration of gold in the rock. He asked for these estimates numerous times during the site tour. De Guzman was happy to oblige, showing a flair for the dramatic. He ran a hand over the rock, then turned to the camera and said solemnly, "This should go about four grams, yes, about four grams." De Guzman must have been barely able to suppress a laugh as he thought of alternative lines like: "What grade would you like it to be, Egizio?"

Unfortunately, the fraud was no joke. Analysts such as Bianchini quickly incorporated de Guzman's eyeball estimates into their calculations, calculations that led to recommendations to buy the stock.

At Busang, Bre-X geologists would inspect the wooden racks filled with core samples and label what they believed to be promising samples as "mineralized," a term geologists use to indicate they believe gold is present. Two-metre sections of this rock were crushed, bagged, and sent to the labs for testing, while the rest of the core was set aside. Making snap decisions on which cores to test was an irregular practice, but in keeping with the push to prove as large a deposit as possible while the company was negotiating with potential partners. "The term mineralization in the drill logs for Busang does provide an initial signal to those involved with the tampering process as to where it would be appropriate to add gold," stated the Strathcona report. Then the bags of crushed rock took a ride in a barge down the Mahakam River to Samarinda.

The Samarinda office was a comfortable place. It had its own fresh-water tower, a satellite dish, and a basketball half-court. Inside, the recreation room was filled with comfortable chairs and a couch, a stereo, and a colour TV. There were pictures of Busang up on the walls. In the middle of it all sat a pool table. "The pool table was de Guzman's passion," said Warjimin, a housekeeper at the office, when interviewed by the *Toronto Sun*. "He was the champion and everyone was afraid of him." He was indeed a champion. At night, de Guzman used the table for another game.

When the sample bags came off the barge from Busang, they had to be trucked to the Samarinda office and its courtyard. Because the lab was overwhelmed, a backlog built up at the office, which is the size of a small bungalow in the suburbs. Bags started to be sent on to a warehouse Bre-X rented in the town of Loa Duri, twenty kilometres away. Every once in a while, de Guzman told the Indonesian workers to bring the bags into the recreation room, where they would be stacked around the pool table. The geologist wanted to "check" the bags to make sure they hadn't broken while travelling down the river, and that the tropical sunlight hadn't caused deterioration in the fibreglass sacks. Checking the bags meant opening them late at night. Several employees told this tale to Strathcona's investigators and Farquharson wrote, "If this step has occurred, we would regard it with great suspicion, as plastic bags contained within a fiberglass bag would not be expected to show any deterioration after only a few months."

Now came the trickiest part of the fraud. De Guzman carefully weighed out tiny amounts of the river gold grains he had bought from Salin and mixed the metal with measured amounts of barren crushed rock from Busang. Farquharson speculated that the blending took place in several bags or buckets, each of which was designed to give a different concentration of gold. Only a few grains of gold needed to go into each plastic bag of core sample to catch the lab's attention and build the Busang myth. When the lab reported a gold concentration of two grams per tonne, it was the equivalent of saying it had picked out two particular individuals in a city of 1 million. When he started salting, de Guzman almost certainly had one bag of material ready that would give a concentration of two grams per tonne, along with a whole series of other bags that would give slightly better or worse grades.

Bags of crushed rock from Busang were lifted onto the pool table, opened, doctored with a scoop of gold and rock mix of the appropriate concentration, given a stir, then sealed up again, according to Farquharson and private investigators hired by David Walsh. John Irvin, manager of the Indo Assay lab in Balikpapan that tested all of Bre-X's rock samples, said that if the measurements are done correctly, the whole scheme is dead easy. "Suppose you have a ten-kilogram bag and you want a reading of five grams [of gold] per tonne. You just measure 0.05 grams [of gold] and flick it into the bag," he said. "We don't check for tiny bits of gold in the bag. You're talking 100 to 400 microns. That all gets crushed." (At this size, the grains are only slightly thicker than a human hair.)

By late 1996, de Guzman was losing all restraint, or getting sloppy. Occasionally, Indo Assay found gold concentrations of ten to twenty grams per tonne, signs of an incredibly rich deposit. Hole number 198 went right off the scale. Long sections of the drill core graded more than 40 grams per tonne, spiking at one point to 64.8 grams. A tiny vein might sport this much gold, though it would be visible to the naked eye, which was not the case in this instance. In a large deposit such as Busang, these concentrations were almost impossible. Strathcona sank a drill only 1.5 metres away from hole 198 and found less than 0.02 grams of gold per tonne.

Perhaps less experienced hands were adding in the gold that night on the pool table. Farquharson and the private investigators are convinced de Guzman did not act alone. He was simply away from the site too frequently to have doctored all the samples that went to the labs. This view is shared by those who worked at Bre-X with the Filipino geologist. "He could not do [the tampering] by himself," said Jonathan Nassey, a senior Bre-X geologist. "There must have been some people helping him do it. He must have instructed somebody there to do it."

The fraud took discretion, nerve, and an intimate understanding of the fictional ore body. "Those involved in the tampering process have a very good understanding of the geology of the Busang property," stated the Strathcona report. It said the criminals "have the knowledge needed to determine the very small amounts of gold required to result in sample assays that would be compatible with the geological interpretation."

However, those with an intimate knowledge of Busang, such as Indo Assay's Irvin, said the scam could have been carried out by as few as two or three individuals, and that a small group of conspirators would explain how the fraud stayed secret so long. Along with Indonesian authorities and the Royal Canadian Mounted Police, the private investigators are questioning every one of the nine senior geologists who worked at Busang. Cesar Puspos, de Guzman's number two at the site, has talked to police from his home in the Philippines. So have co-workers Jerry Alo and Bobby Ramirez. By early August 1997, no criminal charges had been laid in connection with the fraud at Busang.

Why did de Guzman do it? It seems likely that he was driven by a compulsion to gain acceptance for his theories and by greed. For a while, he was successful in finally winning the approval he craved. And before his death he cashed in $4 million worth of Bre-X options. The other obvious question is, *Didn't he know that eventually he would be caught out?* Some observers have speculated that the geologist felt he would eventually prove his radical theory if enough holes were drilled and, in fact, started salting in the hope that real gold would turn up on the very next hole. That's unlikely, since the southeast zone is barren, a fact de Guzman knew better than anyone. De Guzman had known what it was like to have failed at mining and be poor, and he never wanted to go back. In his marriages and in his tangled affairs, he operated far outside the bounds of acceptable behaviour. Clearly, the same loose standards applied to his geology.

The Fatal Flaws of Felderhof and Walsh

In July 1997, John Felderhof faced his critics head on. He knew nothing and saw nothing, he claimed, in a news release put out through his lawyers from his home in the Cayman Islands. "Let me state categorically again that I did not participate in any tampering," Felderhof said. "I was not aware of any tampering with the Busang core samples, and I believed that the systems and personnel in place at Busang were adequate to detect tampering."

Felderhof went on to list twelve reasons for his innocence, among them: he had arranged for his son to work at Busang in the summer of 1997, he continued to hold shares, he had helped Strathcona with the audit in Indonesia, and he had hired reputable labs and outside experts to review Busang at every step in the exploration process. The man who talked up Busang's results at every opportunity also said he was "Bre-X's chief administrative officer in Indonesia, (I was not chief geologist), I was rarely in our Samarinda office and only occasionally on site at Busang." The problem was, he *was* the chief geologist.

As for incredible drilling results such as those for hole 198, "our intention was to resolve these anomalies later, after we completed the entire drilling program, so they could be assessed in the context of the overall pattern." Felderhof again defended his methods, such as using the whole core in testing. And he went back to his theory, explaining that Indonesian rock formations similar to Busang already boasted producing gold mines, and said he would be available to those investigating the fraud.

Felderhof's comments were greeted with scepticism by former Bre-X shareholders. "Oh, really," said Anne Williams of Surrey,

British Columbia. "So now he is just saying the opposite of every-thing that seems to have been obvious." Dermod Travis, spokesman for the Quebec investors suing Bre-X, said the comments were the words of "a man who wishes to hear no evil, see no evil, and speak no evil."

Within the mining community, Felderhof's role at Busang is the subject of endless speculation. Dorothy Atkinson, an experienced geologist and analyst with Pacific International Securities in Vancouver, was the first analyst to pick up on Bre-X, and she met Felderhof on many occasions. Her views are typical of her col-leagues. "To hear him speak, to hear his enthusiasm and excitement, it all seemed so logical, so genuine," she said. "If you could have heard the heart-rending speech he made at the Prospectors and Developers convention, it would have brought tears to your eyes." Then Atkinson started to laugh. "I'm divorced. I've been lied to by men before," she said. "If John Felderhof didn't know what was going on, I can only conclude he was incompetent." As the chief geologist and vice-chairman of Bre-X and a man who spent most of his life prospecting in countries like Indonesia, Felderhof is damned as a crook if he knew what was going on at Busang and damned as a fool if he didn't. Either way, in the end, he has to take responsibility for the fraud.

David Walsh gets far more sympathy from those who know him. Even investors like Karl Zetmeir who lost millions on Bre-X say the chief executive officer was duped along with everyone else. In the summer of 1997, there was no evidence that Walsh knew what his employees did around their pool table when night fell in Samarinda. Walsh promoted Bre-X, firing out press releases, working investors, and raising money half a world away, and had little interest or inclination to learn about geology. That was his fatal flaw and his downfall, and it cost those who believed in him mil-lions of dollars and untold misery. David Walsh should have asked questions from the outset. Of all people, he should have stopped to pinch himself and ask, *Can this really be true?* The titles of Bre-X chairman, chief executive, president, and founder of the company carried a responsibility to shareholders and the mining community. Walsh totally failed to live up to that responsibility.

Reflecting on Fraud

Staring at the Inuit art in his office four months after his trip to Indonesia, Graham Farquharson still finds it difficult to fathom how so many smart people missed the obvious signals that Busang was a hoax. "Look at this," he said, his head shaking in amazement as he pointed to a line in a report on Bre-X by Normet back in 1995. "It states that over 90 per cent of the gold could be separated by a gravity test. That's unheard of." What Farquharson couldn't believe is that Busang's gold literally fell out of the surrounding rock when given a good shake.

The behaviour of locals should also have provided a clue as to what was going on at Busang. Gold can be found in the topsoil of the central zone, and for decades Dayak tribesmen had panned it out of nearby streams, where it is possible to twirl the red soil in a pan and turn up tiny gold grains. No locals bother to pan in the south-east zone, despite the fact that Bre-X's drilling results show that gold-bearing ore extended right to the surface there. When faced with this fact, Felderhof would launch into a theory of how acid in the surface soil destroyed the gold in this unique deposit. When Freeport's Jim Bob Moffett was presented with this theory after conflicting drilling results had appeared, he said, "That's bullshit." The reality, of course, is there was never gold in the southeast zone.

There were many more details an experienced geologist should have caught. No matter how fine the labs ground the Busang core samples, the amount of gold recovered stayed the same. That made no sense. Legitimate gold recovery should improve as the rock sample is ground more finely and more gold is released. But since the salted gold is not *in* the rock, the increasing grinding cannot release any more.

Then there was the composition of the gold grains. As Freeport had noted, Bre-X was finding huge grains, visible to the naked eye, in an underground deposit that should have featured tiny flecks an observer would never notice. In addition, gold and silver always occur together, though the proportions vary. In underground sites such as Busang, the gold and silver stay evenly distributed in a grain. But gold left to weather on the earth's surface, or in a stream bed, goes through changes. The silver is leached out of the exterior, leaving an outer shell of pure gold around an inner mix of metals. Any geology student with decent equipment can spot the difference. In earlier reports done by Bre-X's consultants, details on the composition of Busang's large, pure gold grains were overlooked. "I asked the Kilborn team why no bells went off over the shape of the gold," Farquharson said. "They said they really didn't look at those results, but they had a sheepish look, which they should have had."

Finally, there was the sheer magnitude of Bre-X's claim. Felderhof and de Guzman's unique theories could only go so far. "When they were getting to the point of estimating 200 million ounces, you were talking about 8 per cent of the world's gold in one deposit. Surely at this point someone should have stepped back and asked, 'Can this really be possible, can any deposit grow this quickly?'" Farquharson said. He said closer inspection would have revealed the fraud. "Even in a sophisticated operation, if you're fiddling with the data, at some point, something's not going to work."

The Strathcona president looks back at his experience with the Bre-X fraud and sees a system that failed on three levels. Managers failed in their duty to run the company with integrity, directors were remiss in their duty to watch over the operation, and regulators were negligent in picking up shoddy practices and signs of trouble. The Bre-X story that was just too good to be true turned out to be just that.

CHAPTER EIGHTEEN

A Fable for Our Times

"A gold mine is a hole in the ground with a liar on top."
– *Mark Twain*

All that Glitters

The Bre-X saga is the ultimate example of truth being stranger than fiction. It starts with a justifiably obscure Calgary exploration company – with no revenues or earnings – run out of the basement of a recent bankrupt, its chief executive, David Walsh. At its peak, the market valued Bre-X at $6 billion. The shares went from trading for pennies to $286.50 (on a pre-split basis), back to pennies, and finally to not trading at all. All this on the basis of a single asset that was never independently verified in the far-off jungles of Kalimantan, where many had looked for gold, but few had succeeded.

From the beginning to the end of the story, there were dozens of red flags, warnings to careful analysts and investors that Bre-X was a company to stay away from – even if the gold had been there. What happened to Bre-X would not have happened to a carefully run mining company.

Indonesia has a good system of mining regulation, which culminates in the Contract of Work system. Bre-X's SIPP, or exploration permit, was cancelled in August 1996, and the company was never issued a Contract. This means that a company with a market value in the billions never had clear title to its single important asset. It is one of the many quirks of the story that the official who signed that cancellation did not foresee its far-ranging consequences. "No, I had no idea of the controversy that would be created when I signed the letter," said director general of mines Kuntoro, whose spacious office is in a bland, low-rise building behind five palm trees and a modest hedge. "I just thought it would be better to have some agreement between Bre-X and its partner, and all would be fine and we could proceed." Given the firestorm that followed, "It's ironic."

By the fall of 1996, Bre-X was no longer in control of its fate; the Indonesian government was. The government announced that the company's partner, like it or not, was Barrick. That meant that Walsh couldn't fulfil his responsibility to shareholders. By December, the government had put the fate of the Calgary company in the hands of billionaire businessman Bob Hasan, who concocted an arrangement that no one had predicted and that served Indonesian interests, not shareholders' interests.

There is no escaping the fact that the history of the company is the history of hype and self-promotion. There is also no escape from the conclusion that, unfortunately, it was allowed to get away with it. With no proof, Bre-X radically escalated its estimates for Busang over a two-year period, from a base of 3 million ounces to 200 million. Many analysts were eager, at every stage, to increase the company's already ultra-optimistic forecasts. Everyone lost track of how literally unbelievable the estimates were. Two hundred million ounces of gold has a gross value of $70 billion (U.S.), the equivalent of the gross national product of the Philippines, and larger than that of many other countries. At critical points in the story, Bre-X released ever rising estimates of gold reserves at Busang. Normally, increases are incremental; in this saga, they rose by quantum leaps. "We all got carried away," confessed the CEO of a Canadian mining company, who is rueful about the fact that he and others in the mining community accepted Bre-X's fabulous numbers.

The market values for Bre-X were equally unbelievable. When you pull away the veil, investors were willing to put a $6-billion price tag on an undeveloped piece of jungle that didn't produce one ounce of gold or a cent of revenue. What's more, it was going to take $1.5 billion (U.S.) or so to turn that plot of tropical rain forest into something of value. And that in a country where investors would always have to worry about the whims of the government.

Many analysts, some of whom were geologists, were all too willing to get caught up in the hype. Their research reports are full of phrases such as "I'm just back from Busang, and I have seen the gold." Clearly what they had seen was fool's gold. But the excitement was infectious. For example, Nesbitt Burns, one of Canada's largest and most respected investment dealers, was relentlessly promoting junior mining stocks in countries many of their clients couldn't find on a map. There were a number of buy recommendations in brokerage reports on the stock, with twelve-month targets of $24 or more, the very week that Freeport revealed Bre-X's core samples contained insignificant amounts of gold.

Successful professional investors are forever saying, piously, that the key to a good company is solid management. Did any of these highly paid folks really take a good look at Felderhof and Walsh, whom *Fortune* magazine referred to as the Mr. Magoo of mining? A *Globe and Mail* profile of Walsh, based on interviews and court documents going back to the 1970s, concluded that he was "someone with a knack for taking shortcuts" who had a history of not asking questions when they needed to be asked. As for his colleagues, in the 1980s Felderhof and de Guzman had been involved in heavily hyped explorations activities in Indonesia, run from Australia. When the boom turned bust, Australia tightened its rules for exploration companies. Many of the same cast of characters moved their activities in the 1990s to companies based in Canada, where the regulatory environment was much more friendly. And this time, they knew they wouldn't end up broke.

It was obvious from early in the story that Bre-X was not a company to reveal uncomfortable facts. It was *The Globe and Mail*, not Bre-X, that disclosed the cancellation of the company's exploration permit. In February 1997, Bre-X pretended it had never said it owned 90 per cent of Busang, in clear contradiction to what it had said all along.

Bre-X was suspiciously secretive. Despite the deluge of (often contradictory) press releases and the mass of promotional material the company posted on the Internet, solid information about Bre-X was lacking. In the normal course of events, Bre-X would have gone to the public markets to raise money, which it could easily have done. But that would have meant filing a prospectus approved by regulators, which would have required the company to provide detailed information about its legal, financial, and operational activities.

Since Bre-X raised money through private placements, which don't require the usual documentation because they are exclusively aimed at supposedly sophisticated investors, the only prospectus the company ever filed was a slender document in 1988, when it first went public. And apart from some tightly controlled tours by analysts, Bre-X refused to let others on its site in Busang, to see for themselves. The mysterious fire on the site in January 1997 should also have raised suspicions.

Experienced geologists who toured the site, and there were many, should have been alarmed by irregular practices at Busang, and by the heated defence of these practices by John Felderhof. The decision not to split drill cores or to preserve half the samples was questionable. So was the fact that many mining companies had worked the same ground over the years and found little where Bre-X found so much. A site tour should have included a no-nonsense examination of just how the core samples got to the labs, how long this process took, and the measures in place to safeguard the valuable crushed rock en route. At some stage on the road to placing a $6-billion value on Bre-X, analysts should have demanded independent drilling and assaying at Busang.

Monkey See, Monkey Do

No one comes out of the Bre-X story with an enhanced reputation. No one can claim credit for detecting the fraud, even though it went on for years. The salting operation was uncovered only because an ownership deal was finally reached in February 1997, and one of Bre-X's new partners, Freeport-McMoRan, began its due diligence of the site at Busang, which included fresh drilling. That a massive fraud at the world's hottest mining site could carry on for so long is an indictment of many of those who were involved in the Bre-X story. What made the fraud possible?

First, the herd instinct. "There was a time, as you know, monkey see, monkey do," said mining entrepreneur Robert Friedland, the man behind the huge nickel find at Voisey's Bay in Labrador. "Everyone wanted it [Busang]. It had to be good because Peter Munk wanted it and therefore Placer and so on; that may have undermined fundamental due diligence. Each major thought the other major had done their homework."

But above all, like all fables, the drama has a moral dimension: greed blinded the eyes of everyone, including investors. When shares in Bre-X fell to a couple of dollars from $15 after Freeport said it had found insignificant amounts of gold, thousands of retail investors traded millions of shares over a period of several weeks trying to make a fast buck. They were gambling, pure and simple, and most of them reaped a reward familiar to gamblers: they lost everything. It was as though they had confused an 80 per cent drop in the value of Bre-X shares with an "80 per cent off" sale at a local store.

There were no happy legacies for any of the participants in the Bre-X saga. As a result of the story, those who didn't already know learned that Indonesia was run by an aging autocrat with a squabbling, avaricious family. Like many developing nations, Indonesia could be a few years away from disintegration or a few decades away from becoming a serious economic power. Whatever course the country takes, nationalism is bound to become increasingly important. In the wake of the collapse of Bre-X, the Indonesian government, through mines minister Sudjana, tried to get Newmont Mining Corp. to hand over a 10 per cent share of one of its Indonesian mines. In June 1997, Sudjana proposed drastic revisions to the terms of the next generation of Contracts of Work. On this occasion, however, howls of protest from the foreign mining community forced the minister to beat a hasty retreat.

Corporate Canada did not cover itself in glory throughout the story. Bre-X, a company built on hype and destroyed by fraud, is deservedly gone forever. As for the other most prominent participant, "Barrick burnt a lot of bridges and embarrassed a lot of people, not least of all themselves," said one close observer in Jakarta. The behind-the-scenes deal it cut with the Indonesian government in November 1996 alienated much of the mining community and did nothing to improve its reputation. Having taken part in an arrangement that attracted local and international criticism, Barrick is unlikely to win its way back into the good graces of the government, or the mining community, any time soon. Still, the mining powerhouse is left with the largest landholding of any mining exploration company in Indonesia.

The rest of the gold-mining community continues to struggle, hurt by the Bre-X scandal and the lowest gold prices since the 1980s. By early August 1997, the market value of Placer Dome was not much more than half of what it was at its peak in 1996. Of the players, Jim Bob Moffett's Freeport-McMoRan was the most successful at keeping its reputation in Indonesia intact. When the fraud became apparent, thanks largely to its due diligence, Freeport quickly disavowed its partnership with Bre-X, but maintained its pipeline to the palace of the president.

The story could have played out differently. Whatever their rationalizations, securities and market regulators, who like to use terms like "integrity," should have considered the quality and the assets, not just the awesome numbers, of a publicly listed company like Bre-X. Ironically, Bre-X might not have got away with so much on the much-criticized Vancouver Stock Exchange, which is more loosely regulated than the Toronto Stock Exchange. "In Vancouver, the fraud might have been discovered earlier because there would have been more inherent scepticism," said one veteran executive, whose companies have traded on both exchanges.

The analysts who followed Bre-X have a lot to answer for, as the welter of lawsuits against many of them attests. What value did they provide to investors, as opposed to their firms, given the profoundly flawed advice most of them provided? If investors couldn't rely on regulators or analysts as the Bre-X story unfolded, can they now rely on lawyers to provide them redress? Where will the compensation for the $3 billion that was lost when Bre-X collapsed come from? If there is any certainty in this story, it is that the lawyers will get rich picking the last few bones off the Bre-X carcass.

If Bre-X is a fable, an allegory with a moral, where is the morality in this story? It's hard to find in the litter of a corrupt, authoritarian regime, self-centred first siblings, grasping international mining companies, shortsighted analysts, myopic regulators, greedy investors, and, in the centre of the mess, a fraudulent mining exploration company. Whether it's the story of the Barings Bank or the fall of the Reichmann property empire, the lesson is that investors and other interested parties need to dig beneath the surface. Relying on what they are told or promised is not enough. Nick Leeson wasn't the fabulously successful trader he pretended to be; the Reichmanns weren't the omniscient financial geniuses everyone thought they were; Bre-X was not a company with the find of the century. "I find it difficult to talk about the whole thing, sometimes," a self-pitying David Walsh told Dow Jones at the end of May 1997. "You know, just four years of real hard work went to fantasyland."

Fantasyland indeed.

Acknowledgements

The Globe and Mail broke the Bre-X Minerals Ltd. story on October 4, 1996, with dramatic revelations about problems the Cinderella company had with the Indonesian government, but had failed to disclose. Publication of the story knocked $510 million off the value of the stock in the first five frantic minutes of trading. From that moment on, the paper led the world in coverage as the drama unfolded over the following months. Dozens of *Globe* writers and correspondents around the world contributed to the flood of stories, and three of them went to Indonesia (in one of those cases, it took two diplomatic notes from the Canadian government to get the reporter a journalist's visa). Several of the trips included lengthy visits to Kalimantan, the Indonesian part of the island of Borneo, the site of the famous – or infamous – Busang deposit. *The Globe and Mail* conducted hundreds of interviews on Bre-X, many of them exclusive, among them Paul Waldie's memorable interview of Indonesian billionaire and Suharto golfing buddy Mohammad "Bob" Hasan. Paul tracked Hasan down in a hotel room in Indian Wells, California, where he was staying before teeing off with partner Fuzzy Zoeller in the Pro-Am Bob Hope Chrysler Classic tournament.

According to Info Globe, Globe Information Services' database, Bre-X had been mentioned in more than 1,000 stories by the end of June 1997. More than 200 Bre-X stories had appeared on page A1, the front page of the paper, or page B1, the front page of Report on Business, almost all of them in the relatively short period from the fall of 1996 to the summer of 1997. With one exception, that story count, which is one measure of popular interest, already surpasses the total for any other Canadian business story over the past twenty years. The most heavily covered stories during that period – like Bre-X – involved failure, including the fall of Dome Petroleum Ltd., Edmonton's Principal Group Ltd., Campeau Corp., and Royal Trustco Ltd. The number of front-page stories on Bre-X is destined soon to pass the total of 240 on the collapse of the Reichmann Brothers' Olympia & York Developments Ltd. property empire. Bre-X, however, has already touched and fascinated more people, including thousands of small investors, than that largely institutional story ever did.

We have taken full advantage of our paper's exhaustive coverage of the Bre-X saga and would like to thank all of our colleagues at *The Globe and Mail* who contributed to it. With only a few exceptions, unattributed quotations in the preceding pages are from *Globe* articles or interviews, or from interviews by the authors. We would like to thank everyone who agreed to be interviewed.

This book is a collaborative effort. John Stackhouse, the *Globe*'s development issues correspondent in New Delhi, contributed invaluable material based on the five weeks he spent in April and May in Jakarta and Kalimantan, where he visited Borneo tribesmen. Paul Waldie made an equally valuable and original contribution as a result of his trip to Indonesia and his exclusive interviews, with, for example, Hasan and Indonesian mining official Umar Said. Paul also provided criticisms and suggestions on the manuscript.

Our thanks also to Janet McFarland for interviews she shared with the authors, and to veteran mining reporter Allan Robinson, who co-broke the ownership story, for his comments on several of the chapters. Allan's stories on the fight for possession of Busang were unsurpassed. Michael Den Tandt's reporting helped to unravel the mysteries of Indonesia's geology, while John Saunders' "Big Reads" on Saturdays were a source of inspiration. The early stories that the *Globe* published gained greatly from Mike Babad's skilful editing and suggestions. Celia Donnelly was resourceful in digging up files most of us never realized existed. Particular thanks to Peggy Wente, editor of Report on Business, whose support made all the difference. Our thanks also to *The Globe and Mail*'s editor-in-chief William Thorsell for getting behind the book.

We would also like to thank Avie Bennett, chairman and president of McClelland & Stewart Inc., and Douglas Gibson, publisher; our agent, David Lavin, president of David Lavin Agency Ltd., for spurring us into action; and Wendy Thomas, for her fine editing.

Finally, we would like to thank our wives, Libby Znaimer and Jennifer Bermingham, for their encouragement, support, and tolerance of our unsociable hours.

Any errors of omission or commission are solely the responsibility of the authors.

Douglas Goold
Andrew Willis